CHEAP BASTARD'S® SERIES

THE CHEAP BASTARD'S® GUIDE TO

Los Angeles

Secrets of Living the Good Life—**For Less!**

First Edition

Ashley Wren **Collins**

gpp®
travel

Guilford, Connecticut
An imprint of Globe Pequot Press

All the information in this guidebook is subject to change. We recommend that you call ahead to obtain current information before traveling.

To buy books in quantity for corporate use
or incentives, call **(800) 962–0973**
or e-mail **premiums@GlobePequot.com**.

Text design by Sheryl P. Kober

ISBN 978-0-7627-6003-9

Printed in the United States of America
10 9 8 7 6 5 4 3 2 1

*For Mom, who taught me the beauty of a bargain
and the thrill of calculating your savings when purchasing
something on sale.*

*For Dad, who taught me it's smart to have
at least two dollars in my pocket at all times.*

*For Sissy, who taught me it's totally okay to announce proudly
to an entire room just how little my outfit costs.*

*You all taught me that a cheap bastard is about
being smart **and** classy.*

I love you.

CONTENTS

ABOUT THE AUTHOR

 Ashley Wren Collins is a writer, producer, and actress. Her first book with Lloyd Kaufman, *Produce Your Own Damn Movie!*, is available online and in bookstores everywhere. Ashley holds a BA from the University of Pennsylvania and an MFA from the American Repertory Theater/Moscow Art Theater School Institute for Advanced Theater Training at Harvard University. She has a regular entertainment blog on *The Huffington Post* and is a frequent contributor to *MovieMaker* Magazine. Ashley loves to spend as much time as possible in Los Angeles, though she lives and works in New York City. She's come a long way from the days of eating a fallen Clif Bar off a dirty train platform simply because she had just paid too much for it, though she still upholds all cheap bastard principles. Her website is www.ashleywrencollins .com. She welcomes your thoughts and feedback. Find her on Facebook and follow her on Twitter @wrenashley.

ACKNOWLEDGMENTS

Jerome Henry Rudes of Mistral Artist Management—thank you for your generosity, compassion, wisdom, advice, and support.

To my six hardworking, enthusiastic, and bright research interns, who stuck with me and always made me laugh. Thank you! May the next person who hires you also offer to pay you:

Michelle Johnson, who loves the dollar store more than is actually healthy.

Kammie Daniels, who lives with her belt tightened around her wallet, not her waist.

Annabella Zaklit, who has a place in her heart for Two Buck Chuck and free walks on the beach.

Samantha Moeller, who considers the term "Valet" a synonym for defeat.

Pierce Nahigyan, who has avoided underwear since 2004 in order to cut down on laundry bills.

Rebecca Caldwell, who thanks her student loans for perfecting her penny-pinching game.

To the following individuals who let me crash their pad, watched me type away for hours on end at my computer, fed me, and/or offered great support, ideas, and feedback. Thank you!:

Heather Anglin, David Benson, Lori Bergstresser, Michael Bolton, David Conolly, Christa Fuller, Samantha Fuller, Rob Grader, Georgia Hatzis, Josh Hoffs, Tamar Simon Hoffs, Uma Incrocci, Jaime Keith, Terri Kohler, Jennifer Lafleur, Aida Lembo, Keith Levenberg, Joe Linton, Amy Lyons, Regina Mahoney Lorenzo, Gloria Mahoney, Sylvia Mahoney, Eugenie Mason, Charles Pugliese, Brad Rehak, Jonno Roberts, Jordan Rockwell, Steven Rowley, Ken Simon, Kevin Sirois, Marjorie Soifer, Sydney Strickland, Tony Welch, Kate Willson, Lynn Zelem.

INTRODUCTION:
IT TAKES ONE TO KNOW ONE

"Hey," I called my sister on my cell phone from the street as soon as I emerged aboveground. "I bought a Clif Bar at the bodega because I'm running around to a million appointments today, and I don't have time to eat lunch. It cost $3! I opened it, but the wrapper was tough to pull apart, and it immediately fell onto the platform before I could eat even one bite!" I heard the frustration in my voice.

I rushed on, "I'm not sure if the three-second rule applies to food when it falls on dirty train platforms, but I picked it up and ate it since it was $3."

The air on the other end of the phone was heavy with my sister's patient listening. I wondered how this story sounded now that I was admitting it aloud.

"Anyhow, if I die tomorrow," I said, competing with the noise of the street traffic, "I just wanted you to know why."

She laughed, and I didn't die. That Clif Bar was overpriced to begin with and begrudgingly one of the only quick meal options available to me that afternoon. At 6 percent of my hourly wage at the time and completely uneaten, I blocked any thought of rodents, bugs, or grime running afoot; conveniently decided the "if on the ground three seconds or less, it's still safe to eat" rule also applied in this underground train platform instance; promptly brushed that Clif Bar off; and gobbled it down. And thus, with that Clif Bar episode, my stubborn cheap bastardom, already fledgling for several years, had fully arrived. I had paid for it, and I was going to get the most out of my money by eating the entire thing. *No matter what.*

Growing up and mowing the lawn from the age of 10, babysitting since the age of 11, and on a payroll since 14, I've always known and appreciated the value of earning and spending a dollar. Deciding to take the artistic route both in college and afterward, even as my friends who struggled financially in college went on to great careers with impressive salaries, I learned how to make smart choices that would still allow me to do what I love without going into debt. Many a walk down the street did I spend calculating in my head: "Should I buy the weekly transportation pass or the monthly one? Or does it make more sense with my upcoming schedule to just put $20 on a metro card and not get any pass?"

The economy has been challenging for some time now; our country as well as individuals and families are struggling financially. It's never made more sense for all of us to be cheap bastards. Being a cheap bastard does not mean you are rude, brusque, or ungracious; it means you are smart, efficient, and forward thinking. There's no reason you can't lead a great life, have a great time, and do all the things you want to do while living well within your means and saving pennies, be those pennies real or nonexistent.

You're talking to someone with two Ivy League degrees and nearly six figures of education debt who, in addition to being a writer, actress, producer, and choreographer, has done recruiting for a major airline; worked as a real estate paralegal running closings on houses, co-ops, and condos in New York City and the surrounding area; been a personal assistant to A-list celebrities; and a cater waiter, among many other things. All of these jobs were worked for an hourly wage. I've never had someone else pay my rent, my debt, or my bills. I've lived in Russia, I've seen Japan, England, France, Italy, Turkey, Iceland, Greece, and Africa. No one else has paid my way. I've stayed in hostels and adopted what I call the "Eating in Advance Plan," where I've eaten an especially large (free) breakfast (included with the hostel room charge), with enough food for two meals, in order to avoid having to buy lunch later. (I don't actually recommend you follow my lead in this particular example.)

Why do I tell you all this?

Because it *takes* one to *know* one. The most important thing any hustler or mover and shaker knows is that if you want to be happy, be smart, and succeed, you've simply got to be a cheap bastard. Whether you live in Pasadena or West Hollywood, Burbank or Pacific Palisades, Long Beach or Venice, and whether you're black, white, yellow, brown, purple, or green, I've got you covered. Visitor or native, you can trust me on this journey as I take your life to a whole new level of cheap bastardom. If you follow all of my advice in this book, you will be living quite large in Los Angeles and completely "in the know," going to free museums, concerts, theater, television tapings, and art galleries, as well as taking great classes, hikes, drives, tours, and oh, so much more.

Disclaimer: Parking in Los Angeles is a pain. When I can and it makes sense, I've done my best to provide tips and to help you out by telling you where to park and how much, if anything and if you must, it will cost you. However, if you get ticked off about something parking related, please do not come crying to me. You'll simply have to get over it. It's Los Angeles, and it comes with the territory.

PROLOGUE:
JUST HOW BIG IS LOS ANGELES?

Los Angeles is gigantic. It is one of the most racially diverse cities in the entire world. After New York City, it is the second most populous city in the entire United States, the most populous city in the western United States, and the most populous city in all of California. So, you get it. It's massive.

Los Angeles County alone, at close to 10 million people, is the largest county in all of America, with some 88 incorporated cities and many unincorporated areas. More than one quarter of all Californians call Los Angeles County their home. Larger than Rhode Island and Delaware put together, Los Angeles County borders 70 miles of the Pacific Ocean coast and contains rivers, desert, lakes, forests, islands, valleys, and mountains. The Greater Los Angeles Area, incorporating Los Angeles, Orange, Riverside, San Bernardino, and Ventura Counties, hovers in the area of close to 18 million people.

So perhaps now you understand my dilemma, and appreciate the nature of my mission. I am writing this book for a lot of people. And you are just one of them.

I'm well aware that of all the pleasures living in or visiting Los Angeles has to offer, driving, on a day-to-day basis, is usually not one of them. If you meet someone at a party and he tells you he lives in Los Angeles, see if you don't bring up traffic within the first 5 minutes. Thus, I know how important it is to have cheap options available to you not just anywhere in "Los Angeles" but also near your home or near your work. Because the less time you spend driving, and the less money you spend on gas, the happier you are in achieving the maximum value of your cheap bastard delight in exchange for your input of time and energy.

I think you'll find I've done well by you. You don't have to sit on the 10, the 405, the 101, or the 5 for hours on end to get what you want or what you need. There is a cheaper option closer to you.

I invite you to read this book from cover to cover and see if you don't learn something new about the beloved City of Angels. I know I did. And you know what? With all its traffic, the stereotypes of what some label as a "vapid" entertainment industry, and its endless sunshine without a single noticeable change of season, Los Angeles is, in fact, a pretty darn great place to live. Or visit. It has something for everyone. Be you geek, be you hip, be you old, be you young, be you black, be you white, be you introvert, be you extrovert, cheap options abound. So go ahead, turn the page. I can't wait to learn what you discover.

Entertainment in Los Angeles

TELEVISION:
WHAT RUNS TINSELTOWN

"In Beverly Hills . . . they don't throw their garbage away. They make it into television shows."

—WOODY ALLEN

Entertainment runs Tinseltown. It's what simultaneously drives everyone crazy and makes people love it or hate it. It's also what makes Los Angeles special. Seeing a live television taping is a unique experience not to be missed, whether you're native or not. Seeing your favorite comedy stars, talk show hosts, or game shows is a fun and interactive experience. In general, tapings can last up to 4 hours or more; most shows don't admit children under 10, sometimes no one under 18; tickets are often, but not always, limited to 2 and distributed on a first-come, first-serve basis; and the more popular shows fill up quickly. The fun part is that the studio audience is a very intimate experience; you sit much closer to the action than you would think, and you are likely to walk away with a new appreciation for all that goes into a live taping.

TALK SHOWS

It's Los Angeles, so there's a lot to talk over, argue over, and maybe even file for divorce over. Read on to see how you can be part of the action.

Chelsea Lately
Digital Media Center
12312 W. Olympic Blvd. (near S. Centinela Ave.), Los Angeles
www.eonline.com/on/shows/chelsea

A late night pioneer, being the sexy, smart, and sassy female blonde bombshell that Chelsea Handler is, she will make you laugh as she flirts with her guests and comments on the latest in entertainment news and pop culture. Her show is a half hour format, as opposed to an hour. Chelsea tapes in the afternoon. Visit On-Camera Audiences at www.ocatv.com and click on "Chelsea Lately" on the far left for ticket information.

Conan
Warner Bros. Studios
6564 Forest Lawn Dr., Los Angeles
http://teamcoco.com

Fair-skinned, redheaded, super tall Conan left New York City and rafted across the Los Angeles River (all 5 inches or so of it) to head up *The Tonight*

Show when Jay Leno left. That bombed, Jay threw a tantrum and got his show back, and Conan was out of a job. The country mourned and he came back, this time to TBS. You must be 16 years of age or older and submit your request online. You can ask for up to 4 tickets. Selections are lottery based, with a limited number placed on standby at 10 a.m. each day there is a live taping.

Divorce Court
Empire Studios
1845 Empire Ave. (at Victory Place), Burbank
(877) 311-2222
www.divorcecourt.com/beontheshow

Judge Toler is an alumnus of both of my alma maters, so I can't say a single bad thing about her. You can't get tickets to see *Divorce Court* (the audience is comprised of "paid actors," though the judge herself is very real and a woman of the law), but you can always apply to be on the show . . . if you are getting divorced and at least 18 years of age (but, really, should you have gotten married if you're that young?!) and looking for a cheap way to do it. After all, California can be one of the costliest states to get divorced in; property gets divided up 50/50 here. Fill out the online form and let Judge Toler decide.

Dr. Phil
Paramount Studios
860 N. Gower St. (between Willoughby and Gregory), Hollywood
(323) 461-7445
www.drphil.com

"Get real" with Dr. Phil and let him help you get your life back on track. Dr. Phil rose to fame on the tails of Oprah before launching his own solo career as a talk show host. He does have a Ph.D. in psychology, so at least his insistence that we all "get real" comes from a legitimate place, which is saying a lot . . . in Hollywood. *Dr. Phil,* when in season August through December and January through May, tapes two shows per day on Monday, Tuesday, and Wednesday. You will arrive between 8 and 8:15 a.m., and finish at approximately 1 p.m. Go to his website to request reservations. A member of the audience department will contact you to confirm the date you requested. You can also phone the above number and leave your information, and someone will get back to you. Tickets limited to 4 per person. Must be 18 years of age or older. If the show topic relates to those who are 16 or 17, you can attend with a legal parent or guardian and valid copy of your birth certificate. Street parking only—check signs!

The Ellen DeGeneres Show
4000 Warner Blvd. (at W. Olive Ave.), Burbank
(818) 954-6000
www.ellentv.com

She dances to music and gets her audience on their feet, she dances away from talk of politics, and she dances her way into your heart as she charms celebrities and personalities in her quirky manner. Go to this Emmy winner's website and click on "tickets" to submit a request, and you will be contacted directly by a representative from the audience booking department. Must be 14 years of age or older and can only attend one taping per season. You can also call (818) 954-5929 to check the availability of the limited number of last-minute day-of tickets being released.

Jimmy Kimmel Live
El Capitan Entertainment Center
6838 Hollywood Blvd. (just past Highland Ave.), Los Angeles
(866) JIMMY-TIX (Mon through Fri, 1 to 4 p.m. PST)

Funny man and Emmy winner Jimmy Kimmel tapes his show live at 7:45 p.m., straight from Hollywood Boulevard in the heart of LA's Walk of Fame. Watch Jimmy cozy up to the Hollywood elite in his signature quick-wit style and hear some of the hottest bands today live. Visit www.1iota.com for tickets. Call the number above if you have trouble requesting tickets online. Must be 18 years of age or older.

Judge Joe Brown
Hollywood Center Studios
1040 N. Las Palmas St. (between Melrose and Santa Monica Blvd.), Hollywood
www.judgejoebrown.com

Why do they do these shows? Because they are cheap to produce. All you need is one dynamic judge, and Judge Joe Brown always delivers. Snag a ticket to a taping via www.hollywoodtickets.com, or submit an application

How One Abbreviation (TV) Ended Up in Another (LA)

"Hollywood," the name, is only a little over 120 years old. Nestled against green hills baking in the California sun, the famous white lettered sign has become a symbol of the entertainment industry and the stars themselves that stud our movies, television, and tabloid magazine covers. When originally erected in 1923, the sign read "Hollywoodland," to advertise a new housing development in the hills, and was wired with tiny incandescents that were later sold for scrap during the Depression. Except for a few brief temporary lightings during sign rehabs in 1973 and 1978, the Olympics in 1984, and for one night to shoo in Y2K, the sign remains dark so as not to attract nighttime tourists. From 1923 on, the sign was subjected to deterioration, and in 1949 the Hollywood Chamber of Commerce stepped in and offered to remove the last four letters and repair the rest. It did so, and promptly trademarked the shape of those letters that we now see on T-shirts and souvenirs around the world.

In the early 20th century, New York and New Jersey motion picture production companies headed west for the reliable, sunny weather that works better with film. Of course, electricity and the light bulb were already invented ("Are you smarter than a 5th grader?" I ask), but the electric lights that existed at the time were not powerful enough to expose film, so the best solution was sunlight, something Southern California had in abundance. Additionally, California had a lot of natural, wide open spaces and scenery that would serve as great filming locations. Plus, in addition to being coined the inventor of

online to see if he'll deliver a verdict on air for your case. Maybe you'll get lucky and get someone like the judge I was once assigned for a speeding ticket. He took one look at me, banged his gavel, bellowed, "Merry Christmas!", and then dismissed the ticket.

the modern light bulb, Thomas Edison had also invented the motion picture camera and was pretty darn strict about his patents. Thank- ination of travel between the coasts not being at the y and Edison being based in New Jersey left folks in business better able to escape patent enforcement n thing.

h is credited with shooting the first movie ever shot *In Old California,* a melodrama about Latino/Mexican- rnia in the 1800s. (And you thought the immigration nething new.) Griffith went on to make several more films in Hollywood, unencumbered by bad weather. Word spread, and the entire motion picture industry flocked west. The first studio was built in 1909, and soon Cecil B. DeMille in 1913 and Charlie Chaplin in 1917 had their own studios as well.

The years 1927 to 1948 were considered the "Golden Age" of the Hollywood studio system, which ended when the United States Supreme Court decided movie studios could not own theaters and play only movies produced by their studios with their stars. (Thank you, United States Supreme Court and your ruling to prevent Hollywood monopolization.) Television, to which Groucho Marx once remarked, "I find television to be very educating. Every time somebody turns on the set, I go to the other room and read a book," and David Frost quipped, "Television is an invention that permits you to be entertained in your living room by people you wouldn't have in your home," became the dominant form of entertainment in America by the late 1950s.

Judge Judy
Hollywood Center Studios
1040 N. Las Palmas St. (between Melrose and Santa Monica Blvd.), Hollywood
(888) 800-JUDY (5839)
www.judgejudy.com

Judge Judy has 52 taping days a year. If you have a bone to pick and want her to solve it for you (and not mince any words), fill out the online form.

Judge Karen's Court

Los Angeles Center Studios
1201 W. 5th St. (at S. Bixel Street), Downtown Los Angeles
www.judgekarenscourttv.com

"Stay in your lane," says Judge Karen, repeating her favorite motto time and again to those unfortunate enough to pass in front of her bench. No, she's not referring to your driving on the freeway; she's using traffic metaphors as life lessons. She tells it like it is and wants you to clean up your act. She's a big advocate for family issues, women, and children. Information on the release of tickets for *Judge Karen* morning and afternoon tapings can be found by calling the audience hotline or e-mailing JKCAudience@gmail .com.

Late Late Show with Craig Ferguson

CBS Television City
7800 Beverly Blvd. (at N. Fairfax Ave.), Los Angeles
(323) 570-0059
www.cbs.com/late_night/late_late_show

Described as late night's "best monologue," Emmy-nominated Ferguson does boast a lilting Scottish accent that no other unscripted late night talk show host can lay claim to. Go to www.1iota.com or dial the above number to get tickets.

Lopez Tonight

Warner Bros. Studios
4000 Warner Blvd. (at W. Olive Ave.), Burbank
(818) 954-4101
www.lopeztonight.com

Visit the website above and click on "tickets" to submit a request for the month and date you would like to attend. Allow 2 to 3 weeks lead time. A representative from the audience department will contact you. Standby tickets can be obtained by calling the number above for day-of tickets. Be sure to call before noon PST. Must be 18 years of age or older.

Real Time with Bill Maher

CBS Television City
7800 Beverly Blvd. (at N. Fairfax Ave.), Los Angeles
www.hbo.com/real-time-with-bill-maher

Attend a dress rehearsal of *Real Time with Bill Maher* and watch him work his jokes and hone their delivery to perfection in the perfect blend of cutting edge cynicism fused with current events and politics. A proponent of "New Rules," Bill's dress rehearsal typically lasts about 1.5 hours. Obtain tickets by visiting www.tvtix.com or www.hollywoodtickets.com. Must be 18 or older.

The Tonight Show with Jay Leno
3000 W. Alameda Ave. (near Bob Hope Dr.), Burbank
www.nbc.com/the-tonight-show/tickets

See one of the late night heavyweights entertain America, sweet talk the biggest stars, and showcase musical giants. Go to the website above to fill out an online form with your preferred attendance date and three alternatives. Give yourself a 4- to 6-week lead time. Must be 16 years of age or older. If you're feeling particularly lucky, you can go to the box office for day-of taping tickets. Box office opens at 8 a.m., and the line starts earlier than that. Tickets limited to 2 per person.

GAME **SHOWS**

Are You Smarter Than a 5th Grader?
Sony Pictures Studios
10202 W. Washington Blvd. (near Madison Ave.), Culver City
www.5thgradertvshow.com

Hopefully the answer to the question posed by the title of this show is a resounding "yes," but if you go to a live taping, you may be newly humbled into appreciating America's prepubescent youth. Favorite redneck Jeff Foxworthy hosts, as one adult is pitted against five 10-year-olds, in a battle of knowledge over subjects said adult has already been taught, ranging from music to social studies. Get tickets by going to www.ocatv.com. Groups of 20 or more can attend the show as a fund-raiser and earn money for your group by e-mailing groups@ocatv.com.

Jeopardy!
PO Box 3763, Hollywood, CA 90028
www.jeopardy.com

Before there was life on earth, there was Alex Trebek. To catch the show that popularized responses with an upward inflection, visit www.tvtix.com to get free tickets. Must be 10 years of age or older. You can also write to the PO Box address above, but getting them online will be much faster. If you are brilliantly brainy, you can visit the official website and take the test to find out if you have what it takes to become a contestant.

Let's Make a Deal
Sunset Bronson Studios
5800 W. Sunset Blvd. (at Van Ness Ave.), Hollywood
(888) 706-8767
www.cbs.com/daytime/lets_make_a_deal

Drew Carey's old *Whose Line Is It Anyway?* improv partner-in-crime, Wayne Brady, hosts this iconic classic television game show from the 1960s and '70s. The show has been revamped for modern times, and all studio audience members, who have a 1 in 18 chance of also being a contestant, wear costumes. Visit the website and click on "tickets" for information on the show and ticketing. You will be directed to On Camera Audiences at www.ocatv .com. Groups of 20 or more should e-mail groupbooking@ocatv.com.

The Price Is Right
7800 Beverly Blvd. (at N. Fairfax Ave.), Los Angeles
(800) 852-8909
www.cbs.com/daytime/the_price_is_right

Drew Carey gave this longest-running game show a face-lift into the 21st century when Bob Barker retired, and the daytime game show sensation continues to thrill contestants and audiences of all ages. When in season, *The Price Is Right* tapes two shows per afternoon. Visit the official website and click on "Tickets" for more information on the taping schedule, how to get tickets online, via mail, or at the ticket booth. Must be 18 or older. *The Price Is Right* tapes on the CBS Lot, but you'll have to pay to park at The Grove Shopping Center down the block. Groups should call Guest Relations at (323) 575-2448 Mon through Fri 9 a.m. to 5 p.m. for tickets.

Plain Old Boob Tube Tapings

Um, this is a guidebook. By its very nature it contains the most up-to-date information possible on what to see, what to do, and where to go in Los Angeles. With regards to television show tapings, well, the fact of the matter is that not every sitcom is *Cheers* or *Friends*, meaning they don't all stay on the air forever and ever, and sometimes only for the blink of an eye. Tried and true, seasoned talk shows, game shows, or cheaply produced reality/competition shows that have been around for a while are more likely to stick around. Television shows? I could list them all here and then get hate mail when this book is published that I led you astray. While I consider my character pretty strong, I don't want to risk pissing you off—I mean, we're still at the beginning of this book and I've got a lot of great topics to cover. So if you're looking at these lists and you're whining out loud, "But I wanted to see a sitcom!", I've included a few handy tips and general guiding principles just for you.

Best websites to get free tickets:

Audience Associates is, you guessed it, great free TV taping fun! Visit www.tvtix.com.

Audiences Unlimited offers free tickets to tapings at a wide variety of shows, including those on ABC, CBS, NBC, and Fox. Visit www.audiencesunlimited.com or www.tvtickets.com. Both links point to the same website.

Hollywood Tickets lets you select the show you want to see from the drop-down list on their homepage. Visit www.hollywoodtickets.com.

On Camera Audiences lets you select the show you want to see from their menu on the left. Visit www.ocatv.com.

A great way to search for which television shows tape where and how to get tickets to see them:

Seeing Stars, "the ultimate guide to celebrities and Hollywood," provides detailed information on how to get tickets to tapings at the various television studios, such as CBS, Paramount, and NBC. It is also chock-full of fun facts and figures on everything under the stars. (Get it?!) Visit www.seeing-stars.com.

Wheel of Fortune

Sony Pictures Studios
10202 W. Washington Blvd. (near Madison Ave.), Culver City
www.wheeloffortuneinfo.com

This 25-plus-year-old institution of spinning the wheel in a game of word search meets big puzzle board features Pat Sajak as the host and Vanna White as the letter-turning spokesmodel. (Though now, since it's 2011, she doesn't turn the letters, she simply points at them and they magically "zap" on.) Tickets and information on how to audition to become a contestant (18 or older) can be found on their website. Because, let's face it—you want to win big so you no longer have to be a cheap bastard, and then maybe you'll be able to afford a more expensive guidebook about how to live large in Los Angeles. If you do win it big, since you learned all about how to be a contestant from me, maybe you can treat me to a nice dinner? I also like gift certificates for massages.

REALITY & **TALENT** SHOWS

America's Got Talent

Redondo Beach Performing Arts Center
1935 Manhattan Beach Blvd. (at N. Aviation Blvd.), Redondo Beach
www.nbc.com/americas-got-talent

Gosh, let's hope (America's got talent). Join host Nick Cannon (the dude married to Mariah Carey), and celebrity judges as they watch competitors showcase their dancing, singing, magic, comedy, and more. The show tapes in Redondo Beach, so it's a bit farther out than the other selections. Drive there in a VW van and you can feel like you're reenacting a scene from *Little Miss Sunshine*. The British version of this competition brought the world Susan Boyle. What the American version brings the world is yet to be seen. Check it out live and judge for yourself. A search for tickets will direct you to www.hollywoodtickets.com.

American Idol
7800 Beverly Blvd. (at N. Fairfax Ave.), Los Angeles
www.americanidol.com

Ha! Are you kidding? Not so easy to get tickets. The show is very popular,
but they do love their fans. Put your name on that online waiting list at
www.ocatv.com. *American Idol* is standing room only.

Dancing with the Stars
7800 Beverly Blvd. (at N. Fairfax Ave.), Los Angeles
http://abc.go.com/shows/dancing-with-the-stars

DWTS is also a popular show! Head on over to that online waiting list at
www.ocatv.com. If you do score tickets and happen to have an extra one,
please let me know. My mom would love to join you. You'll enjoy her company. She's very sweet.

So You Think You Can Dance
CBS Television City
7800 Beverly Blvd. (at N. Fairfax Ave.), Los Angeles
www.fox.com/dance

Cat Deeley hosts hip-hop, salsa, quickstep, jive, and all sorts of other dancers as they compete for the title of "America's Favorite Dancer." As this is
a very popular show, you must put your name on an online waiting list at
www.ocatv.com.

FILM:
CHEAP SCREENINGS

"A good film is when the price of the dinner, the theatre admission, and the babysitter were worth it."

—ALFRED HITCHCOCK

Ahhh, the movies. Isn't the phrase "the movies" practically interchangeable with Los Angeles itself? Nearly everyone in this town works in the business, so there are a number of devoted moviegoers out there keeping tabs on what their competitors are churning out and seeing every movie they can in their spare time. It's easy to keep up with the moviegoing Joneses. Whether it's a cheap seat you're on the lookout for, an outdoor summer screening, or the insider track to the film industry you'd love to be in the know about, there is something to suit your taste, interest, and budget. Popcorn not included.

FILM **FESTIVAL** VOLUNTEERING

The film world has become saturated with film festivals in the past 10 to 15 years. Why? Because film festivals are an excellent source of revenue, bringing hotels and restaurants dollars as a city or community hosts several days or a week of events, screenings, and panels. A lot of the festivals in Los Angeles aren't always entirely independent film focused, for they know that if they screen a studio picture or one with a big star in it, it will bring them attention. Eh, it pretty much boils down to opportunity, capitalism, and just plain business. There are still plenty of fantastic films out there that you might not ever get to see if you don't explore the film festival circuit. It will change the way you appreciate films and help you understand the blood, sweat, tears, and years it takes to make a movie. A lot of these film festivals rely on volunteers to help run the show. That's where you enter the picture.

Beverly Hills Film Festival (BHFF)
9663 Santa Monica Blvd., Suite 777, Beverly Hills
(310) 779-1206
www.beverlyhillsfilmfestival.com

The BHFF welcomes some 20,000 attendees for 5 days every April. They are dedicated to independent and emerging filmmakers, but certainly have their share of poolside celebrity panels, special events, seminars, VIP parties, and deal making. Call the number above to get in on the action.

Bicycle Film Festival (BFF)

www.bicyclefilmfestival.com

The BFF in this case is not your "best friend forever," but the Bicycle Film Festival, started as a platform "to celebrate the bicycle through music, art, and, of course, film." By far, this is one of the more unique niche film festivals around. E-mail volunteer@bicyclefilmfestival.com.

Hollywood Film Festival (HFF)

433 N. Camden Dr., Suite 600, Beverly Hills
(310) 288-1882
www.hollywoodawards.com

The HFF runs the gamut from big movies to the little indie engine that could. It is held every year in October. E-mail info@hollywoodawards.com to inquire about volunteer opportunities that match your particular area of interest.

Indian Film Festival (IFFLA)

5225 Wilshire Blvd., Suite 417, Los Angeles
(310) 988-2602
www.indianfilmfestival.org

If Bollywood or Indian films have you hankering for vegetable samosas and eyeing that miniature replica of the Taj Mahal with great longing, The Indian Film Festival could use your enthusiasm. Held at the beautiful Arclight Cinema in Hollywood every April, The Indian Film Festival features programming of narrative and nonnarrative features to support the growing interest in the burgeoning Indian entertainment industry, one of the largest in the world. Call the office number listed above for volunteer opportunities.

Israel Film Festival (IFFLA)

6404 Wilshire Blvd., Suite 1030, Los Angeles
(323) 966-4166
www.israelfilmfestival.com

Held for 2 weeks at the end of October/beginning of November in Los Angeles each year, the IFFLA promises dynamic interaction with filmmakers and people from around the world, not to mention free movie screenings. The IFFLA premieres Israeli features, documentaries, television dramas, and student shorts. It is also held in Miami and New York. E-mail volunteer@israelfilmfestival.org.

Make Friends with Three Letters

If you want to see some of the hottest blockbuster and independent films before they're even released, then it's high time you made good friends with some of your fellow Los Angelenos who have three letters behind their names: **SAG** (Screen Actors Guild), **WGA** (Writers Guild of America), **DGA** (Directors Guild of America), or **PGA** (Producers Guild of America, not the golf championship—though Tiger Woods does provide plenty of entertainment). These unions regularly host private free screenings that feature a talkback session with the producer, director, actors, or writers themselves, and often that union member will have an opportunity to squeeze in a plus one (+1) for the screening and Q&A. Come awards season, if you're a good enough friend, you can watch the latest and hottest movies for free from the comfort of your friend's home as he or she rifles through all of the free DVD screeners of the award-nominated films that come through the mail. You're personable, charming, and capable of holding intelligent conversation—is there any reason why you shouldn't be at the top of the preferred movie-watching companion list?

LA Shorts Fest
http://lashortsfest.com

Great filmmakers have to start somewhere, and they usually start with a short film. See them here before they become famous. Short films are especially great for those of you with short attention spans. Yes, I'm talking to you. Put down that BlackBerry. LA Shorts Fest needs volunteers and interns 12 months of the year, and not just during the weeklong festival in July. E-mail volunteer@lashortsfest.com.

Los Angeles Asian Pacific Film Festival
http://asianfilmfestla.org

The Los Angeles Asian Pacific Film Festival promotes Asian and Asian Pacific American cinema. The festival runs for 10 days at the end of April/beginning of May each year. E-mail volunteer@vconline.org.

Los Angeles Film Festival
9911 W. Pico Blvd., Los Angeles
(310) 432-1240
www.lafilmfest.com

Nearly 20 years old and held every June, the Los Angeles Film Festival presents some 200 feature films, shorts, and music videos from around the world, including some premieres of Hollywood big-budget films. Call the office at the number above to inquire after volunteer opportunities.

Los Angeles Latino International Film Festival
1512 N. Las Palmas Ave., Hollywood
www.latinofilm.org

The Los Angeles Latino International Film Festival is part of the Latino International Film Institute. Every August, the festival presents films, documentaries, and shorts with a wide variety of themes by Latino filmmakers, producers, actors, and writers in a competitive environment. E-mail volunteer coordinator@latinofilm.org to see how you can get in on the action.

Newport Beach Film Festival
4540 Campus Dr., Newport Beach
www.newportbeachfilmfest.com

Eight days of screenings, galas, and events means a lot of volunteer opportunities for you every April. E-mail volunteers@newportbeachfilmfest.com or sign up online.

Old Pasadena Film Festival
Downtown Pasadena
(626) 356-9725
www.oldpasadena.org

The American Cinematheque sponsors this free 3-week movie series that takes place on weekends in July in basements, on walls, in courtyards, shops, and theaters throughout Pasadena's picturesque downtown. All screenings, events, and appearances are completely free. Call the number above sometime in May to sign up!

Palm Springs International Film Festival (PSIFF)
1700 E. Tahquitz Canyon Way, Suite 3, Palm Springs
www.psfilmfest.org

Assist in the theaters, work in the festival office, sell merchandise, help with special events, transport guests, count ballots, and organize credentials as a volunteer with the Palm Springs International Film Festival, held each January. The Shortfest is held in June. PSIFF also hires May/June and December/ January interns. Register online and get ready for those celebrity sightings!

The Pan African Film & Arts Festival (PAFF)
6820 La Tijera Blvd., Suite 200, Los Angeles
(310) 337-4737
www.paff.org

For nearly 20 years, The Pan African Film & Arts Festival has been dedicated to the promotion of cultural and racial tolerance through the exhibition of film, art, and creative expression. Each year in Los Angeles, Atlanta, and Africa, the PAFF presents some 100 films from the United States, Africa, the Caribbean, Latin America, Europe, the South Pacific, and Canada, all showing the diversity and complexity of people of African descent. You may catch a glimpse of such luminaries as Jamie Foxx, Forest Whitaker, Halle Berry, or Tyler Perry. Fill out the volunteer application online in December to be part of the February event in Los Angeles.

The Polish Film Festival
www.polishfilmla.org

For over 10 years every October, The Polish Film Festival has been offering pickled radishes, borscht, pierogi, and films. E-mail info@polishfilmla.org for more information.

Silver Lake Film Festival
2658 Griffith Park Blvd., #389, Los Angeles
(323) 660-1935
www.silverlakefilmfestival.org

Just a little over a decade old and held in April each year, the Silver Lake Film Festival is a non-genre film festival for independent narrative features and documentaries and short films. E-mail info@silverlakefilmfestival.org to volunteer and support independent film, arts, and music.

Central Casting: Be an Extra!

Think the movies are so glamorous that you're just dying to be in one? Being an extra takes a willing, reliable, and professional attitude, as well as a great ability to listen well and take direction when given the first time. (Example: "Cross behind him when I say 'Action!' and greet this woman here like she's your friend you haven't seen in a while.") It is a fairly thankless, but very important job. Think about all the people you see in the background on television and in movies. You don't see them. That's the whole point. What they are doing behind the principal actors and main action is so realistic and natural that you bought and believed it all hook, line, and sinker. On the days you report to set, you will usually be required to bring a few wardrobe options from which the costume designer can choose; if the scene is a period piece or has special wardrobe design needs, they will provide you with what you need.

To be both correct and respectful, the appropriate term is "background" for a movie, as opposed to the slightly more degrading term "extra." To get started, call the registration information line of **Central Casting** (220 S. Flower St., Burbank, CA; www.centralcasting.com) at (818) 562-2755. Central Casting accepts both SAG and AFTRA talent, as well as non-union talent. While there are several agencies with which you can sign up, Central Casting is the best and will have the most opportunities in both film and television. They'll have you bring two forms of I-9 identification, along with a headshot and resume in

Vietnamese International Film Festival (VIFF)
14772 Moran St., Westminster
(714) 893-6145
www.vietfilmfest.com

Try your hand at PR, Guest Relations, Translation, Operations, or the Gala when you volunteer for the VIFF, held for 8 days each April. Visit the website to sign up.

person if you have one. No worries if you don't have a picture; they can take a snapshot right then and there.

Spending time on a real movie or television set is great fun and a wonderful learning experience; you'll find it's not quite as effortless as it seems and you may have some long 10- and 12-plus-hour days. If you're lucky enough, you'll get to see some of the major stars act. One 1-minute scene can take an entire day to shoot, as the crew does the master shot, close-ups, medium shot reverse shot, and any inserts (of props critical to the scene; a letter or gun, for example). You may also find yourself surrounded by interesting people who make their living doing background work. Note: "Interesting" in this case should be translated as "weird," but is obviously subject to individual interpretation.

You will, however, finally get to say you were in the movies and look at those people crossing in frame behind your favorite stars on the big screen with a newfound respect and admiration. If you're unemployed and in between jobs, background work can be a great way to make some cash if collecting unemployment is not an option for you. If you are non-union and work enough times on SAG films where they hand out waivers, though, you'll have to join eventually, and that's a big dent in your budget, so be sure to specify what type of background work you are interested in doing when you sign up with Central Casting. Park on the street and not in the lot. If you get towed, they won't be hiring you.

BARGAIN **FLICKS**

When I say bargain, I mean under $10 for the most part, because let's get real here, movies these days can be expensive. Read on to find out where you can pay less.

American Cinematheque
Egyptian Theatre
Hollywood: Egyptian Theatre, 6712 Hollywood Blvd.; (323) 461-2020
Santa Monica: Aero Theatre, 1328 Montana Ave.; (323) 466-3456
www.americancinematheque.com

With 616 seats, state-of-the-art projection and sound, comprehensive and diverse programming of classic and new movies, indie and mega-budget films, as well as many live Q&A sessions with famous directors and actors, the experience at Grauman's Egyptian Theatre is an unparalleled moviegoing adventure and worth all $11, which is still less expensive than some of the other joints in town. Seniors and students pay just $9. Are you really passionate about movies? Become a member, and enjoy $7 admission fees plus a host of other perks, including 2 free admissions in your birthday month. The Aero location is less grandiose and much more intimate, located in très chic Santa Monica, yet equally stimulating in its cinematic programming.

Culver Plaza Theatres
9919 Washington Blvd. (between Hughes Ave. and Dunn Dr.), Culver City
(310) 836-5516
www.culverplazatheatres.com

For $7 general admission, $5 matinees for all shows before 5 p.m., and $4.50 all day for children and seniors, catching a flick at Culver Plaza Theatres is a bargain. Pair the admission price with a $1.50 Eisenberg all-beef hot dog at the concession stand, or great budget-friendly dining options within walking distance of the theater, and you've got a night out for the record books.

Echo Park Film Center
1200 N. Alvarado St. (near Elsinore St.), Los Angeles
(213) 484-8846
www.echoparkfilmcenter.org

A 60-seat theater features indie, experimental, and documentary film and video from around the world. Thursday night screenings are just $5.

Flagship Theatres: University Village 3
3323 S. Hoover St. (at Jefferson), Los Angeles
(213) 748-6321
www.flagshipmovies.com

Located across the street from the University of Southern California campus, University Village 3 has $7 general admission, $4.50 matinees for all, and $5 screenings for USC students with photo ID at all times. Concession stand prices are lower than usual, and Flagship features "Cool Weekend Late Shows" with crowd-pleasing movies such as *A Clockwork Orange, Best in Show,* and *The Exorcist.* Flagship is also committed to making sure foster families are able to partake in the moviegoing experience. This is a movie theater with heart—how can you not give it a shot?

Highland Theatres
5604 N. Figueroa St. (between N. Avenues 56 and 57), Los Angeles
(323) 256-6383
www.highlandtheatres.com

Two mottos you've got to love: "The Best Price for First Run Movies Anywhere" and "Free Refills on Large Popcorn and Drinks." $6 for adults, bargain matinees for shows before 6 p.m., $4 for children and senior citizens, and $3 Tuesday and Wednesday family discount day all day. Need I say more?

Laemmle Theatres
www.laemmle.com

For the tasteful cheap bastard in you, Laemmle Theatres have offered up the best art house films since 1938. Sign up for the Sneak Preview Club and receive alerts on free screenings, check out Student Sunday Nights for $7 movies and discounts on popcorn, Senior Wednesdays for $4.50 movies after 6 p.m., and New Deal Tuesdays for $7 screenings all day. Purchase of the premiere card will get you $2 off your tickets Mon through Thurs, $1 off tickets Fri through Sun, and 20 percent off all concessions, as well as free popcorn on Thursday. Discounts and deals may change over time, so check website for the most current information. With locations in Beverly Hills (Music Hall 3, 9036 Wilshire Blvd.; 310-478-3836), Encino (Town Center 5, 17200 Ventura Blvd.; 818-981-9811), Pasadena (Playhouse 7, 673 E. Colorado Blvd.; 626-844-6500), Santa Monica (Monica 4-Plex, 1332 2nd St.; 310-478-3836), West Hills (Claremont 5, 6731 Fallbrook Ave.; 818-340-8710), West Hollywood (Sunset 5, 8000 Sunset Blvd.; 310-478-3836), and West Los Angeles (Royal Theatre, 11532 Santa Monica Blvd.; 310-478-3836), there's bound to be one near you!

Landmark Theatres

West Los Angeles: The Landmark, 10850 W. Pico Blvd. (at Westwood Blvd.)
West Los Angeles: Nuart Theatre, 11272 Santa Monica Blvd. (just off the 405)
Westwood: Regent Theatre, 1045 Broxton Ave. (between Weyburn and Kinross)
(310) 281-8223
www.landmarktheatres.com

There are three Landmark Theatres in Los Angeles and the Nuart and Regent offer the best bargain with $8 matinees on all shows before 6 p.m. Mon through Fri and the first screening of the day on Sat and Sun. Seniors and children under 12 are just $8 all the time, and students can tack on another 50 cents to that $8. A Landmark Theatre experience is as traditional and high quality as they come. In the event you are traveling, Landmark Theatres are also located in other major US cities.

Regency Theatre

1003 E. Colorado Blvd. (at N. Catalina Ave.), Pasadena
(626) 229-9400
www.regencymovies.com

Regency Theatres play all the latest and greatest Hollywood new releases. With a $2 admission fee for films starting before and at 6 p.m., $3 evening admission prices, and $8 Saturday midnight screenings, it's clear the Regency Theatre is a movie theater for the times. There are many Regency Theatres located throughout the greater Los Angeles area offering great matinee and senior discounts, but none giving you quite the value for your dollar that this location in Pasadena does. Check website for details. Slide those George Washingtons across the counter and support this theater so they are encouraged to keep on truckin'!

Vista Theatre

4473 Sunset Dr. (at Hollywood Blvd.), Los Angeles
(323) 660-6639

This Los Angeles staple located in the trendy Los Feliz neighborhood shows just one movie at a time, ranging from indies to the big blockbusters. Arrive early to park and greet the massive Egyptian pharaohs flanking the entrance on your way in. Just $6.50 for movie screenings prior to 6 p.m., and $9 for evening shows. Great leg room for Tall Tims and Tanyas everywhere.

Bargains on the Web

On **Craigslist** you can search "free movies" and "events." Scroll through the riff-raff for the good free movie screening opportunities and snatch them up! At www.craigslist.org.

Film Metro is a great website on free promotional screenings listed by city in the United States. Visit www.filmmetro.com.

Free-Flix allows you to watch free movies online without giving a thought to what you're wearing or where you are going to park the car. Visit www.free-flix.com.

Movie2k.to allows you to download and watch newly released movies for free. However, they're not in HD, so the quality is less than stellar. Sort of like watching a movie after you take your contact lenses out. Steer clear of anything rated less than a smiley face and you'll be fine. At www.movie2k.to.

Volition's claim to fame is that they are the "oldest free stuff site on the Internet." Click through a variety of categories to see what strikes your whimsy, one of which is their "Advance Movie Screening Promo," where you can sign up to join their "Movies" mailing list. Online at www.volition.com.

FANCY **SCHMANCY** SCREENINGS

Los Angeles County Museum of Art
5905 Wilshire Blvd., Los Angeles
(323) 857-6010
www.lacma.org

The LACMA has a popular film series and special screenings, as well as retrospectives on legendary film directors such as Ingmar Bergman. Check website for details and purchase tickets online or by calling the box office number above. Screenings tend to sell out, so plan in advance! $10 for general admission; $7 for museum members, students or seniors with photo ID; $5 for the second film in a double feature; $2 Tues matinee, $1 for seniors over 62.

The Old Town Music Hall

140 Richmond St. (at W. Franklin Ave.), El Segundo
(310) 322-2592
http://oldtownmusichall.wordpress.com

Devoted to showing classic silent films in an authentic 1920s movie house with the Mighty Wurlitzer accompanying since 1968, you won't find a theater like this anywhere else. Catch Charlie Chaplin, Mary Pickford, Lillian Gish, and more as they float across the screen in black and white. The Old Town Music Hall also shows other classic films and features live concerts. Admission is only $8 to movie screenings on Fri at 8:15 p.m., Sat at 2:30 and 8:15 p.m., and Sun at 2:30 p.m.

OUTDOOR **MOVIEGOING**

It's LA. The weather is pretty much always fabulous. When it's not, they address it like a national crisis on CNN. All odds considered, the weather for your summer outdoor screening is going to be sublime. Plan on it. A movie under the smog covered stars of Los Angeles is a great summer treat.

Hollywood Forever Cemetery

6000 Santa Monica Blvd., Los Angeles
(323) 469-1181

The Catch: There is a suggested donation of $10. Still, you're outdoors, watching a movie in a cemetery where famous people are buried. You can fork it over for this unique experience. Oh, and parking on the cemetery grounds is $5.

The Hollywood Forever Cemetery has a screening series every summer. A live DJ spins music before and after, turning this scene into a party, if you care to join. Recent screenings included *The Wizard of Oz* and *Night of the Living Dead,* so they do cover a wide range of the film canon. Picnics, pillows, and blankets encouraged; excessive frowning on tall chairs, and no barbecues. Check www.cinespia.org for details.

Moonlight Movies on the Beach
Alfredo's Beach Club
5411 Ocean Blvd., Long Beach
(562) 477-6820
www.alfredosbeachclub.com

On Tuesday, Wednesday, and Thursday in July and August every summer, Alfredo's Beach Club brings you free moonlight movies on the beach. Recent summer screenings included *Grease, Ghostbusters, Ferris Bueller's Day Off, American Graffiti,* and *Shrek.*

Universal CityWalk
100 Universal City Plaza (Universal Center Dr. from the Hollywood Freeway exit)
Universal City
(818) 622-4455
www.citywalkhollywood.com

This faux man-made manufactured construction of a street outside of Universal Studios in Hollywood was originally built in 1993 to encourage foot traffic between the theme park and the movie theater. Colorful and larger than life, you can imagine that it has worked out quite well. There are plenty of stores, restaurants, and minor celeb sightings here and there to keep your attention, but the cheapest thing you can do is attend the fun and free outdoor movie screenings they sponsor every summer. Check website for listings.

Warner Center Park (Warner Ranch Park)
5800 Topanga Canyon Blvd., Woodland Hills
(877) 704-FILM (3456)
www.valleycultural.org

Kick back, relax, and watch a free flick surrounded by the natural beauty of Warner Center Park in Woodland Hills at "Movies on the Green" on Saturday evenings in July and August. Bring your blankets and lawn chairs and delight in the 30-foot professional theatrical screen, watching movies like *Sleepless in Seattle, Butch Cassidy and the Sundance Kid,* and *Field of Dreams.* Parking is $8 per vehicle.

Westfield Century City Mall

10250 Santa Monica Blvd. (at Avenue of the Stars), Los Angeles
(310) 277-3898
http://westfield.com

Skip the shopping at the stores and the major cineplex and opt instead for free movies at sunset every Wednesday evening on the terrace June through September. Recent screenings have included *School of Rock, My Big Fat Greek Wedding,* and *Sixteen Candles.*

COMEDY:
BELLY LAUGHS

"Tragedy is when I cut my finger. Comedy is when you fall into an open sewer and die."

—MEL BROOKS

Jokes, comedy—it's a tough business. Props to the guy or gal who can deliver, 'cuz it ain't easy. Ever been at a party when someone says, "I heard you're funny. Say something funny!"? Uh-huh. You get up there and give it a try. What's that? That's right, I didn't think so. Los Angeles has got some of the best comedy in the country, and a lot of it is free or cheap! Woo-hoo! Amateur and pro comedians usually flock to Los Angeles at some point to tour or test out their material, so take advantage peoples!

COMEDY **CLUBS**

The Comedy & Magic Club
1018 Hermosa Ave. (just past 10th St.), Hermosa Beach
(310) 372-1193
www.comedyandmagicclub.com

On Friday nights you can see 10 Comics for $10. I don't know about you, but that is 2.2 comics per the price of a load of laundry for me. Jay Leno on Sun at 7 p.m. is the big show for $30, but he has to charge so much in order to afford his classic car collection hobby. Because Jay Leno lends his name to this club, you get some of the best in the business, and their tickets usually average $15.

The Comedy Store
8433 Sunset Blvd., Los Angeles
(323) 650-6268
www.thecomedystore.com

The Catch: In general, the shows are free, but there's a 2-drink minimum, with drinks ranging from $6 to $10. Hey, you're on Sunset Boulevard, so they're going to charge you rent just to stand there. However, you've got some of the best comics in the business performing here, so it's worth it.

When you pictured yourself watching comedy in LA, you pictured it here on the Sunset Strip. People like David Letterman and Jim Carrey honed their craft at The Comedy Store. Twenty-one and over, raw, uncut, and unfiltered, but polished. The 7 p.m. Monday night Comedy Store Potluck Show is free up until 9 p.m. Check website for details and call to make reservations. Famous comedians have been known to pop in and take the stage.

> *"My mother never breast-fed me.*
> *She told me she only liked me as a friend."*
> —RODNEY DANGERFIELD

Flapper's Comedy Club
102 E. Magnolia, Burbank
(818) 845-9721
www.flapperscomedy.com

The Catch: 2-drink minimum all around.

$2 Tuesday shows at 7:30 p.m. in the Burbank location. $10 shows in the Yoo Hoo Room (seating capacity 50) twice a night Wed through Sat, plus cheap dinner and drinks. Call ahead and see if they'll swing you 2 shows for the price of just one. Enjoy half-price drinks and appetizers with your comedy while watching the Happy Hour Auditions of local comedians from 5 to 7 p.m. on Wed and Fri. Appetizers range in price from $6 to $10, while entrees will run you $10 to $18, unless you order the filet mignon. Main Showroom seats 225 in Burbank, 100 at the Claremont location (532 W. First St.), which is BYOB with a $5 corkage fee.

iO West
6366 Hollywood Blvd. (near N. Cahuenga Blvd.), Los Angeles
(323) 962-7560
http://west.ioimprov.com

iO West has three main theaters—The Del Close Black Box Theatre (Andy Dick's Theatre), The Loft, and Mainstage. Monday's "Cage Match Omega" and Thursday's "Cage Match" at 11:30 p.m. on the Mainstage are free. In these shows, two teams compete against one another in an improv competition. Winner returns the following week to battle a new opposing team. All other shows range in price from $5 to $10 seven nights a week. Check the website or call. The Del Close Black Box Theatre has "DCT Fridays" at 11:30 p.m., where you can catch different Harold (improv) teams, "The One Hour Improv Festival" on Tues at 10:30 p.m., and "Comedy Lab Live" on Sun at 8:30 p.m., all free. iO West has an open mic on Sun at 10:30 p.m. and "Mystic Mondays" at 10:30 p.m., both free. $3 drink specials. All other Del Close shows are a whopping $5. All shows at The Loft are free. Did you just guffaw and pee in your pants?

The Laugh Factory
8001 Sunset Blvd., Hollywood
(323) 656-1336, ext. 1
www.laughfactory.com

The Catch: No free shows. General admission (first come, first served seating) is as high as $20. Valet is $7. Okay, so it's not cheap and it probably shouldn't be in this book, but they are one of the best places for comedy in LA, so I feel I should mention them on the off chance you get a big bonus at work and go on a little splurge; now you have some options! Just keeping you on your toes to make sure you're reading everything.

Come on, you know you've heard of The Laugh Factory before. What?! You haven't? Are you living in a bubble? Time to get up, get out of the house, and get some comedy into your life. Check the website for details on upcoming shows, and if you can't spring the cash, check out the online comedy videos because then you can laugh for free from the comfort of your own home and in your underwear, and not spend a dime. A second location is in Long Beach at 151 S. Pine St. (562-495-2844 ext. 1).

Spotlight Comedy Club
12215 Ventura Blvd. (at Laurel Canyon Blvd.), Suite 209, Studio City
(323) 377-5550
www.spotlightcomedyclub.com

Laughs in the Valley! Like, totally awesome! The Spotlight Comedy Club features hot, established comedians, as well as up-and-comers, and prides itself on being a throwback to the glory days of comedy with great service, food, and funny. Founder/showroom manager/comedian TK Matteson can be found behind the bar, greeting people at the door, and cracking people up onstage. $10 shows at 7:30 p.m. on Fri and Sat, 1 item minimum, free parking in the underground garage. Check website for details.

IMPROV & **SKETCH**

Ground Zero Performance Cafe
(in the Student Union building on USC's campus)
615 Child's Way (near Figueroa), Los Angeles
(213) 821-1484
www.usc.edu/gz

Part of the University of Southern California, Second Nature, an improv group, presents free improv every Friday at the Ground Zero Performance Cafe. Beverages will run you $1 a drink. Stick to free street parking down around Figueroa Road in order to keep your whole evening a cheap bastard's delight.

Hollywood Improv
8162 Melrose Ave. (between N. La Jolla Ave. and N. Kilkea Dr.), Los Angeles
(323) 651-2583
www.improv.com/ComedyClub/Hollywood

Open Mic on Tuesday at 5 p.m. is free. Sign-up for the comedians is from 4:30 to 4:40 p.m., and each comic gets 3 minutes. All other shows range in price from $7 to $28, with an average of $15. Two-drink minimum. Call and ask about shows, exercising all the phone manners you were taught as a child and explaining you are new in town, and you may score a place on the nonpaying guest list.

"I believe in equality. Equality for everybody.
No matter how stupid they are or how superior I am to them."
—STEVE MARTIN

Second City
6560 Hollywood Blvd. (between Whitley Ave. and Schrader Blvd.), Los Angeles
(323) 464-8542
www.secondcity.com

Chris Farley, Steve Carrell, and Tina Fey are among some of Hollywood's funniest who got their start with the original Second City in Chicago. In LA, you can catch improv, sketch comedy, and more for $5 to $10, or visit www.goldstar.com to purchase even cheaper tickets.

Upright Citizens Brigade Theatre
5919 Franklin Ave. (near N. Bronson Ave.), Hollywood
(323) 908-8702
www.ucbtheatre.com

Amy Poehler, Ian Roberts, Matt Besser, and Matt Walsh took their award-winning comedy sketch show, *The Upright Citizens Brigade,* from Chicago to NYC to perform in 1996. From their success, the UCB comedy training school and theater were born on both coasts. UCB offers some of the best stand-up, sketch, and improv shows 7 nights a week, ranging in price from free to $5 or $10. Check website for details. You can also see a slew of their free comedy videos at www.ucbcomedy.com.

> *"Do you think God gets stoned?*
> *I think so . . . look at the platypus."*
> —ROBIN WILLIAMS

OTHER **VENUES**

Banana Bungalow Hostel
5920 Hollywood Blvd., Hollywood
(323) 469-2500
www.bananabungalowus.com

The Catch: It's free, but the comedy is for guests only.

This is not your typical hostel—it's cute, trendy, and very 21st century with a billiard room, Tiki lounge, and bold-colored private and dorm-type rooms, depending on your needs. The Hollywood location is next door to the Palms Thai Restaurant, which features $5 lunches and $10 dinners. Call ahead to see which night you can catch the funny. The staff also offers great tips on other Los Angeles places to laugh yourself silly. Pros like Marlon Wayans and amateurs alike will tickle your funnybone. An additional location is in West Hollywood at 603 N. Fairfax Ave. (323-655-2002).

Bar Lubitsch
7702 Santa Monica Blvd. (near N. Stanley and N. Spaulding), West Hollywood
(323) 654-1234

Every Thurs at 8:30 p.m., Josh Haness and Josh Weinstein host "The Josh and Josh Show: Stand-up Comedy for Mankind Free of Charge," which presents an eclectic mix of comedians doing their best to make you crack a smile. How can you not love a title that tells you exactly what you are going to get? Twenty-one and over only. Free. Street parking.

"Charlie Brown is the one person I identify with. C.B. is such a loser. He wasn't even the star of his own Halloween special."
—CHRIS ROCK

Big Fish Bar & Grill
5230 San Fernando Rd. (at W. Wilson Ave.), Glendale
(818) 244-6442

Comedy every Tuesday at 9:30 p.m. for those 21 and over! You will see anywhere between 20 and 25 comedians per night. They also have live music and karaoke, but that's not what I'm supposed to talk about here. This is the comedy chapter. Big Fish Bar & Grill is a casual neighborhood bar.

Buchanan Arms Restaurant
2013 W. Burbank Blvd. (several blocks east of Buena Vista), Burbank
(818) 845-0692

The Catch: You pay for dinner, but the jokes will cost you nothing.

Free music and comedy on the first and third Wednesday of every month at 7:30 p.m. Musicians perform first, comedians after 9 p.m. This is a sports bar with English pub food as well, so if fish and chips or roast beef with Yorkshire pudding are your thing, then pip, pip cheerio! "Please sir, may I have some more?" (Ten points if you guessed that last one was from the musical *Oliver!*)

"If you ever start feeling like you have the goofiest, craziest, most dysfunctional family in the world, all you have to do is go to a state fair. Because five minutes at the fair, you'll be going, 'you know, we're all right. We're dang near royalty.'"

—JEFF FOXWORTHY

Cafe Muse
6547 Santa Monica Blvd. (between Las Palmas and Wilcox Avenues), Hollywood
(323) 464-6873
www.cafemusela.com

Open mic night is on Wed at 8:30 p.m. If you're the comedian doing the open mic, show up early to sign up. Located in the heart of Hollywood's Theatre Row, this is a cafe and a coffeehouse started by two theater artists. It's hip and mod, with lots of windows and a casual vibe. They specialize in vegetarian and vegan food, but never fear, they do have a variety of options for everyone. They also have free Wi-Fi. Oh, and free live entertainment every night of the week with a $5 minimum purchase, along with bottomless coffee for $2.50 to $3.50. If you visit their website, you will learn about the 9 muses, so that's like, educational, too. Just call me Thalia, the "blossoming one, the muse of comedy and bucolic poetry."

Casey's Irish Pub
613 S. Grand Ave, Downtown Los Angeles
(213) 629-2353
www.bigcaseys.com

Every Mon at 8 p.m., you can hear professional and amateur comics. Sign up at 7:30 p.m. if you're the one bringing the funny. Save $2 on already cheap mixed drinks, $1 on beer and wine. With a neverending happy hour discount like that, it's almost like you're getting paid to laugh. Casey's is an Irish bar, dark wood bar counter and all, with lots of Irish whiskey, Guinness, and other beers from which to choose.

Coffee Gallery
2029 N. Lake Ave. (at Morada Place), Altadena
(626) 398-7917
www.funkylittlecoffeehouse.com

The Coffee Gallery hosts open mic nights at 8 p.m. several nights a month. They also have weekend shows where you can bring a can of food to donate as your ticket to see the show. Check the website or call for details. Hello?! Doing an easy good deed to hear some jokes? Yes, this counts as free and wins you good karma points. Free parking on Lake Avenue and free Wi-Fi inside. If you are a comedian interested in performing, visit www.comedy-train.net. And this is a coffee house, people. This means your comedy is to be taken with a cup of joe.

Hollywood Hotel
1160 N. Vermont Ave. (at Lexington Ave.), Hollywood
(323) 315-1800
www.hollywoodhotel.net

The Hollywood Hotel hosts comedy every Mon and Thurs at 8 p.m. An intimate space, the lounge in the Hollywood Hotel only seats 37 people, so arrive early to grab your seat. Comedy is free, and there is no drink minimum. Are you laughing yet?

LA Pizza Co
16904 Devonshire St. (just past Balboa), Granada Hills
(818) 366-6888
www.lapizzaco.com

With inexpensive yummy eats of pizza, pasta, and sandwiches, over 20 different beers on tap, and accessible free parking in the Ralph's shopping center at Balboa and Devonshire, you can show up for the Tuesday night show at 8 p.m. for great free comedy. All comedians get 7 minutes in heaven. The website often has additional deals and coupons. Want to perform at LA Pizza Co? Visit www.socalstandup.com. Want to eat, drink, watch, and laugh? If you're over 18, what are you waiting for? I just gave you all the information you need. Is it Tuesday already? Go. Go!

Liquid Zoo
7214 Sepulveda Blvd. (near Sherman Way), Van Nuys
(818) 997-3818

The Catch: That whole 2-drink minimum thing again. However, those 2 drinks are very cheap.

This is a dive karaoke bar that has a free comedy open mic on Wed at 8:30 p.m. Some might find the establishment shady; others might say it has character. Most beers are $4.50, so really, the 2-drink minimum is no biggie. Parking options are solid. Bring cash, as they charge you $2 for credit cards.

M Bar
1253 Vine St. (at Fountain), Los Angeles
(323) 856-0036
www.mbaronline.com

Comedians determine the price of your ticket here, so you're going to fork over anywhere between $5 or $20, plus a minimum of $10 for food. The M Bar does not have a sign either, just to put some pizzazz in your journey to find it. It has a small entrance located on the southwest corner of Fountain and Vine, right next door to El Floridita.

"I blame my mother for my poor sex life. All she told me was,
'the man goes on top and the woman underneath.'
For three years my husband and I slept in bunk beds."
—JOAN RIVERS

Michael's Pub
11506 Oxnard St. North (just past Lankershim), North Hollywood
(818) 980-9762

Free comedy on Tuesday at 10 p.m. Gotta be 21 or over. Comedy can get down and dirty, which means it's not always G or even PG-13. Dive bar with darts, billiards (free all day Sunday), and rock-bottom drink prices. When I say "dive," I mean "dive." There's nothing fancy going on here, and it may look like a rough crowd (but it's not) if you're a high-maintenance type. Michael's Pub has clean bathrooms, a TV screen with sports blaring, and oh, yeah, you can smoke.

Pig 'N Whistle
6714 Hollywood Blvd. (between McCadden Place and Las Palmas in Hollywood), Los Angeles
(323) 463-0000
www.sunseteg.com

Open mic every Wed at 8 p.m. Sign-up starts at 7:30 p.m. $2 cover charge, 21 and over only. Street parking is your best option, as they'll charge you $10 to park behind the bar. Dinner's not super cheap, but it's a Los Angeles landmark located next door to the Egyptian Theatre. Note: When something is considered a landmark, the establishment usually knows it, and as such charges you for it. But, hey—comedy for $2 ain't bad.

Rainbow Bar and Grill
9015 Sunset Blvd. (at N. Doheny), West Hollywood
(310) 278-4232
www.rainbowbarandgrill.com

The Rainbow Bar and Grill is known for being a huge musician hangout for the likes of Lemmy, Guns N' Roses, and other assorted hair bands from back in the day. They also have a comedy open mic night on Mon at 8 p.m. Sign-up starts at 7:30 p.m. A super casual atmosphere with cheap appetizers, pizza, and burgers, the Rainbow Bar and Grill is stuck in the 1980s in decor (note the Ms. Pacman game) and, thankfully, food prices. Shows are upstairs. Park your hiney on a red bar stool and prepare to bust a gut laughing. FYI, they have a sister location in Las Vegas (hello, road trip!).

1739 Public House
1739 N. Vermont Ave. (at Kingswell in Los Feliz), Los Angeles
(323) 663-1739
www.1739publichouse.com

Free comedy on Mon nights at 10:30 p.m., and all meals are $7 or less. There are 64 beers on tap, because comedy is even funnier when slightly lubricated. Free pizza daily during happy hour from 3 to 7 p.m.

"Never tell. Not if you love your wife . . . In fact, if your old lady walks in on you, deny it. Yeah. Just flat out and she'll believe it: 'I'm telling ya. This chick came downstairs with a sign around her neck, LAY ON TOP OF ME OR I'LL DIE. I didn't know what I was gonna do' . . . "
—LENNY BRUCE

COMEDY **WORKSHOPS**

Greg Dean's College of Comedy Knowledge
(323) 464-4355
www.gregdean.com

So if you're reading this and still think you are the funniest person alive and that you can tell a joke that gets a room rolling, check out Greg Dean's free 1.5 hour stand-up comedy workshop held every Mon in Santa Monica at 7 p.m. Learn how to write a joke in 5 minutes. Then, if you really love it, sign up for one of Greg Dean's moderately priced full-blown stand-up comedy classes.

MUSIC:
CATCH A DITTY

*"There are more love songs than anything else.
If songs could make you do something,
we'd all love one another."*

—FRANK ZAPPA

Nearly every musician with dreams of making it big passes through the City of Angels on his or her musical career trajectory, and anything hip, cool, or forward in music happens here first, before spreading across the country and throughout the rest of the world. Because the music industry knows that the visitors and residents of Los Angeles are the tastemakers of the music scene, there are plenty of great deals to be found at various clubs and venues around town. You trust me, don't you? I've got something for each and every one of you, I promise. Los Angeles has some of the best live music in the country. So go ahead, check it out. You won't be able to prove me wrong.

BARS, **CLUBS** & RESTAURANTS

So much to choose from, and only one title to live by. And that title is *The Cheap Bastard's Guide to Los Angeles*. Clubs or places like The Music Box, King King, Largo at the Coronet, Orpheum Theatre, El Rey, Staples Center, and House of Blues just didn't make the cut for this chapter because when you add it all up—the tickets or cover, food or drinks you have to buy, or valet parking you have to suck up—it ain't exactly cheap if you're the one footing your own music celebration. So read below for some choices that are, well, more appropriate for cheap bastards like yourself. And moi.

California Institute of Abnormalarts
11334 Burbank Blvd. (at Bakman Ave.), North Hollywood
(818) 506-6353
http://ciabnormalarts.com

Where can you find an embalmed circus clown at a club founded by a mortician? No, that is not a typo, nor is it a joke. Musical, burlesque, and freak show live events. If you're adventurous in spirit, you've got to check this one out to believe it. And yes, if for any reason that glass case with the dead clown breaks, then run, or the formaldehyde and mercury fumes will get to you. Check website or call for details.

Coffee Gallery Backstage
2029 Lake Ave. (at Morada Place), Altadena
(626) 398-7917
http://coffeegallery.com

Coffee shop fare and folk, country, jazz, bluegrass, classical, oldies, and tribute band music. In other words, no hair bands or techno beats anywhere to be found. Most tickets are $15 to $18, and a few go up from there. Free Wi-Fi ('cause I know you want to be able to check your e-mail while enjoying a cover band playing John Denver's greatest hits). Free Sunday afternoon family bluegrass.

The Echo
1822 Sunset Blvd., Los Angeles

The Echoplex
1154 Glendale Blvd., Los Angeles
(213) 413-8200
www.attheecho.com

Two clubs in one! No-frills club with a laid-back vibe and contemporary bands amidst black walls and old chandeliers. Live music can range from no cover charge to $5 and up, but under $20. (Am I making you feel like you have a bad math problem to solve?) The Echoplex is below The Echo and entered from the alley. The Echoplex also has $4 beers and Down & Derby, a skating night ($5 for rollerskates) where you can skate with your drink. Not a good combination for me (I'm tall; if I hit the floor, it's a long way to go), but maybe it is for you. Keep your patience in searching for a spot on the street so you don't have to pay for the valet parking.

1160 Bar & Lounge
Inside the Hollywood Hotel
1160 N. Vermont Ave. (at Lexington Ave.), Hollywood
(323) 315-1845
www.hollywoodhotel.net

Indie, soul, and funk acts nightly in this swanky teak wood and marble-designed interior that hearkens back to the rollicking 1930s. The venue is intimate, so you'll be swept up into the music, as opposed to straining your eyes to watch someone the size of a pin on the stage. Drinks are cheap, and the crowd is equally swinging and fun, so long as you arrive after 8 p.m. Comedy and cabaret acts on Sun. Wear your spats. Or not.

The Fold
2220 Beverly Blvd., Los Angeles
(213) 908-5344
www.foldsilverlake.com/scheduleindex.html

The Fold books bands, many of them indie or underground, in several venues in Los Angeles, including the Silverlake Lounge, Bootleg, Bordello, El Cid, Home, and King King. Most of the shows at Silverlake Lounge or Bootleg are free or $7 to $10. Check website for upcoming shows and locations.

Harvelle's
1432 4th St. (just off Santa Monica Blvd.), Santa Monica
(310) 395-1676
www.harvelles.com

The oldest live music venue on the westside. Blues, jazz, and then some. Open 8 p.m. to 2 a.m. nightly. Music starts between 9:30 p.m. and 9:45 p.m. Ticket prices range, but many of the shows are just $10. Check online for details.

Michael's Pub
11506 Oxnard St. (at Beck Ave.), North Hollywood
(818) 980-9762

Live music some of the time. Cheap drinks, dart board, pool table, and video games all the time. If you get hungry, there's a 24-hour Taco Bell next door. What more could you ask for?

The Mint
6010 W. Pico Blvd. (1 block from S. Crescent Heights Blvd.), Los Angeles
(323) 954-9400
www.themintla.com

The Mint has been around since 1937. Um, that means it was here before World War II. And it's survived, because it's one of the best places in all of Los Angeles to see live music. Stevie Wonder, Willie Dixon, and Ray Charles are just some of the greats who've made musical magic onstage at The Mint. Plenty of street parking. Tickets start at $10 and go up to about $30, but are always cheaper if you buy them in advance online.

The Other Side

2538 Hyperion Ave. (at Evans St.), Los Angeles
(323) 661-4233
http://flyingleapcafe.com

"Hush up! Don't Tell Mama!" The Other Side, if you haven't already guessed it, is a gay piano bar. Why else would I quote Fred Ebb's lyrics to *Cabaret*? If show tunes and a live piano are your thing, The Other Side is for you. Music starts at 8 p.m. nightly; 9 p.m. on the weekend. Drink specials during happy hour 4 to 7 p.m. Mon through Thurs and noon to 7 p.m. on weekends.

Paladino's

6101 Reseda Blvd. (at Topham St.), Tarzana
(818) 342-1563
www.paladinosclub.com

At Paladino's in the Valley, happy hour runs all day, karaoke croons at 9 p.m. Mon through Wed and Sun at 9:30 p.m. (Tues is live band karaoke), free pool cues up on Sat, free wireless Internet access is available to you all the time, and tribute bands reign supreme, paying homage to some of the greats such as Judas Priest, Metallica, AC/DC, Black Eyed Peas, Led Zeppelin, and The Killers. Cover charge is usually about $10. Check website for upcoming shows.

The Roxy Theatre

9009 Sunset Blvd., West Hollywood
(310) 278-9457
http://theroxyonsunset.com

This is the club where John Belushi partied hard before he died of an overdose and where The Rocky Horror Picture Show debuted before it was *The Rocky Horror Picture Show*. In other words, this club has a reputation for hosting famous musicians and bands on the stage, as well as for partying hard (in case that wasn't clear). Most shows are $5 to $12.

The Satellite

1717 Silver Lake Blvd., Los Angeles
(323) 661-4380
www.thesatellitela.com

Underground independent bands that sound great and you know nothing of yet perform at The Satellite (formerly Spaceland). The key word in that last sentence was "yet." Just ask Beck or Juliana Hatfield. Cover will run you $8 to $20, but Mon nights are cover charge–free.

The Smell
247 S. Main St. (between W. 2nd and 3rd Streets), Downtown Los Angeles
www.thesmell.org

Indie bands for $5 admission. Nonalcoholic beverages and food can be had at the vegan snack bar for super cheap prices. Small and hip venue with art on the walls. Space is tight, so dress in layers or you'll get sweaty. (Hey, I'm looking out for all your needs.) Entrance is around back.

Troubadour
9081 Santa Monica Blvd. (at N. Doheny Dr.), West Hollywood
(310) 276-6168
www.troubadour.com

See them here first and they become famous tomorrow. That's what happened when Joni Mitchell made her Los Angeles debut at the Troubadour on June 4, 1968. The Pointer Sisters made their debut performance in May 1973, Metallica made their Los Angeles headline debut on August 18, 1982, and too many more chart-topping world-renowned singers and bands did just the same. Tickets range in price, many starting as low as $10 or $12, with some going to $20 or $25.

Whisky a Go-Go
8901 W. Sunset Blvd., West Hollywood
www.whiskyagogo.com

Since its doors opened in 1964, this Los Angeles institution has played host to rock and roll's most important bands, including The Doors and Janis Joplin. While the music is very much in the present, the price you'll pay is stuck in the past. Most shows are just $10 or $15, and you can buy tickets at the door without fear that you won't get in. iPhone users can download the Whisky A Go-Go app on their phones; the rest of us can check out their calendar online.

SCHOOLS, CHURCHES & CULTURAL CENTERS

California Traditional Music Society
Center for Folk Music
16953 Ventura Blvd. (at Paso Robles Ave.), Encino
(818) 817-7756
www.ctmsfolkmusic.org

Weekly jams each Sun from 1 to 4 p.m. The first Sunday is old-time, second Sunday is folk, third Sunday is Celtic, and fourth Sunday is bluegrass. Yee-haw! I think I'll take up the banjo. Can I play you a ditty?

First Congregational Church of Los Angeles
Wilshire Center
540 S. Commonwealth Ave. (at W. 5th St.), Los Angeles
(213) 385-1341
www.fccla.org

Home to the Los Angeles Bach Festival each October, a Cathedral Choir, and the largest church pipe organ in the world, The First Congregational Church of Los Angeles has weekly free organ concerts every Thurs at 12:10 p.m. $10 student rush tickets for other music events. Check the online calendar.

Pasadena Presbyterian Church
585 E. Colorado Blvd. (at N. Madison Ave.), Pasadena
(626) 793-2191
www.ppc.net

Pasadena Presbyterian Church hosts The Friends of Music Concert Series, which is an annual series of free high-quality concerts featuring visiting musicians and the church's own five choirs and ensembles, as well as 30-minute free concerts each Wed at 12:10 p.m. For $6 you can get a sandwich buffet lunch with that free concert.

South Bay Chamber Music Society
www.palosverdes.com/sbcms

Established in 1963, The South Bay Chamber Music Society is Southern California's little Lincoln Center. Free chamber music concerts on Fri at 8 p.m. at Los Angeles Harbor College, Music Department Recital Hall, 111 Figueroa Place, Wilmington, and on Sun at 3 p.m. at Pacific Unitarian Church, 5621 Montemalaga, Ranchos Palos Verdes.

FOR **YOUR** OUTDOOR LISTENING PLEASURE

Concerts on the Green
Lou Bredlow Pavilion in Warner Center Park
5800 Topanga Canyon Blvd., Woodland Hills
http://valleycultural.org

For over 35 years, Concerts on the Green has been providing free rock, classical, jazz, R&B, Latino pop, country, cowboy, Dixieland, and folk concerts on Sunday summer afternoons in Warner Center Park. Concerts usually begin at 6 p.m. Arrive early and select your dinner from among 20 different food vendors; bring the kids to the children's play area and keep them entertained until showtime.

Farmers Market
6333 W. 3rd St., Los Angeles
(323) 933-9211
www.farmersmarketla.com

Held mid-October every year, the Farmer's Market Fall Festival features live music of all kinds, from jazz to blues, rock, and Latin. Appropriate for all ages. No headbanging here. They also have free music on Thurs and Fri evenings from 7 to 9 p.m. from Memorial Day to Labor Day and beyond. Get your groove on for the weekend, baby.

Grand Performances
350 S. Grand Ave., Suite A-4, Los Angeles
(213) 687-2159
www.grandperformances.org

"Grand Performances presents free performing arts that reflect the best of global culture and inspire community among the diverse peoples of Los Angeles." Is there anything you disagree with in that statement? Bring your own folding seats, food, and beverages. Runs June through October. Parking will cost you a few bucks.

Hollywood Bowl
2301 N. Highland Ave., Los Angeles
(323) 850-2000
www.hollywoodbowl.com

The Hollywood Bowl has $12 cheap seats for nearly all concerts. Bring a picnic and pair it with a free tour of The Hollywood Bowl Museum before showtime, and you're headed for one awesome night. They will charge you for parking.

Levitt Pavilion Pasadena
30 N. Raymond Ave. (at Douglas Alley), Pasadena
(626) 683-3230
www.levittpavilionpasadena.org

Fifty (count 'em!) free music concerts are presented at the Levitt Pavilion at the historical Memorial Park band shell in Old Pasadena every summer. Music from around the country and around the world. Performances usually start around 7 or 8 p.m. Calendar online.

Pershing Square Summer Concert Series

532 S. Olive St. (at W. 5th St. downtown), Los Angeles
(213) 847-4970
www.laparks.org/pershingsquare

Live free music and films outdoors Wednesday through Saturday in July and August. Please note that if you check this website in the winter, you are instead going to get information on Pershing Square's equally awesome $6 outdoor ice skating and free holiday concerts. Don't get your panties or boxer shorts in a twist. The point is that there are loads of free events in Pershing Square year-round. Just pick a season.

Summer and Music (S.A.M.)

Long Beach
www.summerandmusic.com

Held every June, July, and August, S.A.M. is a sustainable concert series of totally free music held in the East Village Arts District, Rainbow Harbor, and Pine Avenue in downtown Long Beach. Bike valet parking and food trucks are also sometimes available/part of the whole shebang. The rock and roll and the tribute bands lineup nights are awesome! (Don't judge my taste in music.)

Topanga Banjo and Fiddle Contest and Folk Festival

Free Summer Concerts at the Peter Strauss Ranch
3000 Mulholland Hwy. (at Troutdale Dr.), Agoura Hills
www.topangabanjofiddle.org

Four free bluegrass and folk concerts held on the second Sunday of June, July, August, and September from 3 to 5 p.m. at the Peter Strauss Ranch. The actual Topanga Banjo and Fiddle Contest & Folk Festival of music, dance, and entertainment is held in mid-May every year. Entry fee ranges from $8 to $11 if you buy your tickets online in advance. Children under 10 attend for free.

MUSIC **STORES**

Amoeba Music
6400 Sunset Blvd. (at Ivar Ave.), Hollywood
(323) 245-6400
www.amoeba.com

Amoeba Music is the world's largest independent record store as well as a popular live performance venue with free in-store shows. Click on "Live Shows" on the website to get notifications so you don't miss the next one. Locations in Berkeley and San Francisco as well, for when you take that weekend trip up the PCH.

McCabe's Guitar Shop
3101 Pico Blvd., Santa Monica
(310) 828-4497
www.mccabes.com

Guitar store by day, but when the lights go down at night, it's a live music haven. Who, you think, would possibly perform in a venue like this, you ask? Tom Waits, Cowboy Junkies, They Might Be Giants, and Ray Manzarek, to name a few. Tickets range in price from $15 to $25. Open mic night is the first Sunday of each month, and there's many a family friendly event for $8 or so a pop. Musical instrument rentals and lessons on all things string instrument. No alcohol, but plenty of free coffee is served at all concerts.

THEATER:
IN ON THE ACT

"If it's a good script I'll do it. And if it's a bad script, and they pay me enough, I'll do it."

—GEORGE BURNS

"Impossible!" you exclaim. "There can't possibly be any theee-ahy-ter in Los Angeles! In the vacuous wasteland of sun and palm trees, the destination of young film and television starlet pilgrimages everywhere? They do plays? Where they stand up in front of a group of people and say lines and stuff?"

Fortunately, yes! Those starlets, celebrities, and accomplished actors in Los Angeles aren't always just walking the dog, surfing the beach, or stocking up on groceries for their vegan diets or liquid cleanse of the month—they're also sinking their teeth into roles at various first-rate theaters in Los Angeles. Whether it's a volunteer usher gig, a rush ticket, or Shakespeare in the summer, seize the opportunity to appreciate the beauty of live theater—Los Angeles has got some of the best. And when it's live, you never know what might happen.

BE **AN** USHER, **SEE** A **SHOW**!

Volunteer usher opportunities in Los Angeles theaters abound. Often times they involve showing up an hour to an hour and a half prior to curtain, tearing tickets, handing out programs, ushering people to seats, and cleaning up the theater after the audience exits. Dress codes are generally all black or black pants or skirt and shoes with a white shirt. In between these minimal duties, you get to see a great show. You're supporting the arts and giving back to your community. What could be a better combination?

RUSH **TICKETS**

A lot of theaters offer rush tickets, which are perfect for a) the budget-conscious individual or recessionista and b) great for Mr. No Plan Stan and Ms. Last Minute Linda. In general, rush tickets are obtained just prior to curtain for a particular show; hence the rush . . . to the box office. Some theaters offer a general rush price, other theaters offer an even lesser student rush price, and some offer only one or the other. Specifics are included in the listings. Looking for something original to spice up a visit or inject some romance into your evening? Try the excitement of a rush ticket and have something to talk about afterward.

THEATERS

Center Theatre Group
Mark Taper Forum & Ahmanson Theatre at the Music Center
135 N. Grand Ave. (near W. Temple Ave.), Los Angeles
Kirk Douglas Theatre
9820 Washington Blvd. (near Hughes Ave.), Culver City
(213) 628-2772
www.centertheatregroup.com

The Catch: You're forking over $20; however, that $20 was severely discounted and you are seeing high-caliber theater.

The three stages of the Center Theatre Group (CTG)—the Ahmanson, Mark Taper Forum, and Kirk Douglas—present some of the best theater Los Angeles has to offer. Past productions have included *The Glass Menagerie, Leap of Faith* (based on the Steve Martin movie), and *Venice,* a new musical. Up to 3 weeks prior to a performance at any of their 3 theaters, CTG offers $20 "Hot Tix." In general, these are available for every performance, unless it is completely sold out. Seat locations are based on availability. Hot Tix are limited to 2 per person. Hot Tix on-sale dates can be found on the CTG website on each production's show page. They must be purchased via phone by calling the number above, or in person at the box office.

Cerritos Center for the Performing Arts (CCPA)
12700 Center Court Dr. (off the Artesia Fwy.), Cerritos
(562) 916-8501
www.cerritoscenter.com

City owned and operated, The Cerritos Center for the Performing Arts (CCPA) is a premier performing arts and concert facility, offering first-rate performances in theater, dance, and music. The CCPA is hard core, elevating volunteer ushers to the status of "arts ambassador." You're not working for the United Nations, but with this fancy title comes more responsibility. In September every year, the CCPA trains arts ambassadors who then make themselves available to usher for shows 3 times a month. Ushers arrive 1.25 hours prior to curtain and wear black pants or skirt and a white shirt with a black tie or ladies flounce. Blazers and ladies flounces are provided. Call the house manager at extension 8530 if you'd like to become an arts ambassador. The CCPA is looking into offering arts ambassador training at other times of the year.

Falcon Theatre
4252 Riverside Dr. (near N. Rose St.), Burbank
(818) 955-8101
www.falcontheatre.com

Operating year-round, the intimate 130-seat Falcon Theatre was started by director/writer/producer Garry Marshall and his daughter Kathleen. Built in beautiful downtown Burbank (okay, Burbank isn't so beautiful, but the theater is lovely), The Falcon Theatre has produced acclaimed productions of *Death of a Salesman* (starring Jack Klugman) and *Crimes of the Heart* (starring Morgan Fairchild and Faith Ford). The Falcon Theatre also produces great children's theater. Call the box office at the number above to ask about volunteer ushering opportunities.

Geffen Playhouse and Audrey Skirball Kenis Theater
10886 Le Conte Ave. (near Westwood Plaza on UCLA's campus), Los Angeles
(310) 208-6500
www.geffenplayhouse.com

The Catch: You're opening your wallet, but the cost is severely discounted, the quality high, and hey, you may get to see a star onstage instead of just on the boob tube in your family room. If you choose to be a volunteer usher, your evening's not costing you a cent!

Classic plays, musicals, world premieres of original works, and one-person shows are just some of the highlights you might find in a season at the Geffen. Star-studded productions of the past have included such luminaries as Annette Bening, Laurence Fishburne, Joan Rivers, and Alicia Silverstone. In general, The Geffen has 8 shows a week and offers regular rush tickets 30 minutes prior to curtain at $35 per seat. Student rush tickets, available with valid student ID, are available at $20 per seat 30 minutes prior to curtain.

All rush tickets are based on availability. A certain amount of VIP seats are put on hold for every performance. (And Hollywood has a lot of VIPs.) When those are not all taken, they are up for grabs! So sometimes a rush ticket can land you some of the best seats of the house—front and center, up close. If you're interested in becoming a volunteer usher, call the main number and dial extension 115 for the supervising house manager. Volunteer ushers usually sign up for all 5 shows in August before the start of the season, but you can volunteer for one show at a time should you so desire, based on limited availability. Volunteer ushers wear all black and assist the regular usher staff in stuffing programs and scanning tickets, and then grab a seat to watch the show!

Los Angeles Theatre Center (LATC)

514 S. Spring St. (between 5th and 6th Streets), Los Angeles
(213) 489-0994
www.thelatc.org

In particular, the LATC does a wonderful job showcasing works by Latino playwrights or with Latino themes. By becoming a volunteer usher, you receive one free ticket to any show at the LATC. To apply, fill out the Volunteer Usher Packet, which can be found on their website under "About Us," and then "Work with Us," and then send an e-mail to House Manager Adam Jacobo at adam@thelatc.org. Once you receive a confirmation e-mail to attend, you're set!

Orange County Performing Arts Center (OCPAC)

600 Town Center Dr., Costa Mesa
(714) 556-2121
www.ocpac.org

The Catch: Requires manual labor to pull your wallet out from your pocket or purse. But hey, your ticket is discounted and the show is bound to be great at their state-of-the-art facilities. Of course, you can always choose the volunteer usher route and attend for free!

Here is your opportunity to experience firsthand the hotbed of thriving arts in Orange County, and not just its over-tanned reality stars through the vicarious medium of your television. The OCPAC is home to 4 theaters: Sagerstrom Hall, which seats 3,000 people and showcases Broadway shows, ballet, and special performances; the Renee and Henry Sagerstrom Concert Hall, which seats 2,000 and is home to the Pacific Symphony and Orange County Philharmonic Society; Samueli Hall, a 500-seat black box theater that hosts a myriad of different cultural and entertainment genres from children's theater, jazz, and cabaret to rock bands and chamber ensembles; and Founders Hall, an intimate space for small theater productions or meetings. Seniors and students can take advantage of special rush-price tickets beginning 1 hour prior to many performances. Call the box office to find out if a specific show or performance is offering rush tickets: (714) 556-2787.

If you are interested in being an usher at the OCPAC, dial (714) 556-2122, ext. 4278, or go to their website and click on "About the Center," then "Careers at the Center," "Volunteer Opportunities," and then "Volunteer Ushers." Be sure to check out the OCPAC's website to learn about special free performances that are part of the popular "Free for All Series." These shows range from Summer Movie Mondays on the Center's outdoor plaza (bring your picnic dinner and beach chairs), dance performances on the plaza, and other special events that occur throughout the year.

Rubicon Theatre Company
1006 E. Main St. (between N. Ann and N. Laurel Streets), Ventura
(805) 667-2912
www.rubicontheatre.org

Founded in 1998, The Rubicon Theatre presents everything from American classics to modern plays, plays by minorities or classics from other cultures, and new works and musicals. Past productions have included *The Rainmaker, Jacques Brel Is Alive and Well and Living in Paris, Dancing at Lughnasa,* and *Driving Miss Daisy.* There are two tiers of usher opportunities at The Rubicon. You can call the above number and dial extension 239 for the house manager and sign up to be a volunteer usher and see a show for free—there is a point system for number of hours worked. If you're a little more zealous or social, join The Grand Dames ($25 annual membership fee), and get involved in all of the theater's volunteer opportunities, from planning and marketing of special events to welcome preparations for actors and more. The Grand Dames is primarily made up of women, but certainly doesn't discriminate toward any eager men who wish to join. If you are interested in being one of The Grand Dames, call the above number and dial extension 237 for the development coordinator. The Grand Dames see shows for free and enjoy a few other perks here and there, too!

SEASONAL—**BARD** ON **A** BUDGET

The Actors' Gang at the Ivy Substation
9070 Venice Blvd., Culver City
(310) 838-GANG (4264)
www.theactorsgang.com

The Actors' Gang offers free family friendly Shakespeare on Sat and Sun mornings at 11 a.m. in Culver City's Media Park in July and August of every year. Check the website for more details.

Independent Shakespeare Co.
9800-D Topanga Canyon Blvd., #168, Chatsworth
(818) 710-6306
www.iscla.org

The internationally recognized Independent Shakespeare Co. performs the Bard's greatest outdoors in Griffith Park every summer in July and Aug, Thurs through Sun at 7 p.m. Picnics, blankets, chairs, and a good time are all encouraged. All performances take place at the Festival Stage in the Griffith Park Old Zoo, 4730 Crystal Springs Dr., Los Angeles.

Shakespeare by the Sea
777 Centre St., San Pedro
(310) 217-7596
www.shakespearebythesea.org

Shakespeare by the Sea is focused on bringing new, contemporary, and classic works to an underserved, culturally diverse audience in order to ignite imagination, promote literacy, and encourage artistic expression. Every summer, Shakespeare by the Sea performs great works from Willie's canon in an outdoor theater overlooking the Pacific Ocean. Audience members are encouraged to bring a picnic, blankets, and chairs, and to dress warmly. Seating is on a first-come, first-serve basis. Shows run mid-June through mid-August, generally at 7 or 8 p.m. Wed through Sun. Check the website for more details, as show times tend to change depending on performance locations at Point Fermin Park, 807 Paseo Del Mar in San Pedro, and other locations throughout Greater Los Angeles.

The Shakespeare Center
1238 W. First St., Los Angeles
(213) 481-2273
www.shakespearecenter.org

Every summer, The Shakespeare Center sponsors the Shakespeare Festival/ LA. Performances of Shakespeare's classics are offered for free in downtown Los Angeles at the Cathedral of Our Lady of the Angels, 555 W. Temple St., Los Angeles and the South Coast Botanic Gardens, 26300 Crenshaw Blvd., Palos Verdes. General admission is free; reserved seats are $30. Donations of nonperishable items for the Food Bank of Southern California are encouraged.

DANCE:
SHAKE YOUR GROOVE THANG

"To be fond of dancing was a certain step towards falling in love."

—JANE AUSTEN

Absolutely anybody can dance, no matter how old you are, or how little rhythm you feel you have. It's all about having no fear of what you look like. Dance classes can help with that, and shaking your booty in public every once in a while is good for your body and your soul. Los Angeles is a mecca for dancers everywhere, who flock there to train, to study, and to be the next backup dancer for Britney Spears or the Black Eyed Peas. Whether you want to boogie, watch others boogie, or learn how to boogie, and whether you're a beginning lover or advanced lover, your bases are covered in Los Angeles.

BOOGIE **DOWN** AT **STUDIOS**, CLUBS & RESTAURANTS

The Arte Flamenco Dance Theatre and The Center of Worldance
230 W. Main St. (at N. 3rd St.), Alhambra
(626) 458-1234
www.clarita-arteflamenco.com

$12 for a 1-hour class in belly dancing, flamenco, Hawaiian, Tahitian, hip-hop, jazz, Pilates, tap, yoga, or zumba. Prices get even cheaper if you sign up and pay by the month. Plenty of classes for the little tikes, too.

Ballroom Blitz
4878 Eagle Rock Blvd. (at Yosemite Dr. in Glendale), Los Angeles
(323) 258-0029
www.ballroomblitz.org

Sign up for 6 Latin Workout or Ballroom Workout classes for just $50. And those 6 classes don't have to be consecutive. Hello! Does that flexibility not suit your lifestyle just perfectly? I thought so. They also have a buy 1 pair, get another pair free coupon for dance shoes at Very Fine Shoes in El Monte, CA, on their website.

Ballroom by the Bay

1210 4th St. (at Wilshire Blvd.), Santa Monica
(310) 487-0911
www.ballroombythebay.com

Cha-cha-cha for small change. All ages and levels can be found strictly ballroom dancing by the bay for $12 every Wed from 7 to 11 p.m.; $10 for students and USA Dance or Dance Buddies with ID. The price of the dance lesson from 7 to 7:40 p.m. is included in your admission. No partner required,
so what's your excuse for not going?

Bootie

http://bootiela.com

Bootie is dedicated solely to the "mashup," or bootleg song that is, well,
mashed up, and subscribes to the theory that one song is simply not
enough. Using audio editing software, "DJs and mashup artists combine different artists and musical genres to create new and unique songs that are
often greater than the sum of their parts." Technically, none of this music
is legally cleared by the artists, so they host underground mashup parties
in various locations throughout Los Angeles. Visit the website to sign up for
their e-mail list to receive news on the location of the next Bootie LA. Cover
charges range from $5 to $10, depending on your arrival time, and free CDs
are usually given out to first arrivals.

Cancun Olé

5219 E. Beverly Blvd. (at S. Atlantic Blvd.), Los Angeles
(323) 888-8899
www.cancunole.net

Club music on the third Fri of each month starting at 8 p.m. Nightly salsa
and club events as well. $5 cover charge if you slide in prior to 10 p.m., $10
after. $3 domestic beers. This is where the real Latinos go, which means this
is not a tourist trap.

Club Mayan

1038 S. Hill St. (between 11th St. and Olympic Blvd.), Los Angeles
www.clubmayan.com

Live salsa orchestra every Saturday night. DJs spin salsa, meringue, etc., on
the main floor. Check website for the most current information. $12 cover if

you enter before 10:30 p.m., $20 after. (So get there early!) Required formal evening attire, for those of you who like looking all fancy.

Cock n' Bull
2947 Lincoln Blvd. (near Wilson Place and Pier Ave.), Santa Monica
(310) 399-9696
www.cocknbullbritishpub.com

Learn to salsa in the $10 beginner classes at 7:30 p.m. and intermediate at 8:30 p.m. on Tuesday nights at this British pub. Take a break, whip out that laptop, and enjoy the free Internet access as well. (It is not recommended that you surf the Internet and salsa at the same time, unless you are already at an advanced level.) Food starts at $4.25 and up.

The Coffee Depot
3204 Mission Inn Ave. (at Vine St.), Riverside
(951) 222-2263
http://coffeedepot.tv

Salsa social the first Sun of every month starting at 5 p.m., where you can learn how to salsa for free at the largest coffee house in the country. Then come back for more on Mon at 7 p.m. to squeeze in your free swing dancing lesson.

The Dance Family Studio
25 N. Allen Ave. (at Colorado), Pasadena
(626) 568-3764
http://thedancefamily.com

Latin Dance on the first and third Fri of each month for $7, starting at 8:30 p.m., with a free beginner's lesson. The Dance Family Studio will be moving locations soon, so check website for up to date information.

The Dime
442 N. Fairfax Ave., West Hollywood
(323) 651-4421

A small, under-the-radar, underestimated, no-frills dive bar with a laid-back vibe, cheap drinks ($3 beers, $4 well drinks, $5 and up for mixed drinks), great atmosphere, and awesome DJ with a tune for everyone at no cover charge. Party starts at 7 p.m. Get there early to avoid the wait!

Git Your Free Dancin' Online

BallroomDancers.com has a dance directory, classified ads, shopping, message board, and, best of all, free dance videos where all the steps of the major dances for each partner are broken down for you and shown from every angle imaginable. In other words, the videos Fred and Ginger would be making if they were alive today. Check out http://ballroomdancers.com.

Dance Resource Center of Greater Los Angeles is Southern California's "source for everything dance." News, performance calendar, classes, workshops, and auditions. Visit www.drc-la.org.

Eye Spy LA lists all the creative, unique, alternative, and fun things to do in Los Angeles on a weekly basis. This includes entertainment, arts and culture, kid stuff, and other free events. They have a dance calendar (click on "dance" under hot topics on the far left), so you're sure not to miss a thing. Sign up to receive their weekly e-news alerts. Visit http://eyespyla.com.

iDance.net offers nearly 1,400 dance lessons online. Is there not a website for everything? Learn salsa, hip-hop, West Coast swing, tap, jitterbug, and more by purchasing online video dance lessons. Single

El Floridita
1253 N. Vine St., (and Fountain Ave.), Hollywood
(323) 871-8612
www.elfloridita.com

This is a restaurant and a club, but you don't have to do one in order to have the other. Yay! El Floridita delivers on the Cuban experience all the way. Free salsa dance lessons to restaurant customers on Mon and Fri at 8 p.m. ($15 for non-diners), and $5 mojitos on Mon from 7 to 9 p.m. (Because those muscles will feel a little looser and those hips will shake a little better with some mojitos fueling them.)

lessons will run you $1.99, 6 lessons just over $10, 13 lessons just over $21, or for your inner dancing fiend, you can purchase all 65-plus lessons for anywhere between $110 and $130, depending on your instructor. Slow-quick-quick-slow your way over to www.idance.net.

Lafreebee will tell you everything you need to know about free things to do and free stuff in Los Angeles, including those involving your two left feet, or other people's two left feet. At http://lafreebee .com. Make it your homepage.

LearntoDance.com has the goal "to make learning to dance as easy as possible." They have a dance studio locator and free online lessons. Their clips are not embedded, so you have to download them and need Quicktime to view them. Maybe I'm in the wrong line of work writing books and I should do how-to videos for the lawnmower and the sprinkler. Genius! Don't steal my idea. More at www.learnto dance.com.

Salsa & Merengue Society will teach you the history of salsa and merengue and also offers online videos to teach you the fancy footwork involved in each dance. The quality of the videos is a bit prison confessional-like (read: a bit grainy and fuzzy), but the steps are still pretty clear. Visit www.salsa-merengue.co.uk.

Heartbeat House
3141 Glendale Blvd. (at Madera in Atwater Village), Los Angeles
(323) 669-2821
www.heartbeathouse.net

The slogan is "It's what you won't experience at the gym." Community Argentine Tango and yoga classes are just $7. Still-moving seniors over 60 can pay just $5 for a community class. "Hold the ball, paint the wall," as my Tai-chi instructor used to say—those classes are $10. Heartbeat House has an extensive curriculum. It's like sweating to the oldies, but still looking hot in LA in the 21st century.

Ixtapa Cantina
119 E. Colorado Blvd. (and Arroyo Pkwy.), Pasadena
(626) 304-1000
www.cantinaixtapa.com

Free salsa lessons followed by even more bailando on Tues and Sun after 8 p.m. at this Mexican restaurant in Old Pasadena. Affordable appetizers range in price from $4.50 to $12. Que perfecto way to work off that burrito!

Los Angeles Steppers Connection
159 N. Market St. (at Regent St.), Inglewood
(310) 895-5712
www.mylasc.com

Smooth Chicago Style Stepping Sundays, Ballroom Mondays, Salsa Thursdays (2 classes for $15 that night), Ballroom Social Fridays, Line Dancing Saturdays—all for $10 a pop. Ballroom Social Fridays are just $5 if you enter before 9 p.m. Watch out, Gene Kelly.

Monsoon Cafe
1212 3rd St. Promenade, Santa Monica
(310) 576-9996
http://monsoon.globaldiningca.com

Live salsa band every Wed and Sat night, with a beginner salsa lesson at 7:30 p.m., and an intermediate salsa lesson at 8:30 p.m. $12 cover charge.

Odoru Dance Studio
420 W. Avenue 33, #10 (near Lacy and Artesian Streets), Downtown Los Angeles
(310) 486-7716
http://odorudancestudio.com

A new dance studio in the downtown Loft district, Odoru Dance Studio offers dance and exercise classes in the styles of ballet, modern, belly dance, house dance, yoga, and hip-house cardio. Dance your heart out in a no-pressure environment for just $12 per class.

Oil Can Harry's
11502 Ventura Blvd. (at Berry Dr.), Studio City
(818) 760-9749
www.oilcanharrysla.com

This is a gay-friendly country western club where you can two-step, line dance, and sometimes karaoke to your heart's content. Doors open to a $3 cover on Tues and Thurs at 7:30 p.m.; no cover on Fri at 9 p.m. Lessons offered first thing. All domestic beer and margaritas are $2.

Panamerican Night Club
2601 W. Temple St. (at N. Rampart Blvd.), Los Angeles
(213) 386-2083
www.panamericannightclub.com

Beginning at 8 p.m. six nights a week (dark on Tuesday), you can dance the meringue, bachata, salsa, or just shake that booty and feel gooooood listening to that live Latino music. $10 cover charge.

Pasadena Ballroom Dance Association
Grace Hall
73 N. Hill Ave., Pasadena
(626) 799-5689
http://pasadenaballroomdance.com

Swing dances every Saturday night with a live swing band. Starts with a free East Coast swing dance lesson at 7:30 p.m., and then the music revs up at 8 p.m. for 3 hours. Free snacks and refreshments to quench your thirst. No partner necessary. $15 admission.

Sevilla Night Club
140 Pine Ave., Long Beach
(562) 495-1111
www.sevillanightclub.com

Super Salsa at Sevilla! No cover on Tues. $10 for Thurs and Sun (lessons 7:30 to 9:30 p.m.), $8 and $10 on Wed (lessons 8 to 9:30 p.m.). Prices go up as the week goes on. Minors welcome, so long as you sign the Zero Tolerance Drinking Policy. A second location is in Riverside at 3252 Mission Inn Ave., (951-778-0611).

The Sweat Spot
3327 W. Sunset Blvd. (at Micheltorena St.), Silverlake
(323) 953-8089
www.thesweatspotla.com

For $10 in my white tank top and pajama pants with the purple hearts on them, I took Ryan Heffington's Sweaty Sundays class, which was sort of a yoga/jazz/hip-hop fashion show all in one, run by a Caucasian Euro-trashed RuPaul, if RuPaul had a mustache. Ryan Heffington, part performer/choreographer/artist/teacher, teaches this class, and his unbridled enthusiasm and occasional commands of "Look sexy, look hot!" while the sweat pours down your face make you smile, even if you do feel like an idiot. I'm a dancer and I'm in shape, but I hurt for days afterward and loved every minute of my more-than-worth-it $10 workout. The studio offers other dance classes as well. Once in a while they have free events, too.

3rd Street Dance
8558 W. 3rd St. (near S. San Vicente Blvd.), Los Angeles
(310) 275-4683
www.3rdstreetdance.com

Boy do I love . . . let's call them Kara and Henry . . . dear friends of mine who got married, and then danced their first dance at their wedding in one very small, continuous, interminable circle for all to watch. Had they studied at the very popular and fun 3rd Street Dance Studio, they might have mastered their wedding preparation, as well as ballroom, swing, salsa, the Argentine tango, and the Lindy Hop. Alas, they did not. Their loss, and the wedding guests' silent horror and laughter unfolded. $15 (cash only) for single lessons, $96 for an 8-week class (a steal!); private and couples lessons also offered.

Walk In . . . Dance Out
(310) 373-8487
www.walkindanceout.com

Test out your first dance class with Walk In . . . Dance Out before you pay a cent. Six-week courses include 12 hours of practice lessons, averaging $4 to $6 per hour. Major discount if you pay in advance! Break it down in the bolero, hustle, disco, Lindy, 2-step, or Latin style. Locations in Redondo Beach, Playa Del Rey, and Palos Verdes.

Wokcano Restaurant & Lounge

1413 5th St. (near Santa Monica Blvd.), Santa Monica
(310) 458-3080
www.wokcanorestaurant.com

$5 salsa lessons on Tues at 8 p.m. Intermediates start at 9 p.m., after which all are encouraged to take their dancing feelings onto the outside patio. Don't swivel those hips on an empty stomach—fuel your dancing feet early on with the Mon through Fri 4:30 to 7 p.m. happy hour featuring $3 drink specials and yummy sushi, appetizers, and entrees ranging from $3 to $7. Check website for other Los Angeles locations, including Burbank, Long Beach, and Valencia.

Zanzibar

1301 5th St. (at Arizona St.), Santa Monica
(310) 451-2221
www.zanzibarlive.com

Zanzibar offers the best in salsa, rumba, cha cha, bachata, and vintage Latin Jazz. Tumbao Salsa Dura on Monday with lessons at 8 p.m., and intermediate at 9 p.m., taught by world champion Christian Oviedo and featuring DJ Charley. Tu quieres salsa? Si, senor! $5 for all the dancing your feet can take; $10 on the first Monday of the month when they have a live band.

WATCH **OTHERS** BOOGIE **DOWN**

Hollywood Boulevard

(Start at Hollywood and Vine)

As you strut down Hollywood Boulevard to soak up the stars on the Walk of Fame, be sure to take the time to stop and appreciate the lively street life bustling around you, which often includes incredible breakdancing and hip-hop dancers preening their dancing prowess for your free enjoyment.

Keith Glassman Dance and Performance
www.keithglassman.org

Anywhere from 2 to 8 dancers of Keith Glassman's troupe present modern and nontraditional works in unique settings, such as coffee shops, for free. The online calendar has the most up-to-date events.

LA Contemporary Dance Company (LACDC)
4470 W. Sunset Blvd., #553, downtown Los Angeles
www.lacontemporarydance.org

The LA Contemporary Dance Company calendar boasts a host of performances, open rehearsals, showcases, and classes that are either free or cheap ($10 or $15). Hot, sexy, and smoldering, they present a diverse repertoire of modern dance, ballet, and jazz.

Lula Washington Dance Theatre
3773 Crenshaw Blvd., Los Angeles
(323) 292-5852
www.lulawashington.org

The Lula Washington Dance Theatre is an African-American dance company that seeks to explore and express our social and humanitarian plights in the world today. Many of their shows are free. Check the online calendar for the latest and greatest.

World City and Free Dance Downtown
135 N. Grand Ave., Los Angeles
(213) 972-0711
www.musiccenter.org

Admission-free performances on select Saturdays at 11 a.m. and 12:30 p.m. at the W.M. Keck Foundation Children's Amphitheatre at Walt Disney Concert Hall. Tickets for the first show are distributed one hour prior; the second show, 1.5 hours prior. Free Dance Downtown on Friday runs from 6:30 to 10 p.m. in the summer months downtown at the Music Center Plaza. Free dance lessons start at 6:30 p.m. and last throughout the evening; each Friday has a different theme, whether it's ballroom, line dancing, Bollywood, or disco. Donations are encouraged, but not mandatory. The website also has other dance events listed through the Music Center, so click and explore away!

SPECIAL **DANCE** EVENTS

Dance on the Terrace
Westfield Century City
10250 Santa Monica Blvd., Los Angeles
(310) 277-3898
http://westfield.com/centurycity

The Westfield Century City Shopping Mall has free dance lessons and live music Thursdays on the Level 2 Dining Terrace. Sometimes you get a little swing, sometimes a little Spanish Harlem, sometimes even a little Bollywood, but always a good time. Dancing starts at 6:30 p.m., and parking is free for the first 3 hours. Who knew that your shopping experience could be combined with so much culture?

Pasadena Dance Festival
(626) 844-7008
www.lineagedance.org

This would be the United Colors of Benetton if United Colors of Benetton put on dance shows. Every February, you can see dance from around the world at the Pasadena Dance Festival, for free. Following the performance, the dancers will teach you a few of the moves, so you can join in on the fun and celebrate multiculturalism through dance. Sign up for free workshops throughout the day as well.

Saturdays off the 405 at The Getty Center
1200 Getty Center Dr., Los Angeles
(310) 440-7300
www.getty.edu

Free outdoor music and dancing May through October off the 405 at The Getty Center. Bring a picnic and enjoy the DJ and the outdoor setting under the stars (if you can see them through the smog). The night kicks off at 7:30p.m.

Twilight Dance and Music at the Santa Monica Pier
200 Santa Monica Pier, Suite A, Santa Monica
(310) 458-8901
www.santamonicapier.org

Free concerts every Thurs at 7 p.m. from early July through Labor Day every year. Check the online calendar for the impressive lineup of music from around the world. Bee-bop to the tunes on the boardwalk on your way back to the car. Bike valet service (only in Los Angeles!) starts at 6:30 p.m. on event nights.

BOOGIE **DOWN** YOUR **COST** OF **BECOMING** A DANCER

Millennium Dance Complex
5113 Lankershim Blvd., North Hollywood
(818) 753-5081
www.millenniumdancecomplex.com

Call to inquire about work-study scholarships at this professional dance training center for working dancers. Classes are taught by working performers and choreographers. The Pussycat Dolls, Britney Spears, Justin Timberlake, and Michael Jackson have all spent many an hour in this studio. Ballet, hip-hop, jazz, and funk.

Retter's Academy of Dance
5341 Derry Ave., Suite A, Agoura Hills
(818) 889-5774
www.retterworld.com

Retter's Academy of Dance offers 2 scholarships and up to 13 work-study internships to qualified dancers 18 and over. Scholarship includes classes, assistant teaching, office work, performing live, learning how to run a dance studio, assisting on-camera and in choreography, master classes, specialty classes, and live professional performances. Apply via headshot, bio, essays, video dance audition, and 2 letters of recommendation. Work-study interns do co-teaching, assisting, admin/office work, and facilities cleaning.

S Factor
5225 Wilshire Blvd., Suite B, Los Angeles
(323) 965-9685
www.sfactor.com

Sheila Kelley's S Factor has 2 scholarship programs in striptease and pole dancing. Yes! That is correct! Awaken and empower the beauty of the wonderful woman you are on the inside and outside. Work-Study women assist team ambassadors in running the studios, and in exchange, half the cost of your Original Series tuition is covered. You will have to commit to the same dates and times every week, and office or retail skills are a plus. Since 2005, the S Fund contributes $110 or $220 toward the cost of your Original Series session for those facing financial difficulties. Get application information online or call the above number. Additional locations are in Costa Mesa at 2790 Harbor Blvd., Suite 210 (714-434-4991), and Encino at 17253 Ventura Blvd. (818-817-4585).

SPOKEN WORD:
FREE EXPRESSION

*"I think a poet is anybody who
wouldn't call himself a poet."*

—BOB DYLAN

We live in a world where the sight of a true, distinguished gentleman on a park bench turning the pages of a newspaper, novel, or book of poems is extinct, and has been replaced with someone who leaves his phone on the restaurant table and sends text messages during dinner; where people don't gather in smoke-filled salons to debate hot topics of the day, but instead sit transfixed by the blue-light-special glow of their computer screens; a world where a date is not won by filling out a dance card at the society ball or calling on the parents of the girl you've set eyes on, but instead earned in surfing pretty photos and striking up a chat over the Internet. We are consumed, addicted to, and sometimes misled by the very technology we depend upon, thanking it in all of its convenience for its reliability, and cursing it out when it fails us.

No, I'm not submitting my thesis paper for my junior year sociology class. I'm saying that in some ways, in a time when we often pray to get the other person's voicemail when we dial a phone number, the beauty of the spoken word can feel like a dying thing. Fortunately, there are enough great places in Los Angeles where you can still go to hear passages of a book read aloud, debates hotly contested, and the beauty of a poem, already penned or impromptu, performed live. Do something different for a change! You'll be cultural, you'll be literary, you'll be very, very contrary. (Okay, so rhyming is not one of my talents.)

POETRY **READINGS**

Beyond Baroque Literary/Arts Center
681 Venice Blvd., Venice
(310) 822-3006
www.beyondbaroque.org

With sometimes star-studded poetry workshops on Wednesday nights, and a nonstop schedule of live readings as well as free workshops, you can increase your brains cells by the beach—a rare possibility, so take advantage of it while you can! Members get free admission, and some events are totally free or donation only; general admission is $7, and only $5 for students, children, and senior citizens. Free open readings Sun at 5 p.m. If you're particularly jazzed by this listing, stop by on a Fri between 11 a.m. and 6 p.m. to speak with the bookstore manager about volunteer opportunities.

Cobalt Poets at The Cobalt Cafe
22047 Sherman Way, Canoga Park
(818) 348-3789
www.poetrysuperhighway.com/cobalt

The Catch: Free every Tues, but there's a 1-drink minimum. However, they don't serve alcohol, so how expensive can your drink possibly be?

Open readings at 9 p.m. (sign up at 8:30 p.m.) the first Tuesday of every month, featured regulars on the second Tuesday, Valley Contemporary Poets plus featured guests on the third Tuesday, and the Cobalt Classic All Open Reading on the fourth and fifth Tuesday of every month. Note: Not every month has five Tuesdays. Some only have four Tuesdays.

Da Poetry Lounge and The Actors' Lounge
544 N. Fairfax Blvd., Los Angeles
(818) 509-2986
www.dapoetrylounge.com and www.theactorsloungela.com

Since 1998 and every Tuesday night from 9 p.m. until midnight at the GreenWay Court Theater in Fairfax High School, just $5 grants you entry to hear some 35 poets compete in a poetry slam open mic. Winners of the weekly poetry slam form the 5-member team that attends the National Poetry Slam. Brutha Gimel and his 3 co-founders host. If you pony up the $3 suggested donation on the first Wednesday of each month, you can hear 3-minute monologues or 5-minute scenes starting at 8:30 p.m at their actor open mic, held in the same venue, same people, different website. Arrive in the hour before to sign up. Did you follow that?

Emerging Urban Poets at The Santa Catalina Branch of The Pasadena Public Library
999 E. Washington Blvd., Pasadena
http://emergingurbanpoets.blogspot.com

You can perform poetry and listen to others perform poetry every Sat in the back room of the library from 3 to 5 p.m. Now you'll have some fodder

for your Saturday night conversation. Visit http://saturdayafternoonpoetry.
blogspot.com for more information.

The Gypsy Den Grand Central Cafe
125 N. Broadway Ave., Santa Ana
(714) 835-8840
www.gypsyden.com

A cafe and bakery, Gypsy Den features delish freshly made breads, pastries, desserts, soups, chili, salads, sandwiches, pasta, and organic coffee, tea, and beverages in a chill and eclectic bohemian environment. Open mic sign-ups on Mon at 7:30 p.m. and Thurs at 6:30 p.m. Check website for more details on other events. The original Costa Mesa location does not feature live entertainment.

La Palabra at Avenue 50 Studio
131 N. Avenue 50, Highland Park
(323) 258-1435
www.avenue50studio.com

Avenue 50 Studio, Inc. is an arts presentation organization grounded in Latin and Chican culture. They have monthly featured readings. Check website (click on "La Palabra" on the left hand column of the home page) for details.

Moonday Poetry at Village Books
1049 Swarthmore Ave. (near Albright St.), Pacific Palisades
(310) 454-4063
www.moondaypoetry.com

Founded in 2003, poets Alice Pero and Lois P. Jones host an open reading followed by a featured reading the second Monday of every month at 7:30 p.m. Most are held at Village Books in Pacific Palisades; occasionally they branch out to other locations as well, so check online for the latest and greatest details. Arrive early to sign up.

The Moth LA StorySLAM
www.moth.org

For just $8 on the first Wednesday of every month at Zanzibar (1301 5th St., Santa Monica; www.zanzibarlive.com), you can hear true stories told live. Ten stories at 5 minutes each, and you never know what's going to be revealed. Doors open at 7 p.m. and stories commence at 7:30 p.m.

The Rapp Saloon
International Youth Hostel
1436 2nd St., Santa Monica

Open mic every Fri night at 8:30 p.m., not far from the 3rd Street Promenade and next door to Buca di Beppo. Every reader gets 6 minutes of time. Newcomers and seasoned performers alike, as well as any subject or form of expression are welcome. Find The Rapp Saloon on Facebook.

Redondo Poets at The Coffee Cartel
1820 S. Catalina Ave. (Hollywood Riviera), Redondo Beach
(310) 316-6554
www.redondopoets.com

Open mic and a featured poet every Tues at 8:10 p.m. Sign-up with the Redondo Poets starts at 7:50 p.m. All readers get 2 poems or 4 minutes. Free parking and free Wi-Fi. The Coffee Cartel may be the only coffee shop that also serves hot dogs and Hawaiian shaved ice in addition to your standard coffee shop fare.

Tia Chucha
13197-A Gladstone Ave., Sylmar
www.tiachucha.com

Tia Chucha is a cultural center and bookstore dedicated to Xicano history and literature. They sponsor open mic nights of music and the spoken word every Fri from 8 to 10 p.m. They also provide free Internet. In the spring of every year they'll also advertise the Celebrating Words Festival, with a book fair, author readings and panels, spoken word, and more held at Mission College in Sylmar.

Two Idiots Peddling Poetry at The Ugly Mug
261 N. Glassel Ave. (near Chapman University), Orange
www.poetryidiots.com or www.theuglymug.com

Featured and open poetry readings every Wed at 8 p.m. For a $3 cover charge, you're granted 3 poems or 5 minutes, whichever comes first. Co-hosts Steve Ramirez and Ben Trigg want you to remember that poetry reading is fun. Risk-taking is encouraged, as is respect shown for The Ugly Mug by spending some money at their establishment. Smoking permitted on the outdoor patio.

STORY **HOURS**, AUTHOR **APPEARANCES** & BOOK **DISCUSSIONS**

Barnes & Noble
www.barnesandnoble.com

There are some 40 Barnes & Noble locations in all of Los Angeles, and nearly all of them feature free Wi-Fi. The Barnes & Noble in Burbank has an open mic poetry night, and the Encino location has a weekly story time, poetry workshop, and writing group. You probably now feel like you are missing out. You are. Check website for up-to-date details on author appearances and special events.

Book Soup
8818 Sunset Blvd., West Hollywood
(310) 659-3110
www.booksoup.com

Book Clubs

Book clubs are not just for eating, drinking, and gossiping, though none of these things are discouraged. Eager for a literary outlet and maybe even a way to meet new people? The following websites can help you find a Los Angeles book club in a neighborhood on a date and time that's right for you.

www.readerscircle.org: Find any book club in the United States. Type in your LA zip code and find the age group and type of people reading books that might interest you among 60-plus possibilities. Listings provide the e-mail address of the host for you to contact directly. You can also start your own book club via this site and find members, or look up local author events.

www.meetup.com: Search for book lovers and clubs near you. In fact, search for any hobby under the sun to find people like you who want to meet up and do something about it.

Open Mon through Sun from 9 a.m. to 10 p.m., Book Soup has numerous live weekly in-person author events featuring discussions, readings, and signings of some of the best, including today's literary giants or media celebs who've recently penned a tell-all. Check the website for details, park your car for free behind the store on Nella Street, and voila! Tomorrow at the water cooler you get to say, "I went to so-and-so's book reading last night!" Don't you sound fancy?

Borders
www.borders.com

Although some stores throughout the country have closed, there are still multiple locations in the Los Angeles area. The stores feature author appearances, book signings, and story times for kids, too. Check the website for listings of events by location.

Living in Los Angeles

FOOD:
COMPLIMENTARY CUISINE

*"I went to a restaurant that serves
'breakfast any time.' So I ordered French toast
during the Renaissance."*

—STEVEN WRIGHT

I believe that what you eat is who you are. I believe in the vigor of a hearty appetite. Sitting down and eating meals together is one of the most civilized things we do. Beauty comes in all shapes and sizes and we should try to be healthy, of course. (I admit I do love me some jalapeño poppers from time to time.) But live it up, do your best ("Everything in moderation including moderation," per Dr. Edward Taub), and take advantage of the great happy hours, free samples, ethnic food, regular plain ol' American food, food trucks, and more that Los Angeles has to offer. Yum, yum. Bon appétit!

HAPPY **HOURS**

Bar Food
12217 Wilshire Blvd. (between Amherst and Wellesley Avenues),
West Los Angeles
(310) 820-3274
www.barfoodla.com

No, I didn't get the name of the restaurant wrong. That's their real name! Free hot dogs from 3 to 7 p.m. every day, and during happy hour from 5 to 7 p.m., you can get $5 house wine, $6 beers, and food items like burgers, spicy tuna, or chicken pesto for $6 and under. Bar Food has high ceilings with exposed beams coupled with paintings of famous musical artists, so the ambience makes you appear trendy and hip, even if you're not. Free residential street parking.

Cabo Cantina
11829 Wilshire Blvd., Brentwood
(310) 312-5840
www.thecabocantina.com

Happy hour is 7 days a week here, from 4 to 8 p.m.; some of the locations also have a late night happy hour. Taco Tuesday features $4.95 all-you-can-eat tacos, bottomless mimosas, and Bloody Marys Fri through Sun for $9.95 from opening until 3 p.m. (Uh, please have a designated driver if you partake in this liquid pleasure.) $5 foot-long burritos on Wednesday. Free bean and cheese burrito on Monday with purchase of burrito. All-you-can-eat sliders on Monday and Thursday football nights—sliders include rice and black beans, choice of chicken, steak, ground beef, and sautéed veggies. Mega Margaritas for $18. It's like Pancho Villa meets Sancho Panza and Don Quixote attending a medieval banquet know as La Ultima Cena. Additional locations are at 30 Washington Blvd., Marina Del Rey (310-306-2500), 1240 3rd St. Promenade, Santa Monica (310-393-5755), and 8301 Sunset Blvd., West Hollywood (323-822-7820).

Copa D'Oro
217 Broadway (at 2nd St.), Santa Monica
(310) 576-3030
www.copadoro.com

With a solid wood bar and old-fashioned interior, Copa D'Oro is located right in the heart of the 3rd Street Promenade district, serving up $5 cocktails during happy hour 5:30 to 8 p.m. every night, and all night on Monday. Happy hour menu includes discounted paninis and more. Plenty of street and garage parking.

Drago Centro
525 S. Flower St., #120 (between W. 5th and 6th Streets, downtown
Los Angeles
(213) 228-8998
www.dragocentro.com

Named one of the Best Italian Chefs in the US by *Bon Appétit* and *Los Angeles Times* restaurant critic Irene Virbila, Chef Celestino Drago will make mad, passionate Italian love to your taste buds at Drago Centro. The feel is upscale, but they have happy hour all day with bar bites for $3 to $10, and specialty wine, beer, and cocktails for $5 to $7. So you can be a cheap bastard and not look like one. Drago Centro also offers shuttle service every 15 to 20 minutes to the Staples Center, Nokia Theatre and Music Center when there are events at those venues; at the end of the night they'll return you to the City National Bank Plaza. Valet parking.

The Dresden Room
1760 N. Vermont Ave. (near Kingswell Ave.), Hollywood
(323) 665-4294
www.thedresden.com

"Baby, that was money! Tell me that wasn't money," says Trent in the movie *Swingers* (1996), which made The Dresden Room famous. An old-fashioned lounge with American and Continental food featuring live jazz from 9 p.m. to 1:15 a.m. Tues through Sat and classic rock on Sun and Mon, the 5 to 7 p.m. happy hours offer $2 well drinks, $1 off wine and beer, and $2 off appetizers (thus, you spend approximately $4 to $8). Now that's money you're not spending a lot of. Money. (In the awesome sense, not the literal one. Oh, you get it!)

El Chavo
4441 W. Sunset Blvd., Los Feliz
(323) 664-0871
www.elchavorestaurant.com

Okay, see, now I'm writing this listing and jonesin' for some guacamole. Located in the trendy Los Feliz and Silverlake neighborhoods, El Chavo serves up $4 well drinks from 7 to 9 p.m. daily. No reservations; walk-ins only. One of the top 5 happy hours in Los Angeles. Free parking behind the restaurant. Arriba! Arriba!

El Toro Cantina
5364 Wilshire Blvd., Los Angeles
(323) 525-2618

A chill tapas establishment located downstairs from Busby's Sports Bar, the black ceiling, red bar, and bull photos won't please your highfalutin' date or vegetarian, but the nightly happy hour from 4 to 7 p.m (2-drink minimum; after that, drinks are $1) and $1 Taco Tuesdays may win her over—the highfalutin' date, not necessarily the vegetarian. Part of the restaurant becomes a dance floor on the weekend. After chowing down, you can also head next door to Busby's for billiards, table tennis, arcade games, and more (get there before the $10 cover starts at 10 p.m.). Paid lot and street parking.

Figaro Bistrot
1802 N. Vermont Ave. (at Melbourne Ave.), Los Angeles
(323) 662-1587
www.figarobistrot.com

For the cultured palate: 5 to 7 p.m. happy hours feature $4.50 escargot, mussels with cheese, or a beef carpaccio dish for $5, and all wine is under

$6. Great French food and authentic French vibe, oui! It may be Los Feliz, but inside, it's all Parisian antiques and cast-iron chandeliers, mon ami! Metered street parking on Vermont or free parking on residential streets derriere the restaurant. (Okay, okay! My French stinks.)

Good Microbrew & Grill
3725 W. Sunset Blvd. (at Lucille Ave.), Los Angeles
(323) 660-3645
www.goodmicrobrew.com

Sip down in Silver Lake at the Good Microbrew Bar & Grill, where they have the largest selection of handcrafted beers from around the globe, with 24 draft handles, over 400 bottled beers, and 6 microbrews custom made especially for them. Daily happy hour 4 to 7 p.m., with $3 house pints and $5 draft beers. Mystery beer night on Wed from 6 to 10 p.m., with $3 microbrews, drafts, and bottles. Wednesday is very popular, so your best bet is to get there before 8 p.m. to nab a seat. No reservations, and your whole party must be present. Flight of 4 beer tasters is only $3. Lot and street parking.

The Hungry Cat
1535 N. Vine St. (between Sunset Blvd. and Selma Ave.), Hollywood
(323) 462-2155
www.thehungrycat.com

The Hungry Cat is light and bright, with a long bar counter. All cocktails, the daily special, and most draught beers are half off Mon through Fri, noon to 6 p.m. at this seafood establishment nestled in the crook of the action in Hollywood. Woody Allen said, "I will not eat oysters. I want my food dead—not sick, not wounded—dead." But you don't need to agree with him. First hour of garage parking free with validation. Street parking is also possible, but it may try your patience on the weekends. The Hungry Cat also has a location in Santa Barbara at 1134 Chapala (805-884-7402), and in Santa Monica at 100 W. Channel Rd. at the PCH (310-459-3337).

Napa Valley Grille
1100 Glendon Ave., Suite 100, Los Angeles
(310) 824-3322
www.napavalleygrille.com

Located in the heart of Westwood's Financial District just a stone's throw from the UCLA campus, the Napa Valley Grille features $2.50 fish tacos and natural beef sliders during happy hour, as well as $7 Amish Veal Skirt Steak and Frites or Lamb Belly. Is your mouth watering yet? Happy hour is 3 to 7 p.m. and again 9 p.m. to midnight, Mon through Sat; 3 to 9 p.m. Sun. Valet parking or 2-hour free parking on Broxton down the street, with a reasonable flate rate after 6 p.m.

FREE **FOR** ALL

Don't think I don't make a beeline for the free samples at Trader Joe's before I join the checkout line. And don't think, if I really like it, that I don't nonchalantly find a way to take a second one.

And don't think I don't know you do exactly the same thing.

Atwater Village Farmers Market
3250 Glendale Blvd. (at Brunswick Ave.), Los Angeles
(323) 463-3171
www.see-la.org

Free food and produce samples on Sun from 10 a.m. to 2 p.m. Background music often gently hits your ears as you browse, with some musician or performer working his stuff for tips. Plenty of street parking and a mellow Sunday scene. I want that free sample and then a nap on the couch, please. Drool okay, totally understood. Happens even to the beautiful people.

The Cheese Store of Silver Lake
3926-28 W. Sunset Blvd. (at Sanborn Ave.), Los Angeles
(323) 644-7511
www.cheesestoresl.com

In the words of my talented writer friend Kirk McGee, "What if you loved yourself as much as you love cheese?" Well, I'm not afraid to admit it. I do. I love myself as much as I love cheese. At this fine cheese and wine store, you can sample delish cheeses, oil and vinegar with bread, and other assorted delicacies that will leave your palate begging for more.

Fallen Fruit
www.journalofaestheticsandprotest.org/3/viegeneretal.htm

Eve in the Garden of Eden never had it so good. Fallen Fruit is a website that provides a map of all of the free fruit growing year-round on public property in Silver Lake. Oh, yes, such a thing really exists. Any fruit on or hanging over public property is not the sole property of the owner. Hello, my lovely oranges and lemons!

Hollywood Farmers' Market
1600 Ivar Ave. (at Selma Ave.), Los Angeles
(323) 463-3171
www.see-la.org

The Hollywood Farmers' Market is one of the largest and best of them all, held every Sat from 8 a.m. to 1 p.m. Sample all the tasty free morsels. Metered parking or some free parking at the Doolittle Theatre, $2 for the first 2 hours with validation at the Cinerama Dome.

Lark
3337 W. Sunset Blvd. (at Micheltorena St.), Los Angeles
(323) 667-2968
http://larkcakeshop.com

Free coffee or cupcake with a $1.50 purchase on Wed. Hello! Happy birthday to you. Of course, you can also just sample that cupcake without buying a thing . . . but it will taste so good you will end up buying one anyhow. So go ahead. Don't you deserve it?

Silver Lake Farmers' Market
3700 Sunset Blvd. (at Edgecliff Dr.), Los Angeles
(213) 413-7770
www.sunsetjunction.org/index.php/tutorials

Free samples of both produce and cooked food at the Silver Lake Farmers' Market, which is open every Sat from 8 a.m. to 1:30 p.m and Tues from 2 to 7 p.m. Cruise the residential streets enough for parking and something will open up.

Teavana

1153 Glendale Galleria, Glendale
(818) 956-1063
www.teavana.com

Feel like Mary Poppins or Henry Higgins as you sample a spot of tea at Teavana, which boasts an incredibly diverse selection of white, green, oolong, black, herbal, rooibos, and mate tea. Tea is the most widely consumed beverage in the entire world. It also has many antioxidant benefits. Teavana also has a location in the Century City Mall at 10205 Santa Monica Blvd. (310-277-0121).

Trader Joe's

www.traderjoes.com

Whether it's morning, noon, or suppertime, there's always a free sample (with coffee, too) to be had at Trader Joe's. And when you're done, you can purchase the cheap and healthy groceries. Visit the website to find one of one of 50 plus+ locations in the Los Angeles area.

Whole Foods Market

www.wholefoodsmarket.com

Expensive groceries (Trader Joe's is your better option between the two), but you can usually snag some free samples of cheese or pastries and ask to try the olives at the olive bar. Visit the website to locate the store nearest you.

CHEAP **EATS**

Carney's

8351 W. Sunset Blvd., Los Angeles
(323) 654-8300
www.carneytrain.com

For a restaurant housed in an old train car smack in the middle of the Sunset Strip, and with $1 coffee and a Mon through Fri 4:30 to 7 p.m. happy hour with $1.50 domestic beers, as well as hot dogs, hamburgers, and fries ranging in price from $1.40 to $3.20, you can chow down and gawk at the passersby. Cheap entertainment and a full belly—score! Carney's has another location in Studio City at 12601 Ventura Blvd. (818-761-8300).

Clifton's Cafeteria
648 S. Broadway (at W. 7th St.), Los Angeles
(213) 627-1673
www.cliftonscafeteria.com

Since 1935, Clifton's has been serving up home cooking cafeteria style 7 days a week, from 6:30 a.m. to 7:30 p.m. Dine on those mashed potatoes in the serenity of the redwood forest (themed decor) with rock sculpture walls (no climbing!), faux trees, and a waterfall.

Diddy Riese Cookies
926 Broxton Ave. (near Le Conte Ave.), Westwood
(310) 208-0448
www.diddyriese.com

Three cookies for $1 or 35 cents each, $3.75 for a dozen; 45 cents for a brownie, $5 for a dozen. Ice cream sandwiches (2 gourmet cookies of your choice held together by a delicious scoop of ice cream, also of your choice) for $1.50, 1 to 3 scoops of ice cream for $1 to $3. If you live here or have been to Los Angeles more than twice, how can you possibly admit you've never been?

Enzo's Pizzeria
10940 Weyburn Ave. (at Broxton Ave.), Los Angeles
(310) 208-3696

In Westwood on the edges of UCLA's campus, 1 slice will cost you $2.25, or you can pay $5.50 for an 8-inch pizza. Walk to Diddy Riese around the corner to grab some dessert. Great lunch deals and 2-hour free parking down the street. Enzo's has another location at 7261 Melrose Ave. (323-936-3696).

The Frysmith
(818) 371-6814
www.eatfrysmith.com

A food truck so good, I gave it its own entry. Do you like a $4 heaping of gourmet chili cheese fries, vegan chili fries, rajas fries, kimchi fries, or chicken sweet potato? If you don't think you do, you will soon. You must try them all. Be prepared to wait in line.

Philippe's French Dip
1001 N. Alameda St. (at Ord St.), Los Angeles
(213) 628-3781
www.philippes.com

Ten-cent coffee if you drink it inside. All nonalcoholic beverages are 65 cents to $2. Beer is $2.50 to $3.75. Beef Dip, Pork Dip, Ham Dip, Lamb Dip, Turkey Dip—all $5.75 to $6.95. PB & J is $2.10, and cheese sandwiches are $3. Oatmeal and coffee for breakfast for $2. Family-style table fun with sawdust floors and eclectic decor. Free parking in the lot. Why are you not there? Cole's French Dip at 118 E. 6th St. is Philippe's rival, but they recently renovated and while cheap, they did have to pay for those renovations, so, you know, they can't cut quite the same deals as Philippe's.

Pink's Hot Dogs
709 N. La Brea Ave. (near Melrose Ave.), Los Angeles
(323) 931-4223
www.pinkshollywood.com

This Los Angeles landmark is known as the "Hot Dog to the Stars!" Oh, the puns I could do. (I'll spare you.) Always a line, so be prepared to wait awhile. All hot dogs are in the $3 to $5 range, burgers $5 to $7, chili fries for $3.40, onion rings for $2.75, and 70-cent coffee. Oh, boy I do love being tall and thin, but oh, do I miss those pre-teen years when I could eat anything without giving a care in the world to just where it might end up! One visit a month won't kill you. And you can probably squeeze in another if you like, since you're so healthy and fitness conscious now that you are living the LA Vida Loca.

Porto's Bakery and Cafe
3614 W. Magnolia Blvd., Burbank
(818) 846-9100
www.portosbakery.com

Cheese rolls and macaroons for 85 cents, potato balls and guava cheese rolls for 95 cents. How did you not know about this place? A second location is in Glendale at 315 N. Brand Blvd. (818-956-5996).

Socko's Subs
920 Broxton Ave. (near Le Conte Ave.), Los Angeles
(310) 824-1222
www.sockossubs.com

Choose from the skinny, super sub, or giant sub selection. Join the discount club for deals. Will deliver to UCLA students or Westwood area for 50 cents, so you don't even have to take off your pajamas and dress up.

Village Pizzeria
6363 Yucca St. (at Ivar), Hollywood
(323) 790-0763
www.villagepizzeria.net

Giant pizza by the slice for $2.35 to $3.90. Two thin crust pizza slices with 1 topping and a drink for $6.25 until 5 p.m. I nursed the one and only hangover I have ever experienced in my entire life at Village Pizzeria with a slice and iced tea, and was cured instantly. If you're at the Larchmont location at 131 N. Larchmont (323-465-7633) and you pause on the patio to partake of your pizza, you may spot a celeb.

BARGAIN **ETHNIC** DISHES

Crazy Rock'N Sushi
7100 Santa Monica Blvd., Suite 158 (at La Brea Ave.), West Hollywood
(323) 882-8247
http://crazyrocknsushi.com

Happy hour lasts seven days a week here, from noon to 10 p.m., during which sushi rolls are 50 percent off, usually averaging at around $3, with "premium" sushi only a bit more. Every sushi roll under the sun makes an appearance on this menu, so even the choosiest will feel his or her appetite tended to in a more than satisfactory manner.

India Sweets and Spices
3126 Los Feliz Blvd., Glendale
(323) 345-0360
www.indiasweetsandspices.us/

Lunch and dinner combos at this vegan Indian grocery store and restaurant featuring cuisines from northern and southern India range from $4.99 to $6.99, and the Value Combo, Sunday Combo, and individual items such as samosas will cost you even less. India Sweets and Spices has other locations throughout Southern California. Pick up your favorite Bollywood hits and DVDs on your way out.

Kogi
www.kogibbq.com

Yet another food truck so fantastic it warrants its very own entry. "Let me clarify that this isn't fusion food, but Angeleno food. Koreans and Latinos have been living side by side in K-town for generations, so it's only natural that we'd eventually come up with a new flavor profile altogether," says co-owner Alice Shin. Mexican and Korean barbecue in one, made with all fresh ingredients. Roy Choi, Best Chef 2010 according to *Food and Wine Magazine,* created the menu. All items are under $7. Tricks to getting the quickest service after checking their location via Twitter or on their website are to 1) try rainy or cold days; 2) know that Hollywood lines are often short; 3) show up only an hour or two into service at places where the truck goes regularly; or 4) be prepared to wait up to 45 minutes or an hour at new stops.

Mae Ploy
2606 W. Sunset Blvd. (at N. Rampart), Los Angeles
(213) 353-9635

Thai food that will only run you $6 to $10 in hip Silver Lake. Quirky ambiance and authentic taste. I love the shrimp red panang curry and prefer it with brown rice. Parking in back and on street.

Mao's Kitchen
7313 Melrose Ave., Los Angeles
(323) 932-9681
www.maoskitchen.com

Lunch combo from 11:30 a.m. to 5 p.m. of spring roll, entrée, and rice will run you $7.50 or $8.50 for seafood or tofu entrees. If you're eating the Los Angeles diet portion, then you can stretch that $7.50 into 2 meals. A second location is in Venice at 1512 Pacific Ave. (310-581-8305).

Maya's Mexican and Salvadorian Food
1600 N. Alvarado St. (at Berkley Ave.), Los Angeles
(213) 484-0340

A little bit of El Salvador in Echo Park with $1.99 pupusas (except for Mon and Thurs when they are only $1) and $1.25 tacos.

Naga Naga Ramen
46 W. Valley Blvd., Alhambra
(626) 300-0010
www.nagaramen.com

Many Asian cultures believe that eating long noodles symbolizes having a long life. The Alhambra and Pasadena locations have different menus, but everything is $7.50 or under, with most dishes in the $6 range. Lots of vegetarian options. I love the shoyu pork ramen and gyoza. A second location is in Pasadena at 49 E. Colorado Blvd. (626-585-8822).

Nyala Ethiopian Cuisine
1076 S. Fairfax Ave. (in Little Ethiopia at Whitworth Dr.), Los Angeles
(323) 936-5918
http://nyala-la.com

Peruse the markets and thrift stores nearby before ducking in for dinner in this charming establishment. Ethiopian food is always best shared with friends. Veggie and meat combo meals will run you $10 to $15 and leave your belly full and happy.

The Prince Cafe
3198 W. 7th St. (at S. Catalina St.), Los Angeles
(213) 389-2007

A Koreatown staple, this is an old-fashioned hotel lounge bar with a modern bar plopped in the center. Sort of tacky and intriguing all at once. AMC's television series *Mad Men* shoots here, so you know the vibe is up to par if they feel it's good enough to set a swingin' '60s show in. Big drinks and portions of reasonably priced Korean food. The Tong Dak (whole fried chicken) and Kimchi Fried Rice are so delicious, you'll be coming back for more!

Zankou's Chicken
Multiple locations
www.zankouchicken.com

Mediterranean food at a nice price without the sound of the ocean water lapping at your feet, the blue domes of Santorini through your sunglasses, or even a buff Adonis to feast your eyes upon like candy. So, what do you get? Delicious chicken, falafel, shawerma, hummus, tahini, and tabbouleh salad, to name a few. If you're not looking for atmosphere but you are hungry, Zankou will more than fit the bill.

WINE TASTINGS:
FOR THE CULTURED CHEAP BASTARD

*"Wine makes daily living easier, less hurried,
with fewer tensions and more tolerance."*

—BENJAMIN FRANKLIN

If the pennies you've allocated to finance your passion for the red, white, and occasional rosé don't stack up in support of your love of the finest of grapes in their liquid form of perfection, you needn't worry and become convinced that your future wine cabinet is destined to be stocked only with flattened boxes of wine and nothing remotely fitting of a king or queen. Whether it's the free-flowing wine of a tasting at a Los Angeles winery, an art gallery opening, or the incredible special you snagged at Ralph's, there is wonderful wine to be had in cheap bastard style for your taste buds to swoosh, soak, and down in the City of Angels.

WINE **SHOPS**

BottleRock
3847 Main St., Culver City
(310) 836-WINE (9463)
www.bottlerock.net

Part wine retailer, part tasting room and small plates cafe, BottleRock holds Saturday wine tastings from 1 to 4 p.m. $15 to $20 to taste 4 to 5 wines. A discount if you decide to purchase a bottle to go. Now you're ready for Saturday night! Bring it on! BottleRock has a downtown location at 1050 Flower Street, #167 (213-747-1100).

Bristol Farms
1515 Westwood Blvd., Los Angeles
(310) 481-0100
http://bristolfarms.com

Since its opening in 1982, gourmet and specialty food retailer Bristol Farms has been touted by the local media as the "best small market" with the "best deli," "best sushi," "best meat," and "best cooking school." They can also add "best wine tasting" to that list, with their series of ongoing events and deals like two for the price of one. Their online "Wine News" calendar will keep you up to date. Choose among 8 (and counting) Los Angeles County locations.

City Sip

2150 W. Sunset Blvd. (at Mohawk St.), Los Angeles
(213) 483-WINE (9463)
www.citysipla.com

Happy hour Tues, Thurs, and Fri 5:30 to 7 p.m. with $4 select wines and $5 eats. All open bottles are half off by the glass after 9 p.m. on Sun, so swing by for a nightcap! They also offer half-price wines and cheap wine and cheese flights from time to time.

Colorado Wine Company

2114 Colorado Blvd. (near Casper Ave. in Eagle Rock), Los Angeles
(323) 478-1985
www.cowineco.com

Colorado Wine Company is a wine store specializing in bottles $25 and under. They cater to any wine lover, regardless of the level of knowledge. On Wine Cellar Wednesday from 4 to 11 p.m. and Thurs until 9 p.m., you can pick any bottle off the shelf and they'll pour it for $6 to $12 for the glass, and you can order in food. Colorado Boulevard's new culinary row has great order-in possibilities, from Tommy's to Casa Bianca, Brownstone Pizza, Lemongrass, The Oinkster, Dave's Chillin-N-Grillin, The Taco Spot, and Larkin's Joint. Kick off the weekend on Fri from 5:30 to 8 p.m., where you get 5 wines and artisanal cheeses from Auntie Em's for just $15. Hello, my friend Mr. Bargain! You can also get the pick-me-up you desperately need after the Monday you just had on Tuesday, where wine is poured by the glass or served 4 at a time with more gourmet cheese, from 4 to 9 p.m. Call ahead for the featured wines of the night or sign up online to receive their e-mail list. Wrap up your weekend with a lazy Sunday tasting of 2 whites and 2 reds and some cheese, for just $12 from 1 to 4 p.m. Pretty soon you'll be humming "Bottle of red, bottle of white . . . " from Billy Joel's "Scenes from an Italian Restaurant." Only you'll be in a great wine shop. Not an Italian restaurant.

55 Wine

3111 Glendale Blvd. (at Glenfeliz Blvd. in Atwater Village), Los Angeles
(323) 662-5556
www.55degreewine.com

55 Wine can boast the title of #1 Wine Bar, according to City Search. Even with their name and that title, they also happen to sell just as much beer.

Wine tasting hours are Tues through Fri 6 to 10 p.m., Sat 5 to 11 p.m., and Sun 5 to 10 p.m.; beer can be partaken of Thurs through Sun during those hours. All beer tastings are $15 for 5 flights, and wine tastings, depending on the region, cost, and caliber, will run you $10 to $30 for 3 wines, with a full glass of your favorite of those 3 wines. They've also got a great small menu of savory pizzas, cheeses, and more. Look online, e-mail events@55degreewine.com, or call ahead for the latest schedule.

Red Carpet Wines and Spirits

400 E. Glenoaks Blvd. (near N. Jackson St.), Glendale
(800) 339-0609
www.redcarpetwine.com

The staff at the family-owned Red Carpet Wine is down-to-earth, friendly, and knowledgeable about the wine they sell and pour. The Wine Bar was given a makeover recently, expanded hours, and the Enomatic Serving System, which allows your wine to be opened and tasted without the danger of oxidation. $1 pours on Mon; $2 pours Tues through Thurs. Their website also recommends wines by price category.

Silverlake Wine

2395 Glendale Blvd. (at Brier Ave.), Los Angeles
(323) 662-9024
www.silverlakewine.com

Every Mon or Thurs from 5 to 9 p.m., you can lessen the burden of the start or end of your work week by sampling 3 wines in one particular category (be it by grape, winemaker, or region, for example) for just $12. Wines are served with different cheeses, olives, and bread, and no reservation is necessary. Feeling a bit more sophisticated? Wind down the weekend on Sun at 3 p.m. with 4 wines and an aperitif for $20. Each wine is expertly paired with an hors d'oeuvre, sure to whet your appetite and allow you to sneak in a happy, satiated snooze before Sunday night football.

Vendome Wine and Spirits

9153 W. Olympic Blvd., Beverly Hills
(310) 276-9463
www.vendometolucalake.com

Cheap Wine (The Non-Headache-Inducing Kind)

Whether it's to complement the pasta and salad dinner you've whipped up in the kitchen for the new flame you're digging, the bubbly bath you promised yourself, or the brilliant "blind wine tasting" your fancy friends asked you to attend (and bring a bottle), there are plenty of cheap bottles of wine to be had for $10 and under. Several supermarket-type chains will be your surefire bet so as not to send you breaking a sweat if you feel stressed by the assignment. I'm a big proponent of cheap wine that won't send you in search of the Advil or puckering your lips, so you can trust my advice.

BevMo! has a nickel wine sale from time to time, where if you buy 2 bottles of the same wine, the second bottle is only 5 cents. Yes, that's right. A nickel. Nearly 200 bottles are part of this sale, and prices start as low as $8. Score! BevMo! also has wine tastings. Visit www.bevmo.com for a location near you.

Ralphs has affordable wines and some 50-plus locations in Los Angeles to choose from. At www.ralphs.com.

Trader Joe's—If you've haven't heard of "Two Buck Chuck," the nickname for Charles Shaw wines at $1.99 a bottle, I'm not sure what rock you've been living under. They've got Cabernet Sauvignon, White Zinfandel, Merlot, Chardonnay, Sauvignon Blanc, Shiraz, and some Pinot Grigio as well, so you're covered with reds and whites. The Bronco Wine Company buys surplus grapes from California growers in order to produce Charles Shaw, so you're also supporting your local economy. (Though not all batches of surplus grapes are tremendous . . . no two bottles of wine are alike.) Friends don't let friends drink White Zinfandel, but if you do, I won't tell. Check online for one of a billion locations (okay, I'm exaggerating, but only a little) near you. At www.traderjoes.com.

Whole Foods does not have Two Buck Chuck, but they do have a great selection of affordable wines, including Three Wishes, Two Buck Chuck's $2 competition. Find a location near you at www.wholefoods market.com.

Vendome holds Wednesday tastings from 5 to 8 p.m. at $1 per pour. Don't let that bang for your buck go to your head if you're driving. Beer tastings on Sat are 2 to 5 p.m., with 15 beers for $10. Tastings are sometimes suspended during the busy holiday season, so call ahead. Two additional locations are at 906 Granite Dr., Pasadena (626-396-9234), and 10600 Riverside Dr., Toluca Lake (818-766-9593).

Wally's Wine and Spirits
2107 Westwood Blvd. (at Mississippi Ave. in Westwood), Los Angeles
(310) 475-0606
www.wallywine.com

There are tastings on Sat from 1 to 4 p.m., usually for just $10! Includes cheese and bread, and they'll give you a discount if you decide to purchase some of what you tasted. Wally's also offers wine courses on particular regions.

Wine Expo
2933 Santa Monica Blvd. (at Stanford St.), Santa Monica
(310) 828-4428
www.wineexpo.com

Wine Expo hosts tastings every night in the wine bar. A flight of 3 will run you $8 up to $18, depending on your selection. The "Latest" tab on their website has the list of wines in each flight so you can prepare your taste buds accordingly. Roberto, the manager, is a bit of a music geek as well—you'll probably want to purchase a bottle of wine and get him to beef up your iTunes library.

The Wine House
2311 Cotner Ave., West Los Angeles
(310) 479-3731
www.winehouse.com

Test drive the automated in-store tasting area with 32 different selections, ranging from $1 to $5 a pour. The Wine House also offers some 290 or so varieties of wine for sale under $10. My personal tip? When invited to dinner at someone's house, pick up a bottle of one of the reds of Francis Ford Coppola (yes, that film director who also happens to make great wine). Depending on the year, it will cost you between $10 and $15, but taste like 3 times that, and you'll be elegant and oh so sophisticated.

WINERIES

Yes! Los Angeles has wineries! Wine—I'm sorry—wind through them to sample some of the best. Now you can't say you didn't know. I have not included any that fall outside of a cheap bastard budget.

D'Argenzio Winery

1204 W. Burbank Blvd. (at N. Mariposa St.), Burbank
(818) 846-VINO (8466)
www.dargenziowine.com

The winery is in Sonoma, but lucky for you Southern Californians, they have a second tasting room and wine bar in Burbank. Wine tastings will run you $10 for 5 to 6 wines. Open to the public Mon through Thurs noon to 5 p.m., and Fri and Sat 6 to 8 p.m. Closed Sunday.

Rosenthal—The Malibu Estate

26023 Pacific Coast Hwy., Malibu
(310) 456-1392
www.rosenthalestatewines.com

Fourteen hundred feet above the mystical fog of the Malibu-Newton Canyon AVA, grapes produce Cabernet Sauvignon, Merlot, and Chardonnay. If you want to taste their wine, you'll have to stick to the public tasting room on the PCH. $15.

San Antonio Winery and Restaurant

737 Lamar St., Los Angeles
(323) 223-1401
www.sanantoniowinery.com

This winery has been around since 1917. You can now pick your jaw up off the floor. In fact, there used to be more than 100 wineries that lined the Los Angeles River Basin. (Yes, there's a Los Angeles River, too.) Complimentary tastings of 3 free samples from a selected list. Artisan series tasting of 3 wines for $8, or 4 wines for $10. Free tours of the winery on the hour Mon through Fri noon to 2 p.m., or Sat and Sun 11 a.m. to 4 p.m.

WINING & **DINING**

Il Moro
11400 W. Olympic Blvd. (entrance and valet on Purdue Ave.),
West Los Angeles
(310) 575-3530
www.ilmoro.com

On Tues from 5 to 8 p.m. for just $15, you can sample wines and gourmet finger food created by the chefs at this Northern Italian eatery. Beer tastings are held during the same time slot on Thurs.

Lago
231 Arizona Ave., Santa Monica
(310) 451-3525
www.lagosantamonica.com

Lago offers some serious deals for wine-o-philes and hop-heads alike: $4 house wines and $3 beers in the bar and restaurant every day from 4 to 7 p.m., and in the bar only in the same time slot on Sat and Sun, and Tues all night. Small bites at the bar are fancy, succulent, and won't break the bank. Lago's menu focuses specifically on the cuisine of Bellagio on Lake Como in northern Italy.

Left Coast Wine Bar & Gallery
117 E. Harvard St. (at S. Maryland Ave.), Glendale
(818) 507-7011
www.leftcoastwinebar.com

Kick back for a double welcome whammy of live jazz and 4 flights of wine for just $15 on Tues at 8 p.m. Take in the original fine art that surrounds you as you detect the fruit and wood traces in that red you're sipping.

The Mercantile
6600 W. Sunset Blvd. (at Seward St.), Hollywood
(323) 962-8202
www.themercantilela.com

W is for wine on Wednesday. Saunter into The Mercantile, and enjoy 3 half glasses of wine for just $16 at this wine bar, cafe, and small gourmet market under chef Kris Morningstar.

Seven Bar Lounge

55 W. 7th St. (at S. Main St. downtown), Los Angeles
(213) 223-0777
www.sevenrestaurantbar.com

Sample free tastes from a different winemaker every month at Seven Bar Lounge. Check out those legs! (The legs on the wine . . . don't go there, buddy.) Wine-tasting events on the second Thurs of the month just prior to the Downtown Art Walk, from 5:30 to 7 p.m. Reasonably priced bites for the cost of the name. $7.

The Standard

550 S. Flower St. (at 6th St. downtown), Los Angeles
(213) 892-8080
www.standardhotels.com/los-angeles

Partnering with Silver Lake Wine, The Standard Downtown offers wine every week in their hotel lobby from 5 to 8 p.m. A live DJ, snacks, and 3 flights of boutique wines, all for $20.

Vertical Wine Bistro

70 N. Raymond Ave. (upstairs, north of Union St.), Pasadena
(626) 795-3999
www.verticalwinebistro.com

Great deals on appetizers, cocktails, beer, and wine during happy hour, which runs Tues through Sat 5 to 7 p.m., Tues through Thurs 10 p.m. to midnight, and Sun night all night. Show proof of your San Gabriel address with ID or a business card, and you'll find yourself sipping a complimentary glass of Prosecco with any food purchase! Join the birthday club for free online and receive a $25 gift certificate on your birthday, good all birthday month long. Happy birthday to you, indeed.

Wine Detective

146 S. Lake Ave., #109 (near Cordova St.), Pasadena
(626) 792-9936
www.winedetective.com

Happy hour every day from 4 to 7 p.m., with house wines for $5 and select food 20 percent off. If you're feeling so bold as to open a tab, you'll get a tasting card, which entitles you to taste any of their 16 whites or 32 reds on

Connecting with Wine Lovers Online

It's the modern age and the 21st century, so you can connect to your fellow wine aficionados and stay hooked into the latest wine events all for the cost of your Internet connection. I haven't featured any of the food- and wine-type festivals offered in and around Los Angeles, as their fees do not fall under the cheap bastard category, but I have included the Los Angeles-centric wine websites you need to know about, should you find your enthusiasm escalating toward an unbridled passion.

I'll Drink to That is networking for wine enthusiasts. Talk business and drink wine, killing two birds with one stone. Access the networking site through the main blog at http://illdrinktothat.info.

Learn About Wine is your source for wine education and events in Southern California. Have I admitted that I am absolutely hopeless when it comes to opening a wine bottle? Lucky for you, founder Ian Blackburn has been drinking wine for a living since 1995. Many of his events are held downtown. Visit www.learnaboutwine.com.

Local Wine Events is a website of wine events by city, worldwide. Yes, yes, it's true. The largest and most comprehensive calendar of food, wine, beer, and spirits events you'll ever see. Sign up for free notifications via e-mail, or post an event. Browse the Wine Q&A, blogs, books, magazines, and more. Visit www.localwineevents.com.

Meetup.com features a multitude of Los Angeles–based wine fan groups you can (wait for it, wait for it) meet up with to drink and

display. A glass of Casanova Di Neri Brunello di Montalchino, once labeled "the best wine in the world" by *Wine Spectator,* is only $4.50.

TAKE **YOUR** WINE **WITH** A **SIDE** OF **ART**

At art galleries, openings, and special events around town, you have an exciting opportunity to enrich yourself both culturally and viticulturally.

talk wine. (Anything beyond that is up to you.) Choose from The San Gabriel Valley and LA Metro Wine, Gay Winos, Hollywood Food and Wine, Women and Wine, The Santa Monica WLA Wine and Poker group, West LA Wine and Social Lovers Group, West Los Angeles Wine Enthusiasts, and more. At www.meetup.com.

Wine Berserkers is "a forum community for those gone berserk over wine." You know you're in trouble when the new prized centerpiece of "art" on your coffee table is a bowl full of wine corks. Discuss wine, read tasting notes, and glean all the information you would ever need or want to know at www.wineberserkers.com.

Wine Searcher can help you locate that wine bottle by name, vintage, state, and currency from its database of nearly 20,000 wine stores. You can view all matching wines, exact matches, exclude auctions, or read auctions only. Yes, can you believe they actually have wine auctions? Visit www.wine-searcher.com.

Wine Tasting for Los Angeles (WTFLA) has, among several things, everything you need to know about free wine tastings and awesome happy hours all over Los Angeles, such as the fact that The Olive Kitchen + Bar (8462 W. Sunset Blvd.; www.theolivekitchen bar.com) in West Hollywood has 50 percent off all wine, beer, and appetizers or 3 wines, cheese, and charcuterie for $15 on the first Wednesday of each month from 7 to 9 p.m. Be in the know at www .wtflosangeles.org.

Expand your horizons gazing at a beautiful piece of art, and sip some free wine to make it all go down even better.

Brewery Artwalk, held once in the fall and once in the spring, hosts an open studio weekend in which some 100 artists share their work with the public. Look at the art, appreciate it, question the artists directly about it, drink some wine, and purchase a piece at great studio prices. More information at www.breweryartwalk.com.

Downtown Los Angeles Art Walk is held the second Thurs of each month from noon to 9 p.m., in the financial and historical Downtown district. This self-guided tour, which started in 2004 and has flourished as much of Downtown has cleaned up, encompasses more than 40 galleries and museums spread throughout Downtown's many subdistricts, including Bunker Hill, Little Tokyo, and Gallery Row on Main and Spring Streets in the Historic Core. About 10,000 visitors regularly take the tour. If you're in a gallery and it is serving wine, you are freely welcome to it, so raise a glass and engage in some lively art discourse. Visit www.downtownartwalk.org for more details.

First Fridays at Abbot Kinney are held the first Friday of every month from 6 to 10 p.m. on Venice's Abbot Kinney Boulevard. You can check out the art, shops, music, and, of course, the wine. Visit www.abbotkinneynow .com for more information.

Miracle Mile Art Walk is held the third Saturday of January, April, July, and October. Your taxes will tell you that's once a quarter, folks. There are 40 galleries within 4 square miles of each other on Melrose, La Brea, and Beverly Boulevard, and at least as many bottles of wine and free sips to be had. Visit www.miraclemileartwalk.com.

NELAart Second Saturday Night is held, as the name suggests, on the second Sat of every month from 7 to 10 p.m. at Eagle Rock and York Boulevards in Highland Park. Tool around the neighborhood to explore some two dozen galleries, alternative arts spaces, and arts organizations. You will need your car. Get the latest at www.nelaart.com.

St. Elmo Village is an artists' collective founded the year they put a man on the moon (1969). At 4830 St. Elmo Dr., you can listen to live jazz and African drumming, and partake in some wine. There's more information at www.stelmovillage.org.

BEAUTY SERVICES: CHEAP IS IN THE EYE OF THE BEHOLDER

"Beauty is in the eye of the beholder and it may be necessary from time to time to give a stupid or misinformed beholder a black eye."

—MISS PIGGY

I was the girl who, when we paired off at slumber parties to do makeovers, no one wanted to be my partner. When I declared Vanessa looked absolutely beautiful after I had finished with her, the rest of Lindsay's pajama-clad guests peered at me dubiously. When I did a play nearly 20 years later, in a cast including over 10 women, I alone was given a private makeup tutorial. If I vacation with my girlfriends, I can get ready for a night out—shower, makeup, and all—in 35 minutes, while everyone else toils for 1.5 hours. I frighten houseguests when they ask for a hair dryer and I can't produce one. Thus, you might say beauty isn't my strong point. Heck, I only just learned how to do my hair after all these years. However, we are modern women, and a modern woman in Los Angeles comes with certain expectations to look good all the time. And I am an expert at how to do that without breaking the bank—whether it's your hair, your nails, your face, or just all over you. Read on for some of the best-kept secrets in town.

BEAUTY **SCHOOLS**

Stylists don't come out of the womb knowing how to cut hair. They, too, have to go to school first, and practice on real-life people such as you. In the cases where I've gone to beauty schools and been worked on by a student, I've always ended up with a great color or cut, and sometimes that great color or cut is one of the best I've ever had. Cuts or color are supervised by professionals, so it's not like they'll have their way with you and then send your head of hair, forever scarred, out into the real world. Your appointment may last a little longer than usual, as the student will have to review his or her work with the teacher before you depart.

The Catch: *Beauty school services cost money, but they do cost far less than a full-service salon. Call ahead for hours and details. And hey, don't be so cheap that you don't leave the standard 20 percent personal services tip. Students need to eat, too, and you don't want to wreck your karma by being a too-cheap bastard.*

Aveda Institute Los Angeles

10935 Weyburn Ave. (at Westwood Blvd.), Los Angeles
(310) 209-2000
www.avedainstitutelosangeles.com

Haircuts start at $19 and color starts at $25. The Institute offers manicures, pedicures, and makeup application lessons, and more. They run specials from time to time, so check the website for details. Closed Sun.

Marinello Schools of Beauty

Multiple locations
www.marinello.com

Haircuts start at $4.99 and color starts at $17.95. Menu and prices vary by location. Bring a friend and get $3 off any service.

Sassoon Academy

321 Santa Monica Blvd. (at 4th St.), Santa Monica
(310) 255-0011
www.sassoon.com

Cuts start at $22 on weekdays, $26 on weekends, and color starts at $26. If you would like to be a hair model (sessions last 3 to 5 hours) and are between 18 and 50 years of age, call (888) 757-5100, ext. 1, to book an appointment.

Simi Valley Adult Cosmetology School

3340 Los Angeles Ave. (at Crater St.), Simi Valley
(805) 579-6275
www.simi.tec.ca.us/files/cosmetolpar.asp

Haircuts start at $8, and color starts at $10. This school uses Redken and Clairol coloring products. A predisposition (PD) test for $2 is required 24 hours prior to any color services. What does this mean? They test a small part of your hair to make sure the color comes out the way you are hoping it will. They offer facials and nail services as well. Cash only, closed Sun and Mon, with no chemical services after 2 p.m. on Sat, or 7 p.m. during the week. No appointment necessary.

West Valley Occupational Career Center
6200 Winnetka Ave., Woodland Hills
(818) 346-3540
www.wvoc.net

The Cosmetology Department offers free haircuts on Mon and half-price services for those 55 and over every Tues and Wed.

CUTS **FOR** LESS

Think there's no way your current budget can accommodate a high-end salon cut or color? Think again. Whether it's a high-end salon, a chain, barbershop, or being a hair model, it's time you expand your imagination to include some of the steals below, and you'll officially be known as Thrifty Tresses all around town.

Alexander's for Hair
11515 W. Pico Blvd., Los Angeles
(310) 473-0462
http://alexandersforhair.com

Formerly Reeder's Barbershop, Alexander's for Hair offers a "Hero's Special" that gives a 20 percent discount to firefighters, police, and military Mon through Fri 2 to 5 p.m. Must present ID. They also offer special care for your kids while you get your haircut on a Sunday; your first visit is only $20 for a deluxe cut; and, if you refer a stylist or barber whom Alexander's hires, your monthly haircuts are free during the entire time he or she works there.

C the Salon
12050 Ventura Blvd., C101 (at Laurel Canyon), Studio City
(818) 763-4005
www.cthesalon.com

Be a hair model on Tues night at 5:30 p.m., and a junior stylist will cut those locks for $20, or color them for $30.

Cool Cuts 4 Kids
515 N. Grand Ave., Suite G (at Valley Blvd.), Walnut
(909) 595-7272
www.coolcuts4kids.com

For $18.95, your child can watch cartoons, a movie, or play a video game while getting his or her hair cut. If you were anything like me as a child and constantly moved your head and talked so much that your bangs turned out crooked, then this salon should feel like a miracle invention. Join the rewards club and receive notices on special sales and promotions.

The Fade Inn Barber Shop
5633½ Hollywood Blvd., Los Angeles
(323) 467-7270
www.fadeinn.com

The Fade Inn is a neighborhood barbershop specializing in low tapers, fades, razor shaves, mohawks, fauhauks, and graphic designs, so you can be as classic, downtown, or valley as you like, whatever best suits your style. Most cuts are around $15.

Frédéric Fekkai
440 N. Rodeo Dr., Beverly Hills
(310) 777-8700
www.fekkai.com

Free cuts on Thursday and free color on the third or fourth Sunday of each month, so long as you agree to cut off at least 2 inches of your hair and try something new. Frédéric Fekkai is the crème de la crème of salons. All processes are supervised. Go to http://beafekkaimodel.com to upload a photo and fill in a questionnaire for consideration to be a hair model. An additional location is in West Hollywood at 8457 Melrose Place (323-655-7800).

Floyd's 99 Barbershop
Multiple locations
www.floydsbarbershop.com

Originally opened in Denver, Colorado, Floyd's 99 Barbershop is not your garden variety barbershop, with the music cranked high while your locks are clipped. Prices for men and women's haircuts range from $15 to $34.

Gamine Silverlake

2845 W. Sunset Blvd. (and Historic 66), Los Angeles
(213) 413-8808
www.gaminesilverlake.com

This trendy high-end Silverlake salon offers half-price haircuts to first-time clients on Tues, Thurs, and Sun, a limited number of complimentary haircuts by assistants; and certain color services at reduced rates. Assistant cuts and services are completed under the supervision of an experienced stylist, and since assistants are very diligent about doing work your tresses will be thrilled with, there's nothing to fear but your beautiful self staring back at you from the mirror when the job is done. Call ahead for details.

The Hive

1402 Micheltorena St. (at Sunset Blvd. in Silverlake), Los Angeles
(323) 665-1028
www.thehive.la

Located in hip and trendy Silverlake, if you follow The Hive on Twitter and Facebook, you can keep up to date with their latest specials and discounts. You can also get a free haircut by referring 5 friends.

Mastercuts

2700 Colorado Blvd., Suite 113 (in Eagle Rock Shopping Center), Los Angeles
(323) 257-1105
www.mastercuts.com

No frill, no fuss, and no appointment necessary at this salon chain specializing in cuts for the whole family. When you find a good stylist at Mastercuts, stick with him or her, tip well, and you'll never have to pay a fortune to keep those ends healthy again. Believe me, unless you're a supermodel (yes, of course you're gorgeous, darling), no one can tell the difference between a $15 and $100 haircut, so why should you pay more? Adult cuts start at $16.95.

Rudy's Barbershop

Multiple locations
www.rudysbarbershop.com

Applicable adjectives are as follows: cheap, sexy, walk-in only, flanked by hip and modern art and music in a casual environment. No, that's not your date I'm describing; it's Rudy's Barbershop, which started in Seattle, Washington,

Bang for Your Beauty Buck

Sometimes, beauty really is just at your fingertips. Check out these sites to get the best beauty bargains in Tinseltown.

http://coupons.laweekly.com/los-angeles/deals—Click on "Health & Beauty" to find deals on body, dental, hair, massage, spa, waxing services, and more.

www.craigslist.com—Type in "free haircut" or "free massage" and see what you yield. A lot of cosmetologists are looking to build their portfolios and thus may offer their services for free . . . at your own risk . . . but free.

www.freecycle.org—Sign up and join a group in your region, surf message boards for free items, or post items to be donated. No cost for any of the items, so everything, whether it's makeup, chair, or nail polish, is free. You must, however, post something for free in order to get something for free.

www.groupon.com/los-angeles—Not only can you find great deals on beauty services, but also you can find great deals on restaurants, entertainment, and more. Log on every day to check the most up-to-date details.

http://livingsocial.com—Deals on spas, restaurants, and events in Los Angeles e-mailed to you daily.

www.spafinder.com—Wellness Week is every September, so log on to find great deals up to 50 percent off.

www.spaweek.com/deals—Spa Weeks run in September and then again in April. During these weeks you can get treatments for a flat rate of $50 at participating spas around the country. Visit the site and sign up to receive alerts.

Polish That Won't Hurt Your Purse

Los Angeles has a number of nail salons that feature mani-pedis for $23 and less. Here are a few of them listed by neighborhood, so take your pick.

Beverly Hills
Amy Nail Design, 245 S. Robertson Blvd.; (310) 652-2446

Culver City
Top Nailine, 308 Fox Hills Mall; (310) 390-8788
World of Nails, 10811 Washington Blvd., #110; (310) 838-5943

Hollywood
C'est La Vie, 1253 Vine St.; (323) 466-4730
iNails, 5900 Hollywood Blvd., Suite C, and 5419 Hollywood Blvd., Suite A; (323) 962-3652 and (323) 463-3158; www.inails.com
Lynda Nails Salon, 1727 N. Vermont Ave., Suite 110; (323) 663-7215
Nailism, 5638 Hollywood Blvd.; (323) 466-2328

Pasadena
De Lacey Beauty Shoppe, 48 S. De Lacey Ave.; (626) 577-4809
Dian Nails, 2044 E. Colorado Blvd.; (626) 793-4994
Elite Nail, 1820 E. Colorado Blvd.; (626) 744-9946

Silverlake
Nails Station, 3038 Rowena Ave.; (323) 667-1688
Vina Nails, 4362 Fountain Ave.; (323) 660-4571

and Portland, Oregon, before opening up in Los Angeles in 2006. Choose from one of 11 locations and counting; shop their unusual merchandise (T-shirts, CDs) while you wait. Prices start at $15 and run up to $30 for a cut.

Supercuts
Multiple locations
www.supercuts.com

Studio City
Natural Nails, 11709 Moorpark St.; (818) 763-6217
Ventura Nails, 12080 Ventura Place, Suite 1; (818) 762-2918; www.venturanails.com

Venice
Lincoln Nails, 713 Lincoln Blvd.; (310) 399-7277
Spring Nail Spa, 2492 Lincoln Blvd.; (310) 827-0115

West Hollywood
Joyful Nails, 8229 Santa Monica Blvd., Suite 102; (323) 848-9116
LA Beverly Hills Nails, 8327 Beverly Blvd.; (323) 852-0405
Lanny Nails, 8317 Beverly Blvd.; (323) 653-3370
Nails and More, 468 N. Doheny Dr.; (310) 271-9800
Wonder Nails Salon, 309 N. Fairfax Ave.; (323) 651-4188

Westwood
Bisou Nails, 1281 Westwood Blvd., Suite 100; (310) 444-9091
Christine's Nails, 1361 Westwood Blvd.; (310) 478-7811
MB Nails, 2180 Westwood Blvd., # 1N; (310) 475-4266
Milan Nail Spa, 1567 Westwood Blvd.; (310) 478-6999
Star Nails, 1317 Westwood Blvd.; (310) 445-5689
V T Nail and Spa, 1411 Westwood Blvd.; (310) 312-5657

Wilshire
Lovely Nails, 11918 Wilshire Blvd.; (310) 478-9814
Wilshire Nails, 609 S. Western Ave.; (213) 380-7375
Wilshire Pro Nails, 11968 Wilshire Blvd.; (310) 820-0379

A national chain and one of my personal favorites. Log online to get their many locations in Los Angeles, West Hollywood, Burbank, Studio City, Culver City, Sherman Oaks, or Santa Monica. Haircuts start at $15, sans the hair wash or style and blowdry. I like to go, have them wet my hair with a spray bottle, perfect my layers and make those ends healthy, and then I pay, tip, and slip out the door and head home to wash and style it myself for the day.

Visage Aveda Salon

517 S. Olive St. (between 5th and 6th Streets downtown), Los Angeles
(213) 228-0008

The salon is located inside the Millennium Biltmore Hotel, and your haircut is free if you purchase color or highlights. You can also snag 20 percent off other salon services such as nails, waxing, facials, and massage.

The Yellow Balloon

1328 Wilshire Blvd. (at 14th St.), Santa Monica
(310) 458-7947
www.yellowballoonsm.com

Prices range from $17 to $25. Coupons are sometimes offered on their website. If this is your kid's first haircut, they will take a Polaroid and issue a certificate, so you will remember the big day. I think my mom still has the foot of my hair they cut off when I was 9 years old.

FREE **SAMPLES** & MAKEOVERS

Bloomingdales

10250 Santa Monica Blvd., Century City
(310) 772-2100
www.bloomingdales.com

At Bloomie's make-up counter, you can find a cosmetologist who appears talented and friendly to you, and sit down for your free makeover. You may be encouraged and tempted to try some of the products they use on you, but even if you don't buy them, at least your face can give them a test drive. An additional location is at 8500 Beverly Blvd., West Hollywood (310-360-2700).

Kiehl's

720 Americana Way, Glendale
(818) 553-1955
www.kiehls.com

Kiehl's has been around since 1851 and has everything you need for your skin or hair. Browse the store for something you want to give a whirl, and they will send you home with a free sample. When you buy an item in the store, they'll send you home with 3 free samples. And then you can blame me for being officially hooked. Log on for more information. Additional locations are at 189 The Grove Dr., West Hollywood (323-965-0569), and 100 N. Robertson Blvd., Mid-City West Los Angeles (310-860-0028).

Nordstrom
189 The Grove Dr., West Hollywood
(323) 930-2230
www.nordstrom.com

Will you gravitate to Lancome, Estée Lauder, MAC, or Clinique? Take your pick, the world is at your feet . . . or should I say your face? A second location is at 10830 W. Pico Blvd., Los Angeles (310-470-6155).

Sephora
Multiple locations
www.sephora.com

Why Sephora hasn't existed since the invention of the mirror, I'll never know. What genius to have nearly all beauty brands known to man under one roof. Free makeup applications in the store, plus free samples, whether you are at the store or buying online. Get a Beauty Insider card and score even more free stuff.

DISCOUNT **MASSAGE** SERVICES

California Healing Arts College
12217 Santa Monica Blvd., Suite 206, West Los Angeles
(310) 826-7622
www.chac.edu

Dubbed as one of the top ten massage therapy schools in the United States in *Massage for Dummies,* the California Healing Arts College offers 50-minute massages for $25 to first-timers, and $35 every session thereafter.

CloudMover Day Spa

7368 Center Ave. (at Gothard St.), Huntington Beach
(714) 890-0900
www.cloudmover.com

Massages range in price from $40 to $110, depending on the treatment and length of time. CloudMover calls itself "the affordable professional day spa," and offers a line of skin care, facials, body treatments, and waxing services in addition to massage. Check the website to stay up to date with their current specials and promotions.

Healing Hands Wellness Center

303 S. Crescent Heights Blvd., Los Angeles
(323) 782-3900
www.healinghandswc.com

Healing Hands Wellness Center offers massages at $55 for one hour, or $80 for 90 minutes. Fifteen percent off all massages Mon through Fri 10 a.m. to 2 p.m. at the above location only. Healing Hands often runs a new patient bonus that includes a free 30-minute massage with the purchase of an acupuncture or chiropractic treatment. A second center is located in Larchmont at 414 N. Larchmont Blvd. (323-461-7876).

The Massage Garage

3812 Main St. (south of Venice Blvd.), Culver City
(310) 202-0082
www.themassagegarage.com

"We fix bodies" is the Massage Garage's motto. How can you not love that? Thirty-minute test drive for $32, 1 hour tune up for $48, or a 90-minute overhaul for $74. First-timers get a one-time $42 rate any Tues, Wed, or Thurs. If it's your birthday and you can prove it, you get $5 off. Facials, too.

The Massage Place

Multiple locations
www.themassageplaces.com

Choose from Swedish, thai, deep tissue, sports, shiatsu, reflexology, or pregnancy massage. They are able to offer low rates of $37 for 30 minutes, $47 for 60 minutes, and $67 for 90 minutes because there is no spa atmosphere.

Take it from someone who knows. You don't need all the fancy stuff. All you need is one amazing massage. Choose from 1 of 9 Los Angeles locations.

Rescue Massage Center

412 S. Pacific Coast Hwy. (just south of Torrance Blvd.), Redondo Beach
(310) 540-6406
www.rescuemassagecenter.com

At Rescue Massage Center, you can get a 30 minute massage for $45, 1 hour for $55, or 90 minutes for $88. Choose from deep tissue, thai, and relaxation. Savings go up if you purchase a massage package.

Shiatsu Massage School of California

2309 Main St. (at Strand St.), Santa Monica
(310) 581-0097
www.smsconline.com

Shiatsu ("shi" meaning finger and "atsu" meaning pressure) is a traditional hands-on therapy originating in Japan. Used properly, it can relieve muscle pain, nausea, anxiety, stress, and depression. Spa trainees administer 1-hour massages for just $30. Can't you feel that neck pain disappearing already?

REAL ESTATE:
FROM LIVING TO
LIVING IT UP

*"I figure if I have my health, can pay the rent
and I have my friends, I call it 'content.'"*

—LAUREN BACALL

How often have you been to a bar, met someone you find attractive or interesting, only to have the first question out of said attractive or interesting individual's mouth after "What's your name?" and "What do you do?" be "Where do you live and how much is your rent?" and you find yourself realizing, once again, that it's completely socially acceptable to announce proudly the full figure of your bargain apartment to a roomful of total strangers. I spent a year after graduate school living in a new sublet every 2 to 3 months; one of those moves I schlepped all of my belongings by myself on multiple trips via public transportation. Fed up with the gypsy lifestyle, I called up an ex-boyfriend with a killer apartment on a Saturday in 2004. He said he thought I was reliable (I am) and I could move into the vacant spare bedroom without a security deposit (I did). "When were you thinking of moving in?" he asked. "Tomorrow?" I replied. It's 7 years later and I'm still there. At $675 for rent and utilities per month, I'm not leaving until marriage or Steven Spielberg calls. I mean, he waters the plants while I'm away and makes hot apple cider in the "fall" and "winter." (It's LA, we know those seasons are optional terminology here.) I share all of this because I know how incredibly important it is to live in a happy, safe, and healthy environment. Where you rest your head at night and what walls you look at on a day-to-day basis can buoy or cloud your life. Follow my advice for budget-friendly hostels, apartment renting, co-op living, green resources, and more, and you'll be happy.

HOSPITABLE **HOSTELS**

Just because you're watching your pennies, it doesn't mean you should skimp on the life experience and necessity to take a vacation every once in a while. Airfare and lodging are usually the biggest ticket items. A lot of hostels offer shared or private rooms with amazing wallet-friendly deals.

Backpackers Paradise Hostel
4200 W. Century Blvd., Inglewood
(310) 419-0999
www.backpackersparadise.com

It's $19.99 for a room with 20 dorm beds, $23.99 for 8 dorm beds, and $25.99 for a room with 4 dorm beds. Two and 3 bedroom suites and suite cottages also available. Free continental breakfast, dinner buffet, champagne, tea, coffee, and cake, as well as airport shuttle and Wi-Fi. A/C, swimming pool, pool table. Must be under 30 years of age and have a valid international passport at check-in.

Banana Bungalow

603 N. Fairfax Ave., West Hollywood
(877) 666-2002
www.bananabungalowus.com

Beds from $20 and up in an 8- to 16-person dorm and shared bath with even cheaper weekly rates. Private rooms have one queen-size bed or a queen and two bunk beds. Free Wi-Fi, Mac computer use, breakfast, pool table, basketball area, bike rental, parking, foosball, table tennis, tiki garden, and patio. Hip and mod design, so you are stylin'! Inexpensive dining and entertainment options within walking distance. Call or e-mail westhollywood@bananabungalowus.com or the Hollywood location at hollywood@bananabungalowus.com (5920 Hollywood Blvd., Hollywood; 887-977-5077).

CouchSurfing.org

www.couchsurfing.org

Not a hostel. Log onto couchsurfing.org and find a couch of a friendly stranger to crash on! Free to join, it's a nonprofit organization that runs on donations. Applies to other cities, too. Find a free place to stay, read reviews, meet a new friend. Sort of totally frightening and utterly, utterly fascinating. You try it and then tell me all about it.

Hollywood & Highland Hotel & Hostel

7038½ Hollywood Blvd., Los Angeles
(323) 464-3122
www.hh-hostel.com

Must be over 18 but under 35, have a valid passport or driver's license, and check in before midnight. Rooms are $25 and up, depending on whether you take a 4-, 6-, or 8-bed arrangement. Breakfast included.

Orbit Hotel & Hostel

7950 Melrose Ave. (at N. Hayworth Ave.), West Hollywood
(323) 655-1510
www.orbithotel.com

Six- and 8-bed mixed dorms or private rooms starting at $18 and up. Private rooms also available. Free coffee and tea all day, free movie night, dinners for $6 at the cafe. No curfew, free parking, billiard tournament, comedy night, DJ night, security lockers, common room, and barbecue area. Discounted tours and shuttles. Must have passport. What? Aren't you sold yet?

Venice Beach Cotel

25 Windward Ave., Venice
(310) 399-7649 or (888) 718-8287
www.venicebeachcotel.com

A room with a view of the ocean in the heart of Venice Beach. Oceanfront lounge/bar, free boogie board and paddle tennis rentals. Are you already rollerblading there in your mind? $22 a night for shared rooms or $52.60 for a private room; everything from 6-person share rooms to private suites. Security locker in room. Must bring valid passport to check-in, no exceptions. Call or e-mail reservations@venicebeachcotel.com for more information.

FOR **RENT** & CRAZY **CO-OPS**

Apartment searching can suck days off your life. Best to minimize the pain as much as possible, balancing the act of paying as little as you can for the absolute best apartment that falls somewhere in the range of both your vision and your means. Here are some of Los Angeles's best resources:

Affordable Housing Online

www.affordablehousingonline.com

Search for low-income apartments in LA and get everything you need to know about the housing grant application process and Section 8 housing, the voucher program providing assistance to low-income families.

Apartments.com
www.apartments.com

Search by zip code, corporate or short term, property name, number of bedrooms, rent minimum or maximum. Place an ad and access landlord resources, too. Voila! See what happens as you roll the Magic 8 Internet Ball of your housing future.

Craigslist.org
www.craigslist.org

Come on, do I really need to explain here? Great listings and self-postings sometimes accompanied by photos, but the apartments tend to go quickly and the listings are not managed; they're simply, well, there. But I have found great sublets on Craigslist before and had good roommate situations. But then again, I have the unfortunate trait of being able to get along with anyone.

Fellowship for Intentional Community
www.ic.org

Ecovillages, cohousing communities, residential land trusts, communes, student co-ops, urban housing cooperatives, intentional living, alternative communities, cooperative living, and more. Search by city/state and region.

Los Angeles Eco-Village
117 Bimini Place, #221 (at W. 1st St.), Los Angeles
(213) 738-1254
www.laecovillage.org

"Demonstrating higher quality living patterns at a lower environmental impact" and providing "education, training, and consulting for more sustainable neighborhoods: socially, economically, and ecologically," Los Angeles Eco-Village is a 40-member group of approximately 500 people within 2 blocks, 3 miles from downtown Los Angeles. Kid-friendly, with a weekly organic food buying co-op that serves the 'hood. If you are interested in becoming a member, you have to be able to demonstrate your sincerity and enthusiasm. $10 fee for a tour.

To Obtain or Not To Obtain Renter's Insurance, That Is the Question!

I know, I know. Maybe you went to that pricey school but are now paying those hefty tuition loans back with major interest as you devote yourself to the low-paying but emotionally rewarding job you found as a social worker. Or maybe you didn't go to college, but still work hard for your money. Either way, you've probably managed to accumulate the stuff we all seem to accumulate in this day and age. Stuff meaning that of a technological or digital sort: an iPod, cell phone, computer, printer, television, DVD player, maybe even a scanner, an expensive snowboard for that one trip you took to Lake Tahoe years ago and blew your birthday cash on, or that mountain bike your last boyfriend gave you.

And while you haven't pursued the American dream of owning a piece of property, you still have stuff. And gosh darnit, it's your stuff. So what if you get robbed, or there's an earthquake, or a fire? What will you do then?

Consider getting renter's insurance to protect those things you just can't live without, so you don't have to worry about "what if." Visit sites like www.statefarm.com, www.geico.com, www.nationwide .com, or www.esurance.com, and get started on that very adult and responsible research project of purchasing renter's insurance. Then please remind me to do the same once I clear off my desk with my expensive computer and all-in-one copier/scanner/printer. Okay, okay! Dialing now.

Move.com
(800) 978-7368
www.move.com

Search for apartments and homes for rent. Specify number of bedrooms, bathrooms, and pet friendly residences. Calculate your free moving quote. I'd love a really big and real closet in the bedroom. Oooo, what is that like? I can hardly remember.

Rent.com
www.rent.com

Apartment and home listings by city and state from your low end to your high end price range and number of bedrooms.

Technicolor Tree Tribe
http://technicolortreetribe.wordpress.com

Student housing co-op near USC. Community-style living with a focus on activisim and the eco-friendly. Sunday potluck meetings, vegan cooking groups, skill-building workshops. Pet friendly. Peace, dude.

University Cooperative Housing Association
500 Landfair Ave., Los Angeles
(310) 208-8242
http://ceo.lacounty.gov/ccp/cel.htm

For UCLA, UCLA Extension, Santa Monica College, and other accredited university students only. You have to work 4 hours per week, but will pay only $1,350 to $1,700 for 11 weeks, depending on how many roommates you have. Price includes food and utilities, and rooms are fully furnished. Hello, Student Budget Friendly Living! Nice to meet you.

VacancyList.net
http://vacancylist.net

Search by city, state, zip, area code, number of bedrooms, and amount you are willing to pay. Filter by date available or amount you can afford.

RESOURCES **FOR** RENTERS & **OWNERS**

Hey, man, today's stock market is up, down, and all around. Unemployment is high and jobs can be tough to come by. What do you do when faced with paying rent or a mortgage without a job, or with a new job at a salary far less than what you normally command? There is help out there, so don't be shy, and seek it.

The Beehive
http://losangeles.thebeehive.org

The Los Angeles branch of a Washington D.C.-based nonprofit organization committed to improving people's lives by teaching them how to succeed economically, no matter where they fall on the income bracket. How to avoid credit counseling scams, fix your finances, find affordable housing, know your renter's rights, and more.

ClearPoint Credit Counseling Solutions
6001 E. Washington Dr., Suite 200 (Banco Popular building), Los Angeles
(323) 869-5100
www.bydesignsolutions.org

Not-for-profit organization with free and low-cost services to help you get out of debt, repair your credit, file for bankruptcy, renegotiate repayment rates, take a workshop, and buy/save for a home. Meet with a credit counselor for an hour to devise a budget and set financial goals. Check out the blog pointers on boosting your credit score.

LoanSafe.org
www.loansafe.org

Forum for help with mortgage, debt/credit, loan, and rent issues. Sign up to receive free mortgage and foreclosure guidance.

LoanWorkout.org
http://loanworkout.org

Free e-book, link to information and government help on foreclosure, as well as a search engine to look up Los Angeles-pertinent information.

Los Angeles Neighborhood Housing Services, Inc.
3926 Wilshire Blvd., Suite 200 (at S. St. Andrews Place), Los Angeles
(888) 89-LANHS or (888) 895-2647
www.lanhs.org

The LANHS is dedicated to establishing, protecting, and preserving lifelong homeowners. Regional housing counselors and legal assistance partners are at your disposal to help families faced with the reality of losing their homes. Public interest attorney groups are available to counsel victims of real estate fraud, and conduct workshops for budgeting and credit recovery, borrowing smart, home buyer education, reverse mortgage education, and foreclosure prevention. A free downloadable sample financial hardship letter to request loan modification with a back payment and late fee waiver is available on the website.

GOING **GREEN**

California Cash for Appliances
www.cash4appliances.org

Recycle your old appliances for cash! Must be with a certified recycler. Fill out that rebate form and get a rebate check in the mail. Buy an eligible appliance from your local retailer or contractor during the rebate period. Program continues until the money runs out. Sort of like karaoke. I do it until the songs I sing well run out.

Discounted Composting Bins from LA Department of Public Works Environmental Programs Division
900 S. Fremont Ave., 3rd floor annex (at Orange St.), Alhambra
(888) CLEAN LA
http://dpw.lacounty.gov/epd/sg/bc_bins.cfm

Now you can compost, and in turning your organic waste into a rich and fertile soil, you will never need to purchase potting soil again. $40 will get you a backyard bin and $65 will get you a worm bin. Take workshops on composting, worms, water/firewise gardening, and grasscycling. Find out when the next Smart Gardening workshop is. If you somehow ever learn how not to kill an orchid, please share your knowledge with me. Thank you.

Energy Savers
www.energysavers.gov

Information on federal tax credits and rebates for energy efficiency, renewable energy and energy-saving tips, as well as a plethora of tips on how to go green and save money in landscaping, appliances, designing, and remodeling.

Energy Star
www.energystar.gov

Tax credits for energy-efficient appliances; how to apply and how to get them. Tips on how to make your home more energy efficient (don't keep appliances you aren't using plugged in!), and a rebate finder that lists rebates you may be eligible for.

Flex Your Power
www.fypower.com

Find out how to make your house more energy efficient and cut your power bill. Save money and help the environment and search by zip code for rebates in your area and financially friendly eco-tips. Check out online literature on how to go green and get rebates while doing it.

Light Bulb Depot
7029 Paramount Blvd. (at E. Washington Blvd.), Pico Rivera
(562) 948-3111 or (800) 315-2852
www.lightbulbdepot.com

Daily deals and sales on bulbs; free shipping when ordered by the case. Environmentally friendly stock and LED light bulbs, too!

Los Angeles Department of Water and Power
PO Box 51111, Los Angeles, CA 90051
(800) 342-5397
www.ladwp.com/ladwp/homepage.jsp

The LA Department of Water and Power has a Low Income Refrigerator Exchange Program. Check to see if you qualify to receive an energy-saving refrigerator to replace your old model and explore up to $500 worth of incentives offered for creating and using solar power in your home. Can you please ask my roommate not to defrost the freezer right after I go grocery shopping? Like clockwork. I go food shopping, and all of a sudden he's inspired. The LADWP also has a tree planting workshop, water conservation rebate hotline, compact fluorescent light bulb distribution program, and more. Poke around this incredible website and see what money you're missing out on keeping.

1000 Bulbs
www.1000bulbs.com

Check out the list of the most ecologically friendly light bulbs on the market, and nab some overstock. Yes, they ship them to you, and no, amazingly, they don't break.

ARE **YOU** BEING **SERVED?**

If you're detail-oriented, praised for the perfect professional voicemails you leave and e-mails you write, and tired of slaving away in an office 40 hours a week, then maybe it's time you think about transforming into The Nanny or Mr. Belvedere. What will I do when I'm rich? Buy an expensive mattress and hire a cleaning lady. Oh, to dream . . . Los Angeles has some of the wealthiest people in the world, who employ a lot of personal assistants, nannies, and housekeepers, so read on to find out how to become one!

California Concierge
22647 Ventura Blvd., #165, Woodland Hills
(818) 883-8550
www.calconcierge.com

$500 a month for 8 hours or $2,200 a month for 40 hours buys the customer a personal assistant (you) who will run errands, return messages, and perform household duties. Responsibilities may range from picking up groceries, running to the dry cleaners, and getting the auto inspection sticker, to overseeing household renovations, paying bills, and procuring tickets. If your middle name is "Organized" or "Attention to Detail," call the number above to submit your candidacy for consideration. Can I call you Mr. Step and Fetch It?

Hire a Helper
(866) 994-4473
www.hireahelper.com

Hire a Helper employs landscaping, moving, cleaning, or home improvement helpers at a cost of $10 to $20 an hour for the customer. If you're pretty handy, give them a call or e-mail them at new-helper-support@hireahelper.com.

House Sitters America
www.housesittersamerica.com

Log on and register for $30 to create a house sitter profile that will stay active for 1 year. All cases are individually negotiated between you and the homeowner, but in general you do not pay to live in their house. Assignments range from 1 day to 4 months, and sometimes 6 to 12 months or even 3 years.

The Rent a Wife
(323) 644-2850
www.therentawife.com

Want to run someone else's errands, file paperwork, walk their dog, make things pretty, or plan a party? Start your exploration of the personal assistant world by becoming a wife, and get paid for it, yet have none of the hassle. Call The Rent a Wife. Clients purchase 5 hours a month for $200, 10 hours a month for $380, 15 hours a month for $450, or $50 an hour for same-day service; when they sign up for a package, they get a free 30-minute consultation and a $50 coupon. Call or e-mail through the website now. I will say this: As a personal assistant, every day is different, and you're certainly not working on your office tan under the fluorescent bulbs.

Sandra Taylor Agency
280 S. Beverly Dr., Suite 200, Beverly Hills
(310) 205-2810 or (818) 788-7599
www.sandratayloragency.com

The Sandra Taylor Agency provides housekeepers, nannies, cleaning ladies, certified nurse's assistants, companions for the elderly, butlers, secretaries, chauffeurs, estate managers, and more. There are fees connected to live-in nanny help. Salaries for English-speaking, nondriving nannies and housekeepers start at around $400 per week and go up from there . . . and have you thought about the free lodging and food that comes with that salary?

Sittercity
www.sittercity.com

For a free 7-day trial, 1 month for $35, 3 months for $70, or $140 per year, you can find nannies, babysitters, pet sitters, and senior care in your area. Search by zip code and browse in-depth bios for applicants. Post a job, receive applications and interview applicants, and hire the best match for you. Or be the best match for someone else and join now. As someone who spent years working in human resources (there are few jobs I haven't had), I give you these two tips: 1) A good handshake and smile say a lot; 2) A follow-up personalized note or e-mail say even more. If you want it, go after it.

CHILD'S PLAY:
CHEAP ACTIVITIES

"Your modern teenager is not about to listen to advice from an old person, defined as a person who remembers when there was no Velcro."

—DAVE BARRY

"Mom, I'm bored!" is an all-too-familiar declaration that falls on the ears of many a busy parent. "Then find something meaningful to do," was always the response my mother gently retorted. No one ever tells you, "You know what? One day you'll be all grown-up and never in your life will you be bored again because there will always be something to do, whether that's paying a bill, doing the laundry, cleaning the house . . . " I know, I'm sorry. Now I have you pining for those carefree summer days when the 4th of July felt like it was eons into the summer, and you had light-years ahead of you until you had to return to school again.

Los Angeles has a plethora of resources for babies, children, and parents, as well as activities, from museums to after-school programs, youth clubs, and music schools, to keep your child entertained and make a positive impact at the same time, so you'll never have to listen to, "Mom, I'm bored!" again. Turn to these pages for answers and inspiration when you feel at a loss, challenged, or in need of support or access to a list of fun stuff your child can do.

ARTS & **CRAFTS**

Barnsdall Friends of the Junior Arts Center
4814 Hollywood Blvd. (between N. Edgemont and N. Berendo Streets),
Los Angeles
(323) 644-4629
http://barnsdallarts.org

Free family art workshops on Sun from 2 to 4 p.m. Check the online calendar. Free art workshops in Griffith Park on Sat, April through October. Ragan Art Academy for children ages 12 and up to enroll in a full 2-year art program in the visual arts, where they learn the techniques of drawing, design, painting, and sculpture. Students can also opt to take one class at a time. Financial aid is available.

LACMA NexGen
5905 Wilshire Blvd., Los Angeles
(323) 857-6000
www.lacma.org

The nation's only free youth membership program is offered at the Los Angeles County Museum of Art. Free general admission to anyone under the age of 17 with an accompanying adult. Reasonably priced art classes and programs for kids and teens are available. Art camp for children ages 6 to 9 and 10 to 13. Financial aid for classes and camp is available. Call the art class registrar at (323) 857-6139 or the education department for more information at (323) 857-6512.

LA Kids
(213) 485-4841
www.laparks.org/dos/sports/lakids.htm

At over 100 participating recreational centers across Los Angeles, the Department of Recreation and Parks provides free, challenging physical, educational, and social activities for youth in low-income areas. Activities include dance, piano, golf, soccer, softball, tennis, volleyball, gymnastics, boxing, tennis, drama, cheerleading, tutoring, swimming, and more. Call for more information.

Los Angeles Music and Art School (LAMusArt)
3630 E. 3rd St., Los Angeles
(323) 262-7734
http://lamusart.org

LAMusArt has a dynamic and affordable program for youth in music, dance, drama, and visual arts. Student musicians age 12 and over, after an audition and interview, can participate in the Los Angeles Philanthropic Committee for the Youth Arts Orchestra. Boys and girls ages 7 to 16 can audition and interview to sing with the LAMusArt Choir, performing at school and community events. Children ages 7 to 14 are eligible to participate in a 4-week summer camp at a reasonable rate. Financial assistance is given to those who qualify.

Silverlake Conservatory of Music
3920 Sunset Blvd. (at Hyperion Ave. at Sunset Junction), Silverlake
(323) 665-3363
www.silverlakeconservatory.com

Founded by the Red Hot Chili Peppers' bassist, Flea, children can study music at the Silverlake Conservatory with exceptional teachers at a reasonable price. Silverlake offers scholarships as well as free lessons and instruments for deserving children.

Studio City Recreation Center (Beeman Park)
12621 Rye St. (at Beeman), Studio City
(818) 769-4415

The Studio City Recreation Center offers gymnastics, soccer, tae kwon do, ballet, tap, and hip-hop for the 3 to 6-year-old set, cooking and sewing for pre-teens, and guitar, flag football, basketball, and tennis for the older kids. Prices average at $65 for 8 weeks of classes. This facility also has summer and spring camp programs to keep the kids out of trouble. Adults can delight and get fit in yoga, tennis, and tae kwon do.

Venice Arts
www.venice-arts.org

Administrative Office & Classrooms
610 California Ave., Venice
(310) 578-1745

Gallery & Workshop Annex
1702 Lincoln Blvd., Venice
(310) 392-0846

Venice Arts encourages the creation and sharing of personal and community stories through photography, film, and multimedia. Ages 6 to 9 can participate in their Art Discovery program, and ages 10 to 18 can take photography, digital arts, and media arts classes taught by professional artists in a small and nurturing environment while having access to the use of cutting-edge equipment. Free workshops are held year-round at various schools, parks, and public housing developments.

Zimmer Children's Museum
6505 Wilshire Blvd., Suite 100, Los Angeles
(323) 761-8989
www.zimmermuseum.org
Hours: Closed Mon and Sat; Tues through Thurs 10 a.m. to 5 p.m.; Fri 10 a.m. to 2 p.m.; Sun 12:30 to 5 p.m.
Admission: $8 adults; $5 children ages 2 to 17; free to children under 2 and grandparents on Tues when accompanying a child.

Geared toward children ages 8 and under, the Zimmer Museum's hands-on exhibits offer tots and tikes thought-provoking snippets of important cultural awareness and sensitivity issues, from global citizenship to community responsibility. Classes, family programs, and field trips create an interactive experience where your child will learn to play well with others and be curious, generous, and creative. Some exhibits have Jewish cultural themes but are not religiously or culturally exclusive. Play at the Water Table and learn how to take care of Planet Earth; drive an ambulance, learn about doctors and nurses, or answer a call for help in "People Helping People," and learn about the gift of compassion. The museum also accepts volunteer applicants, and youth volunteers can earn credit toward community service hours.

FUN **PARKS**

Whether it's Disneyland, Magic Mountain, or Knotts Berry Farm, Los Angeles has got some great theme and amusement parks that will keep you entertained all the good long day. Their websites will offer discounts for you to purchase your tickets ahead of time; sometimes they also run 2 for 1 deals or perks via AAA or Costco. Below are some of the best deals offered that will fit well within your cheap bastard budget.

Disneyland
1313 S. Harbor Blvd., Anaheim
http://disneyland.disney.go.com

It's hard not to love Disneyland. Come on, isn't it time you tap into your inner child? It's okay if you don't want to mention how much you love it. I won't give away your secret. Follow @DisneyParks on Twitter, where they sometimes run contests for free tickets. If and when they do, you have to act fast. Make good friends with a park employee, and he or she can get you and two others in for a day. Best of all, admission is totally free on your birthday! Where's your party hat?

Knott's Berry Farm
8039 Beach Blvd., Buena Park
(714) 220-5200
www.knottsberryfarm.com

Thrill rides, children's rides, family rides, and water rides. I love the Ferris wheel! Free admission for 2 weeks in December if you bring a $15 toy for the Toys for Tots Drive. Online your admission is reduced to $34.99, AAA members can save 30 percent, military and veterans plus one guest get in free November 1 through Thanksgiving, and Social Services and County Welfare employees plus one get free admission on select dates in November and December.

Magic Mountain
26101 Magic Mountain Pkwy., Valencia
(661) 255-4100
www.sixflags.com/magicmountain/index.aspx

Flume rides and wooden roller coasters are my favorite, but Magic Mountain is happy to turn you upside down and all around so you can scream your head off. What's the best way to get that cost lowered? Go near Christmas-time for $15 with a present in hand for the Toys for the Holidays Drive, or bring a can of food during Thanksgiving week, and you're in! If you use your Discover card, you get a 5 percent discount on regular admission, and once in a while, your Coke can will run a "buy one, get one free" admission deal, so be on the lookout as you quench your thirst.

STORY TIME

Blue Chair Children's Books
177 N. Glendora Ave. (at Meda Ave.), Glendora
(626) 335-8630
www.bluechairbooks.com

Free story time every Mon at 10:30 a.m., as well as Music Merriment on Tues at 10:30 a.m., Wed at 10 a.m., and Fri at 10:30 and 11:30 a.m. Music Merriment includes finger play activities, singing, dancing, and drumming, and occasionally some basic music theory and terminology.

Children's Book World
10580½ W. Pico Blvd., Los Angeles
(310) 559-BOOK (2665)
www.childrensbookworld.com

Open since 1986, this full-service children's bookshop in West LA stocks over 80,000 titles and hosts storytellers, author readings, and musical performers every Sat at 10:30 a.m. Check the website or call for the most up-to-date events.

The Cow's End Cafe
34 Washington Blvd., Venice
(310) 574-1080
www.thecowsendcafe.com

Free sing-along for kids every Thurs morning from 10:30 to 11 a.m. Great for kids up to age 3. Tips encouraged.

Lawndale Public Library
14615 Burin Ave. (at 145th St.), Lawndale
(310) 676-0177
www.colapublib.org/libs/lawndale/index.php

Story time every Sat at 2 p.m.

Lomita Library
24200 Narbonne Ave. (at 242nd St.), Lomita
(31) 539-4515
www.colapublib.org/libs/lomita/index.php

Free story time for toddlers ages 3 and under 9:30 to 10 a.m. every Wed. Free preschool story time for ages 3 to 5 from 10 to 10:30 a.m. every Wed. Includes stories, songs, art activities, and finger plays for children.

Platt Public Library Pre-School Storytime
23600 Victory Blvd. (at Platt Ave.), Woodland Hills
(818) 340-9386

Stories, songs, and finger plays for ages 3 to 5 on Wed, 10:30 to 11 a.m.

Pottery Barn Kids: Book Club at The Grove

189 The Grove Dr., Los Angeles
(323) 549-9344
www.thegrovela.com/los_angeles/entertainment/kids_calendar.php

Story time every Tues at 11 a.m. for kids of all ages.

Read Books Eagle Rock

Used Books & Newstand
4972 Eagle Rock Blvd., Los Angeles
(323) 259-9068
www.readbookseaglerock.com

Readings for kids ages 1 to 5 every Sat from 11 to 11:30 a.m.

Redondo Beach Public Library

303 N. Pacific Coast Hwy. (at Diamond St.), Redondo Beach
(310) 318-0675
www.redondo.org/depts/library/default.asp

Family Pajama Story Time on Thurs evenings at 6:45 p.m., plus story time on Tues for babies at 11 a.m., and toddlers at 11:30 a.m. Check website under "Children's Department" for more details.

Vroman's Bookstore

www.vromansbookstore.com

Bookstore: 695 E. Colorado Blvd., Pasadena
(626) 449-5320
Hastings Ranch: 3729 E. Foothill Blvd., Pasadena
(626) 351-0828

In operation since 1894, Vroman's is Southern California's largest independent bookstore. Check the online calendar or call for kid story times and events, both at the bookstore and the ranch.

AFTER-SCHOOL **PROGRAMS** & YOUTH **CLUBS**

After-School All-Stars
6501 Fountain Ave. (at Wilcox Ave.), Los Angeles
(323) 957-4426
www.la-allstars.org

All-Stars, supported by such celebrities as Kobe Bryant, has a three-tiered approach to their program, focusing on the visual and performing arts; health, nutrition, and physical fitness; and leadership, character development, and community service learning. They also offer homework assistance and sponsor summer youth camps.

All Peoples Christian Center
822 E. 20th St. (at Stanford Ave.), Los Angeles
(213) 747-6357
www.allpeoplescc.org

All Peoples Christian Center offers after-school youth social and academic programs in South LA for children ages 6 to 18 in order to encourage students at a young age to graduate and pursue higher education. Family work social services, counseling, crisis intervention, and parenting classes are also held in both Spanish and English. All Peoples Christian Center also hosts Camp Joe Ide Summer Camp, which allows 60 children ages 8 to 12 to experience nature in the San Bernardino Mountains for 1 week each summer.

Boys & Girls Club of Hollywood
850 N. Cahuenga Blvd. (at Willoughby Ave.), Hollywood
(323) 467-2007
www.bgchollywood.com

Daily homework help, in addition to a technology lab, Career Launch and Money Matters workshops, leadership building programs, sports, fitness, and recreation classes, an art studio program, and music classes through UCLA.

Center for the Arts, Eagle Rock
2225 Colorado Blvd. (near Rockland Ave.), Los Angeles
(323) 226-1617
www.centerartseaglerock.org

After-school arts programs at various elementary and middle schools throughout Northeast Los Angeles, as well as winter and summer art camps targeted toward nontraditional and underserved audiences. Free animation classes for ages 10 to 14 in a special 30-week program. Check website for more details. They also host a music festival every fall.

826LA
http://826la.org

826LA West
SPARC Building
685 W. Venice Blvd., Venice
(310) 305-8418

826LA East
1714 W. Sunset Blvd., Echo Park
(213) 413-3388

A nonprofit writing and tutoring center dedicated to supporting kids ages 6 to 18 with their creative and expository writing skills, and to helping teachers inspire their children to write. After-school tutoring programs from 3:30 to 5:30 p.m., as well as evening and weekend workshops covering things like SAT preparation and character sketching. In-school tutoring and field trips. Student work is published in anthologies.

Immanuel United Church of Christ
1785 E. 85th St. (at Glendale Ave.), Los Angeles
(323) 234-3633

The church sponsors a youth group, open gym, homework help for school-age children, a youth basketball team, Head Start program, counseling, and parenting classes. Emergency food and clothing are available. Thrift shop on the premises; donations welcome. Staff speaks Spanish and Samoan. All services are free.

LACER Afterschool Programs

1718 N. Cherokee Ave., Suite A (near Hollywood Blvd.), Hollywood
(323) 957-6481
www.lacerstars.org

Arts- and literacy-based after-school programs that encompass visual art, music, dance, film, academic support, sports, and enrichment activities for underserved middle school and high school students.

YMCA

www.ymcala.org

Fitness classes, after-school programs, youth summer day camps, child care, parenting classes, support groups, and more. Each location offers different services and programs. All are reasonably priced. See the website for a complete listing of YMCA locations in the Metropolitan Los Angeles area.

RESOURCES

Action Parent & Teen Support

11372 Ventura Blvd., Studio City
(818) 763-9556

Free weekly support groups for parents and adolescents, with a focus on families dealing with low self-esteem, depression, drug and alcohol abuse, running away from home, and pregnancy. Individual and family therapy is also offered on a sliding scale, as is low-cost drug testing.

Asthma & Allergy Foundation of America (AAFA)

Los Angeles Chapter
5900 Wilshire Blvd., Suite 710, Los Angeles
(213) 937-7859

Breathmobiles

Arrowhead Regional Medical Center, (909) 498-6277
Children's Hospital of Orange County, (714) 532-7571
Mattel Children's Hospital UCLA, (310) 794-5561
USC Medical Center, (323) 226-3813

The Asthma & Allergy Foundation of America is dedicated to controlling asthma and allergic diseases for millions of sufferers. The California chapter of the AAFA is the largest one. Breathmobiles, or allergy clinics on wheels, were developed to decrease morbidity and mortality rates in disadvantaged children. Since 1995, the Breathmobiles have treated over 120,000 children. Allergists, nurse practitioners, respiratory therapists, and patient service workers at Breathmobile clinics provide diagnosis, treatment, and education to high-risk inner city schoolchildren with asthma or allergies. Free educational programs and brochures on asthma and allergy topics.

Autism Society of America
Los Angeles Chapter
8939 S. Sepulveda Blvd., Suite 110–788, Los Angeles
www.asa-la.org

The Autism Society of America offers an information and referral service that provides monthly parent support groups, a library, resource files, and more.

Beach Cities Health District (BCHD)
514 N. Prospect Ave. (lower level), Redondo Beach
(310) 318-7939

Medical, dental, and mental health care for eligible residents of Hermosa, Manhattan, or Redondo Beach. Counseling, support groups, referrals, and more. Serves the uninsured and underinsured. Most services are low-cost or free.

Because I Love You
(818) 884-8242
http://bily.org

For 30 years, Because I Love You has been supporting parents with troubled kids of all ages with behavioral problems including drugs, runaways, truancy, verbal and physical abuse, curfew, dress codes, and problem friends. Call or check the website for a BILY group near you, or to access their comprehensive list of websites for parents, free publications, addiction resources, anger management tools, and pamphlets in downloadable form.

Big Brothers Big Sisters of Greater Los Angeles and the Inland Empire

800 S. Figueroa St., Suite 620, Los Angeles
(213) 481-3611
www.bbbslaie.org/

At-need or at-risk girls ages 6 to 18 (or up to 21 if pregnant or parenting) are matched to volunteer Big Sisters, who act as positive role models and provide friendship, companionship, and guidance on a one-to-one basis. Fatherless boys ages 6 to 12 are paired up with adult male volunteers who are over 18, have a driver's license and proof of auto insurance, and act as Big Brothers.

Breakthrough Parenting Services

12405 Venice Blvd., #172 (at S. Centinela), Los Angeles
(310) 823-7846
www.breakthroughparentingservices.org

Open enrollment on parenting classes offered 50 weeks a year for parents with everyday problems. Support for parents with custody disputes. Free eNewsletter on divorce. Serves West LA. Fees are on sliding scale.

Community Guidance Counseling Center

Temple Beth Hillel
12326 Riverside Dr. (at Laurel Grove Ave.), Valley Village
(818) 762-4817

A nonprofit mental health service center open to all community members, regardless of race or religion. Assists with problems in raising children, and teens who face challenges in coping with life. Fees on sliding scale based on ability to pay.

Dy-Dee Diaper Service

40 E. California Blvd. (at Edmondson Alley), Pasadena
(626) 792-6183
www.dy-dee.com

It is estimated that by the age of 2.5 years, a child has spent over 22,000 hours in diapers, and parents have changed those diapers over 13,000 times. Since 1938, Dy-Dee Diaper Service has been delivering cloth diapers and supplies to Los Angeles and Orange Counties, including Pomona, Ontario,

San Bernadino, Thousand Oaks, and Simi Valley. Cloth diapers decrease the likelihood your child may develop diaper rash, they are slightly less expensive than disposable diapers, and even more so if you wash them yourself. Are you converted yet?

Family Focus Resource Center
California State University at Northridge
18111 Nordhoff St., Northridge
(818) 677-5575
www.csun.edu/~ffrc

The Family Focus Resource Center serves those in the San Fernando and Santa Clarita Valleys and offers free services to families with special needs. Call to make an appointment Monday through Friday with any of their full-time Spanish-speaking staff, or e-mail family.focus@csun.edu.

La Leche League
(877) 4-LALECHE
www.lllusa.org

The mission of La Leche League USA is to help mothers to breast-feed through mother-to-mother support, information, encouragement, and education. There is a small membership fee that is nominal, considering all the money you'll save using the knowledge you gain and the wonderful resource that is your body, rather than forking over the bucks for formula. Visit the website to find a local group near you.

Los Angeles County Public Social Services / Toy Loan Program
2615 S. Grand Ave., 2nd floor (at W. Adams Blvd.), Los Angeles
(213) 744-4344

The Toy Loan Program is designed to build character, integrity, and a sense of responsibility in children. Toys are loaned freely, and there are no fees associated with this program.

Los Angeles Valley College Family Resource Center
5800 Fulton Ave. (at Oxnard St.), Valley Glen
(818) 778-5612
www.lavc.edu/child_development/frc.html

The Los Angeles Valley College Family Resource Center has a free baby clothes exchange program where you can bring in the baby clothes ages 0 to 3 that your child has outgrown and exchange them for ones that you need. They also have a great lending library of parenting books.

Maud Booth Family Center
11243 Kittridge St. (at Klump Ave.), North Hollywood
(818) 980-2287

Maud Booth Family Center offers comprehensive services for families with children up to 11 years of age, including health, mental health, nutrition, parental involvement, social services, and advocacy. Child care is available, and they serve breakfast and lunch. Bilingual staff.

The Pump Station & Nurtury
1248 Vine St., Hollywood
(323) 469-5300
www.pumpstation.com

Voted as "The Best of LA" by the readers of *L.A. Parent Magazine* 2010, The Pump Station was started nearly 30 years ago by two women who were Lamaze teachers, RNs, and mothers. The website alone offers many educational breast-feeding videos and information, and they offer free weekly sling clinics on how to "wear your baby" and the benefits of doing so. Additional locations are at 245 Wilshire Blvd., Santa Monica (310-998-1981), and 2879 Agoura Rd., Westlake Village (805-777-7179).

Richstone Family Center
Center for Positive Parenting
13634 Cordary Ave., Hawthorne
(310) 970-1921
www.richstonefamily.org

Dedicated to preventing and treating child abuse, the Richstone Family Center has after-school programs, parenting classes, family activity days, counseling, and support programs for South Bay, Centinela Valley, and Southeast LA residents. Bilingual staff and fees on sliding scale.

UCLA Parenting and Children's Friendship Program
300 UCLA Medical Plaza, Los Angeles
(310) 825-0142
www.semel.ucla.edu/socialskills

Founded in 1982, the UCLA Parenting and Children's Friendship Program teaches parents techniques on increasing cooperation and reducing conflict within the home and at school. They also have social skills training for children ages 7 to 12 who have difficulty making and keeping friends.

Pacific Asian Counseling Services (PACS)
8616 La Tijera Blvd., Suite 200 (at W. Manchester Ave.), Los Angeles
(310) 337-1550

PACS offers counseling, case management, outreach, education, advocacy, and consultation for individuals and families in Asian Pacific communities. Staff speaks English, Vietnamese, Chinese, Japanese, Khmer, Samoan, Tagalog, Korean, Taiwanese, and Spanish. Fees on sliding scale.

EDUCATION:
HEAD OF THE CLASS

"Why don't they pass a constitutional amendment prohibiting anybody from learning anything? If it works as well as Prohibition did, in five years Americans would be the smartest race of people on Earth."

—WILL ROGERS

I know it's there in the back of your mind, gently scratching at you like a persistent hangnail—your burgeoning desire to learn how to meditate, to write that play you always dreamed of, or to sew a quilt like the one your granny made for your bed when you were a kid. Will it make you feel better if I 'fess up to some of my secret desires? Here is a short list of just some of the things I wish I knew more about: knitting, African tribal dancing, and gardening. Armed with these New Year resolution-like intentions, I am fortunate to have the wonderful resources Los Angeles has available at my feet. You want it, you name it, you think it; Los Angeles has it. All you need to do is get up off your couch!

ARTS, **CRAFTS** & DANCE

The Alliance of Los Angeles Playwrights (ALAP)
7510 Sunset Blvd., #1050, Los Angeles
(323) 957-4752
www.laplaywrights.org

For nearly 20 years, the ALAP has nourished and supported the Los Angeles playwright community (no, it's not only TV writers and screenwriters out here), from novices to established playwrights. Just $40 to join ($20 if you're a student), and you can participate in events like the Annual Reading Festival, featuring rehearsed readings of members' plays, workshops, professional panels, and networking events.

The Celtic Arts Center
5062 Lankershim Blvd., #3003, North Hollywood
(818) 760-8322
www.celticartscenter.com

Monday brings free Irish Gaelic Language lessons at 7 p.m., followed by free Céilí (folk) Dance lessons at 8 p.m., followed by a free Celtic music jam session beginning at 9 p.m. That's a lot of free loving Irish! Check website for location.

Jennifer Knits

108 Barrington Walk, Los Angeles
(310) 471-8733
www.jenniferknits.com

Free knitting instruction available with every purchase, as well as a happy hour with all vino, snacks, knitting classes, and wisdom free to those using Jennifer Knits products on Tues from 5 to 7 p.m.

LynBrown.Com Quilt Blog

http://lynbrown.com

Lyn is a quilting guru, lecturer and instructor within the North Orange County Community College District. She offers 5 free weekly classes in the art of quilting in Anaheim, Yorba Linda, Buena Park, Fullerton, and Cypress. Open enrollment. E-mail SwanPub@aol.com to sign up. Be sure to read her "New Student Supply List" so you're all set for your first class. Can I please put in my order now for my very own homemade quilt?

Southern California Haiku Study Group

The Pacific Asia Museum
46 N. Los Robles Ave. (at E. Union St.), Pasadena
www.socalhaiku.org

Free haiku workshops on the third Sat of each month from 2 to 4 p.m. Haikus have 17 syllables total, with 3 lines of 5, 7, and 5 syllables, respectively. Here is my haiku for you: City of Angels/LA's got it all for cheap/This book you should keep.

Wildfiber

1453 14th St., Suite E, Santa Monica
(310) 458-2748
www.wildfiber.com

Wildfiber is a yarn lovers' paradise; inside you'll feel you've hit the pot of gold on the other side of the rainbow (literally, since they have every color and color combination of yarn known to man). Wildfiber has a number of 3-hour, 1- to 4-week knitting classes such as "Knitting for Beginners and Beyond," "Fixing Mistakes," and "My First Top Down Sweater." Classes start at $40 and up (plus materials), in their old laundry building just north of Broadway.

THE **LOS** ANGELES **PUBLIC** LIBRARY

Whether it's a hardback, puffy letter paperback, magazine, video, CD, DVD, or audiobook (on cassette or CD), the Los Angeles Public Library has a wealth of resources available to you (including free lectures and classes), so long as you can prove you are a resident of the state of California via a photo ID or driver's license issued by the DMV, or a combination of 2 IDs (passport, school ID, or other government-issued ID) and provide proof of current address (credit card statement, property tax receipt, or bill with current postmark). Save yourself the price of that book you'll read once and then will sit unloved on your shelf, and take that book out of the library for free! Return it and get another! Come on! They didn't make you learn the Dewey Decimal System for nothing in grade school. For a complete list of the Los Angeles Public Library's 70-plus locations and their telephone numbers, please see Appendix C on p. 302.

Central Library
630 W. 5th St. (between S. Grand Ave. and S. Gaffey St.), Los Angeles
(213) 228-7000
www.lapl.org
Hours: Closed Mon and Sun; Tues and Thurs 10 a.m. to 8 p.m.; Wed, Fri, and Sat 10 a.m. to 5:30 p.m.

Pass under the painted ceiling and atrium chandeliers in the lobby and delight in the smell of the books. Take a tour—self-guided or once daily; special programs for children, young adults, and ESL students. You can also call to request a tour of the Maguire Gardens directly outside the Flower Street entrance. Don't you feel smarter and more learned already?

County of Los Angeles Public Library
www.colapublib.org

Their website has an excellent searchable database for events by branch location, date range, and topic. With a kagillion locations, you'll have to check Appendix D on p. 305 for one near you.

GOVERNMENT **LIBRARIES**

LA Law Library (Main)
301 W. 1st St. (between Hill St. and Broadway), Los Angeles
(213) 785-LALAW (2529)
http://lalawlibrary.org
Hours: Closed Sun; Mon through Fri 8:30 a.m. to 6 p.m.; Sat 9 a.m. to 5 p.m.

Bursting to the gills with nearly 1,000,000 books and documents, the LA Law Library was established in 1891 to provide information to the legal community, government officials, and the public. It is the second largest public law library in the United States. The Law Library derives its income from a portion of the filing fee charges paid by parties of civil litigation in the Superior Court of Los Angeles County. So you can thank our litigious society for the law library. And I should know. I worked for an attorney for 4.5 years and I've spent too many an hour convincing the courts I am not Alicia Collins born on August 19, 1981, and trying to shirk jury duty for the umpteenth time. See Appendix E on p. 311 for listings of other locations in courthouses and branches of the public library.

PRIVATE **LIBRARIES**

A private library is not a public library, which means that it is under the care of private ownership, and has a select, target audience for whom its resources are made available. This select, target audience is usually not the general public at large. Often a private library has a particular focus in its collection. Read below for some of what Los Angeles has to offer in this arena and how you can score an invitation to the stacks.

The Getty Research Institute Library
1200 Getty Center Dr., Suite 1100, Los Angeles
(310) 440-7390
www.getty.edu/research/library
Hours: Closed Sat and Sun; Mon through Fri 9:30 a.m. to 5 p.m.

An extensive collection of nearly 900,000 volumes of books, periodicals, and auction catalogs as well as prints, maps, photographs, manuscripts, optical devices and archival collections focusing on the history of art, architecture, and archaeology, with an emphasis on western European art and culture in Europe and North America. The Getty Research Institute Library also has a burgeoning collection of works on Latin America, Eastern Europe, and Asia. Check website for details on the three levels of reader privileges granted to visitors and members of the scholarly and museum communities. At the basic level, you'll likely qualify as a "Plaza Reader." I'll just call you Michelangelo. Or Mary Cassatt. If that's not really your thing I can just call you by your first name, but, you know . . . art . . . it does a mind good.

Jewish Community Library of Los Angeles
Children's Division
6505 Wilshire Blvd., Los Angeles
(323) 761-8648
www.jclla.org
Hours: Closed Mon, Fri, Sat, Jewish holidays, observances, and national holidays; Sun noon to 4 p.m.; Tues through Thurs noon to 6 p.m.

The Jewish Community Library contains more than 30,000 Jewish books, movies, music, and archives, as well as a myriad of family programs and literary activities for adults, many of them free. The library also books events featuring storytellers, musicians, acting troupes, authors, illustrators, and parenting experts. Library cards are free for all, with no residency requirement. Free visitor parking on the west side of the building. Oy gevalt!

LA84 Foundation Sports Library
2141 W. Adams Blvd. (at S. Gramercy Place), Los Angeles
(323) 730-4646
www.la84foundation.org
Hours: Closed Sun; Mon, Tues, Thurs, Fri 10 a.m. to 5 p.m.; Wed 10 a.m. to 7 p.m.; first Sat of every month 10 a.m. to 3 p.m.

The LA84 Foundation Sports Library has one of the world's most comprehensive collections of sports information and is free to all. There are some fees associated with the circulation of materials and any reference question that takes longer than 10 minutes to answer. Who pitched a perfect game for the New York Yankees on July 18, 1999, when they played the Montreal Expos? That would be David Cone. Who was there? That would be me. Which piece of information is not in the library? Take a wild guess.

Los Angeles Family History Library

10741 Santa Monica Blvd. (between Selby Ave. and Manning Ave.),
Los Angeles
(310) 474-9990
www.lafhl.org
Hours: Closed Sun; Mon, Fri, Sat 9 a.m. to 5 p.m.; Tues, Wed, Thurs 9 a.m. to
9 p.m.

Originally started by The Church of Jesus Christ of Latter-day Saints in 1964,
the Los Angeles Family History Library contains everything you ever wanted
to know about your family, ancestry, and genealogy. Why does your grand-
mother like lima beans and corn, but not when presented together as suc-
cotash? Perhaps your research will unlock that mystery for you. The library
is free to nonmembers and has state-of-the-art technology, as well as a
large collection of resources including microfilms/fiches, books, and free use
of fee-based websites like http://ancestry.com. They also offer genealogy
courses and classes in person and online for small registration fees. Thank
you, Mormons!

ONE National Gay and Lesbian Archives

909 W. Adams Blvd., Los Angeles
(213) 741-0094
www.onearchives.org
Hours: Closed Sun and Mon; Tues and Fri 1:30 to 5:30 p.m.; Wed and Thurs
3:30 to 9 p.m.; Sat 11 a.m. to 5 p.m.

ONE National is the largest research library on gay, lesbian, bisexual, and
transgendered heritage. There is no charge to use the collection. You can
also check out the gallery and museum open on Fri, Sat, and Sun for the
suggested donation of $5 at their 626 N. Robertson Blvd. address in West
Hollywood. Wave your rainbow loud and proud, my dears. It's about time we
have an impressive collection on LGBT history and concerns.

The Writers Guild Foundation Shavelson-Webb Library

7000 W. 3rd St. (at S. Fairfax Ave.), Los Angeles
(323) 782-4544
www.wgfoundation.org/library.aspx
Hours: Closed Sat and Sun; Mon, Tues, Wed, Fri 11 a.m. to 5 p.m.; Thurs 11
a.m. to 8 p.m.; closed the last Fri of every month.

Open to WGA members and the public with the flash of your photo ID, this
screenwriting-focused library has an impressive collection of produced film,

television, and radio scripts, DVDs, and other materials related to screen-writing and screenwriters. Just shy of 30 years old, the library houses some 25,000 items and counting.

UNIVERSITY **LIBRARIES**

Many public and private universities in Los Angeles allow nonstudents to read, study, browse their collections, and take advantage of the Wi-Fi on their computers free of charge. Here is a sample listing of some of the heavy hitters and what they have to offer. Many of the phone numbers are general university numbers, but they will happily connect you to the appropriate library instantly.

California Institute of Technology (Caltech)
1200 E. California Blvd., Pasadena
(626) 395-6811
www.library.caltech.edu

Caltech is home to the Sherman Fairchild Library, Millikan Library, Dabney Library, Astrophysics Library, and the Geology & Planetary Sciences Library. Check website for individual hours of operation. Borrowing privileges beyond the Caltech community are extended on a selective basis.

California State University—John F. Kennedy Memorial Library
5151 State University Dr., Los Angeles
(323) 343-3988
www.calstatela.edu/library
Hours: Closed Sun; Mon through Thurs 8 a.m. to 9 p.m.; Fri 8 a.m. to 5 p.m.; Sat 10 a.m. to 6 p.m.

You are free to go to the library and use the resources in-house as often as you like. Should you wish to check items out, you can become a "Friend of the Library" for just $35/year.

California State University Northridge—Oviatt Library

18111 Nordhoff St., Northridge
(818) 677-2285
http://library.csun.edu
Hours: Mon through Thurs 7:45 a.m. to 11 p.m.; Fri 7:45 a.m. to 5 p.m.; Sat 11 a.m. to 5 p.m.; Sun noon to 8 p.m.

Again, all those library resources are free for you to use, but if you want to check any materials out, you'll have to invest in a Friends of the Oviatt Library membership at $50/year. A family can join for $70/year and receive two library cards.

Charles R. Drew University of Medicine and Science— CDU Health Sciences Library

1731 E. 120th St., Los Angeles
(323) 563-4869
www.cdrewu.edu/library-information-services
Hours: Closed Sun; Mon through Thurs 8 a.m. to 9 p.m.; Fri 8 a.m. to 6 p.m.; Sat 9 a.m. to 4:45 p.m.

Borrowing privileges are limited to Charles Drew University of Medicine students, but they are more than happy to host your visit and offer you use of all of their materials and resources.

Loyola Marymount University

1 LMU Dr., Los Angeles
(310) 338-2700
www.lmu.edu/libraries_research.htm

Loyola Marymount University is home to the William H. Hannon Library and the William M. Rains Law Library. Check website for hours. Anyone can do research at either library free of charge, but you must enter before 8 p.m. The William H. Hannon Library has extended overnight hours on the first floor. Library cards for nonstudents will run you $300 per year here, so get that studying, researching, quiet time, and xeroxing done on-site.

Mount St. Mary's College—Charles Willard Coe Memorial Library

12001 Chalon Rd. (between N. Grace Ln. and N. Bundy Dr.), Los Angeles
(310) 954-4000
www.msmc.la.edu/academics/libraries.asp

Hours: Mon through Thurs 8 a.m. to 10 p.m.; Fri 8 a.m. to 4:30 p.m.; Sat 9 a.m. to 5 p.m.; Sun 10 a.m. to 10 p.m.

The Special Collections section of the library consists of rare books and early editions of the Bible, theology treatises, devotionals works and Classical writings, as well as 18th, 19th, and 20th century art books and literature, all open to students, faculty, staff, and qualified researchers. Borrowing (again, books that are not part of the special collection) and computing privileges will cost you a $25 library card, good for 1 year. The J. Thomas McCarthy Library on the Doheny campus of Mount St. Mary's College is located at 10 Chester Place, Los Angeles (213-477-2750) and is open Mon through Thurs 8 a.m. to 9 p.m. and Fri through Sun 10 a.m. to 10 p.m.

Pepperdine University
24255 Pacific Coast Hwy., Malibu
(310) 506-7273
www.library.pepperdine.edu

Pepperdine is home to the Payson Law Library and the Drescher Graduate Library. There are also graduate campus library locations in Encino and Irvine. Check website for hours. You can look at books for free, but checking them out will cost you $100 for a Friend of the Library card, good for 1 year. So get everything done you need to get done while on-site, and then enjoy a beautiful drive on the PCH as you head home.

University of California Los Angeles (UCLA)
405 Hilgard Ave., Los Angeles
(310) 825-4321
www.library.ucla.edu

UCLA is home to the Arts Library, Louise M. Darling Biomedical Library, College Undergraduate Library, Richard C. Rudolph East Asian Library, Hugh & Hazel Darling Law Library, Eugene & Maxine Rosenfield Management Library, Music Library, Charles E. Young Research Library, the Science and Engineering Library, Southern Research Library Facility, Southern Regional Lab Facility, UCLA Lab School Library, and the William Andrews Clark Memorial Library. Check website for individual hours of operation. If you want borrowing privileges, you'll have to purchase a fee card at $100/year at the Louise M. Darling Biomedical Library, Charles E. Young Research Library, or the College Undergraduate Library. The fee card enables you to check out up to 5 circulating items at a time.

University of Southern California (USC)
University Park Campus
Los Angeles
(213) 740-2311
www.usc.edu/libraries

USC is home to an Accounting Library, Asa V. Call Law Library, Helen Topping Architecture & Fine Arts Library, Crocker Business Library, Cinema Arts Library, Doheny Memorial Library (their main library at ext. 2924), Gerontology Library, Grand Avenue Library, Leavey Library, Music Library, Norris Medical Library, Hoose Library of Philosophy, Science & Engineering Building, Special Collections Department, and the Von Kleinsmid Center Library for International and Public Affairs. Check website for hours. All libraries are accessible to the general public. A $125 card for non-USC folk will grant you 6 months of borrowing privileges. I think you can take care of everything while you're there, don't you?

YOUR **SPIRITUAL** SELF

Falun Dafa Practice Sites in Los Angeles
www.falundafa.org

All Falun Dafa practice sites offer on-the-spot free instruction in this spiritual movement based on Buddhist and Taoist teachings. To learn more about Falun Dafa or access free audio and visual materials for download, visit the website. For a comprehensive list of Los Angeles-area practice sites, check out www.its.caltech.edu/~falun/LA_practice.html.

Kadampa Meditation Center
1492 Blake Ave., Los Angeles
(323) 223-0610
www.meditateinla.org

Kadampa Meditation Center offers drop-in classes, beginner meditation courses at $12 a class, programs for kids and families, short and long retreats, and an in-depth study of Buddhism and meditation. Locations all over Los Angeles; visit their website for more information.

Peace Awareness Labyrinth & Gardens

3500 W. Adams Blvd., Los Angeles
(323) 737-4055
www.peacelabyrinth.org

Peace Awareness Labyrinth & Gardens is home to the Movement of Spiritual Inner Awareness, which teaches Soul Transcendence and practical spirituality, as well as the Peace Theological Seminary and College of Philosophy, which offers master's and PhD programs, along with classes on the Internet and retreats. Best of all, meditation techniques, Spanish language, soul dancing, and free-form writing are just some of the suggested donation workshops they offer on a weekly or regular basis. Click on "Events" on their homepage for more details.

Sahaja Meditation in Los Angeles

19530 Ventura Blvd., Tarzana
(866) Y-SAHAJA (972-4252)
www.sahajayogala.org

Introductory meditation classes, workshops, walk-ins, and special events in 15 centers around Los Angeles. Do you see the light? Stop thinking about how much laundry you have to do. Breathe . . .

Shambhala Meditation Center of Los Angeles (SMCLA)

963 Colorado Blvd., Los Angeles
(323) 255-5472
http://la.shambhala.org

Free guided instruction and dharma talks at their Eagle Rock Center and Westside group. Classes and programs in meditation, Buddhist, and Shambhala teachings. Check website for details.

Sivananda Yoga Vedanta Center

13325 Beach Ave. (between Glencoe and Redwood), Marina del Rey
(310) 822-9642
www.sivananda.org/la

Swami Vishnudevananda, disciple of spiritual teacher Swami Sivananda, came to the west in the late 1950s to open the first Sivananda Yoga Vedanta Center, established to spread peace, health, and joy through yoga. Today, there are more than 60 locations throughout the world, which have trained more than 26,000 teachers. The Marina del Rey location was founded in 1971 and offers Satsang ("company of the wise"), wherein you can participate in free silent meditation, mantra chanting, a reading, and discourse Mon through Sat at 6 a.m, Wed at 7 p.m., or Sun at 6:30 p.m. Guest lecturers sometimes make an appearance, and all are invited to eat soup together following. Satsang knows no prejudice on the basis of race, creed, or faith. To deepen your Kirtan (mantra chanting) practice, join in on the Satsang chants taught for free on alternating Saturdays from 4 to 6 p.m., where you will learn call-and-response, rhythm, and more.

Vedanta Society of Southern California
1946 Vedanta Place, Hollywood
(323) 465-7114
www.vedanta.org

Vedanta is one of the world's most ancient philosophies and the foundation for Hinduism. Vedanta, however, is universal in application and equally relevant to all countries, cultures, and religious backgrounds. In fact, it strives to show that all religions teach the same basic truths about God, the world, and our relationship to one another. The Vedanta Society offers services, lectures, classes, retreats, seminars, and workshops on ancient and broad religious philosophy. Free interviews with Swami Swahananda and Swami Sarvadedvananda are available by appointment. In addition to the Hollywood location, there are Vedanta centers in South Pasadena, other parts of Southern California, and throughout the world.

HEALTH & MEDICINE:
AN APPLE A DAY

"My doctor gave me six months to live, but when I couldn't pay the bill, he gave me six more."

—WALTER MATTHAU

I used to think people who live without medical insurance are crazy. Then I became one of them. With the amazing resources Los Angeles has to offer, it is possible to take good care of yourself with free or inexpensive medical care. Here's how.

FREE **OR** LOW-COST **HEALTH** CLINICS

As you peruse these listings to find a clinic in your neighborhood that will meet your needs, it is helpful to know that most clinics have sliding scales, low- to no-cost rates, or accept the Medi-Cal or similar insurance plans. Go armed with a good magazine or book; they don't call it the waiting room for nothing. When making an appointment for your needs, flag your calendar to schedule that appointment far in advance, so you're not stuck pouting on the other end of the phone at their lack of availability over the next 2 months.

AltaMed
10418 Valley Blvd., Suite B, El Monte
(626) 453-8466
www.altamed.org
Hours: Mon and Wed 8 a.m. to 7 p.m.; Tues and Thurs 9 a.m. to 7 p.m.; Fri 8 a.m. to 5 p.m.; Sat 8 a.m. to 1 p.m.

AltaMed has been offering primary care medicine, geriatrics, women's health, family planning, pediatrics, and screenings through its community clinics, senior care programs, and health and human services for the entire family over the past 40 years. Their various 43 combined Los Angeles and Orange County locations feature adult health day care services, senior case management, program of all-inclusive care for the elderly, disease management programs, health education, youth services, and HIV/AIDS care and substance abuse treatment, serving more than 100,000 families a year with more than 650,000 annual patient visits. AltaMed's user-friendly website or customer service (877-462-2582) can help you find a location, doctor, or clinic in your area.

Arroyo Vista Family Health Center

6000 N. Figueroa (at N. Avenue 61 in Highland Park), Los Angeles
(323) 254-5221
www.arroyovista.org
Hours: Mon through Fri 8 a.m. to 7 p.m. and Sat 8 a.m. to 4:30 p.m. Call 2
weeks in advance to make an appointment.

The Arroyo Vista Family Health Center provides affordable, quality health care services to patients with or without insurance, regardless of their ability to pay. Services offered at no cost include pregnancy tests; health education; diabetes classes; and childhood, flu, and pneumonia vaccinations; as well as dental, vision, height, weight, blood pressure screenings, and more. The financial screening team can meet with you to discuss sliding scale fee options. Additional locations in Lincoln Heights are at 2411 N. Broadway (323-987-2000), El Sereno at 4837 Huntington Dr. N. (323-225-0024) and 4815 N. Valley Blvd., Suite C (323-222-1134), and Loma Drive at 303 S. Loma Dr., Suite 202 (213-201-5800).

Chinatown Service Center

767 N. Hills St., Suite 400 (at Alpine Street in Chinatown), Los Angeles
(213) 808-1700
www.cscla.org
Hours: Mon through Fri 8:30 a.m. to 5 p.m.

Since 1971, Chinatown Service Center is the largest community-based nonprofit Chinese-American health and human services organization in Southern California, dedicated to serving immigrants, refugees, and others in aiding in the physical adjustment to American life. Physical exams, diagnosis and treatment for illnesses, lab tests, immunizations, and basic eye care are provided in English and various Chinese dialects. The main office is located at the address above, and several other satellite offices throughout Los Angeles provide youth and child development services.

Clínica Monseñor Oscar A. Romero Community Health Center

123 S. Alvarado St. (near Beverly Boulevard in Pico Union/Westlake),
Los Angeles
(213) 989-7700
www.clinicaromero.com

Hours: Mon through Thurs 8 a.m. to 8 p.m.; Fri and Sat 8 a.m. to 5 p.m. Call up to 2 months in advance for an appointment. Dental and counseling hours vary.

The Clínica Monseñor Oscar A. Romero provides medical, dental, counseling, and health education services to adults and children. Their newly opened children's clinic farther down on South Alvarado offers free physical exams and immunizations, as well as assistance with Medi-Cal or WIC enrollment, or in changing a medical plan. Hours differ at the children's clinic and at the Boyle Heights location at 2032 Marengo St. (323-987-1030), where they also have an alcohol and substance abuse treatment program. The clinic will work with you to determine payment.

Community Health Alliance of Pasadena
1855 N. Fair Oaks Ave. (at E. Tremont St.), Pasadena
(626) 398-6300
www.chapcare.org
Hours: Mon through Thurs 8 a.m. to 7 p.m.; Fri 8 a.m. to 4 p.m.; Sat 8 a.m. to 1 p.m.

Keep those pearly whites pearly with Community Health Alliance's dental care. Behavioral health services and medical care coverage including cholesterol checks, cancer screenings, disease screenings, vision and hearing tests, family planning, lab and radiology, blood pressure screenings, medicine, and prescriptions. Alternate locations at 1800 N. Lake Ave. and 3160 E. Del Mar Blvd., both in Pasadena and reachable via the same phone number as listed above.

Compton Central Health Clinic
201 N. Central Ave. (at E. 150th), Compton
(310) 635-7123
www.comptoncentralhealthclinic.org
Hours: Mon and Wed 9 a.m. to 7 p.m.; Tues and Thurs 9 a.m. to 5 p.m.; Fri 9 a.m. to 6 p.m.; Sat 9 a.m. to 3 p.m.

Immunizations, laboratory services, radiology, and primary care, including medical diagnosis as well as pharmacy services. The Compton Central Health Clinic also offers vaccinations.

Eisner Pediatric & Family Medical Center

1530 S. Olive St. (at Venice Blvd. in the Fashion District), Los Angeles
(213) 747-5542
www.pedcenter.org
Hours: Mon through Sat 8 a.m. to 4:30 p.m. Evening clinic hours vary by department.

The Eisner Pediatric & Family Medical Center has a multilingual staff that provides infant, toddler, children, adolescent, and women's care, along with mental health and dental needs services. They accept Medi-Cal, Healthy Families, CHDP, PPP, FPACT, private insurance, and cash. Some services are free.

El Dorado Community Service Center

4023 Marine Ave., Lawndale
(310) 675-9555
www.eldoradocsc.org
Hours: Mon through Fri 8 a.m. to 4:30 p.m.

This cluster of service centers scattered throughout the Los Angeles area offers general family practice, gynecology, pre- and post-natal care, pediatrics, family planning, mental health services, and narcotics treatment. Check out the website for information on all of their area locations.

Hollywood Walk-in Clinic

6430 Selma Ave., Hollywood
(323) 848-4522
http://hollywoodurgentcare.snappages.com
Hours: Mon through Fri 9 a.m. to 5 p.m.; Sat 10 a.m. to 4 p.m.

Urgent medical care services treating things like lacerations, abscesses, abrasions and minor burns, suture removal, cast check, coughs, bronchitis, earaches, sinusitis, sore throats, STDs, drug testing, allergic reactions, asthma, TB tests, vitamin B12 shots, physicals, and more. Although the cost is $69 for a general medical visit, considering that same visit to the ER will run you hundreds more, it's a steal.

The Saban Free Clinic

8405 Beverly Blvd. (at Orlando Ave.), Los Angeles
(323) 653-8622
www.thesabanfreeclinic.org

The Saban Free Clinic offers a variety of services, from primary, preventive, and specialty care for adults and children, to prenatal, OB/GYN, optometry, diabetes, asthma, high blood pressure, pharmacy/medication needs, HIV testing, STD diagnosis and treatment, cancer screenings, chiropractic care, mental, and dental services. They provide short-term therapy, crisis intervention, and group classes for teens on Mon at 4:30 p.m., and group classes for parents of elementary school-age kids on Tues at 7 p.m. For a complete list of locations, see Appendix A on p. 296. To make an appointment, call (323) 653-1990 Mon through Thurs from 7:30 a.m. to 5 p.m. and Fri 7:30 a.m. to 4:30 p.m. If you have no insurance, it's free, so long as you can prove you are a resident of Los Angeles County.

South Central Family Health Center

4425 S. Central Ave. (at 45th St. in the Furniture and
Decorative Arts District), Los Angeles
(323) 908-4200
www.scfhc.org
Hours: Mon through Fri 7 a.m. to 7 p.m.; Sat 7 a.m. to 6 p.m.

Primary care on a sliding scale based on your income if you don't qualify for other programs. South Central offers physicals, preventive health services, sick visits, diabetes, blood pressure, and cholesterol screening, chronic disease and STD disease screening and treatment, food and nutrition counseling, assistance with low-cost medications, and more.

Venice Family Clinic

Multiple locations
www.venicefamilyclinic.org

To make an appointment at any of the Venice Family Clinic locations, call (310) 392-8636 Mon through Thurs 8 a.m. to 5 p.m. and Fri 8 a.m. to 4 p.m. Be patient. They get nearly 500 calls a day, and there are no walk-ins. The Venice Family Clinic is the largest free clinic in the nation. The clinic provides comprehensive primary health care, specialty care, dental and eye care, mental health services, health education, child development services, domestic violence intervention, HIV/AIDS, women's health, and more, as well as public insurance enrollment to more than 24,400 patients, including more than 6,000 children, who make over 103,000 visits annually. Prescription medications are provided at no charge.

Donating Blood, Plasma, Platelets & Your Time

My father used to donate blood to make the rent in the 1960). Now that we're in the 21st century, you can find many places where they'll pay you to donate platelets or plasma. Why is that? Because donating platelets and plasma is more time-consuming and involved. What? Is your 6th grade science failing you and you can't remember what platelets and plasma are? Here's your refresher: Plasma is a fluid of blood and lymph in which platelets are suspended; platelets are tiny bits of protoplasm. They aid in clotting, thus helping hemophiliacs and burn victims, to name a few. Here is a list of centers where you can donate and help the less fortunate. I'll be the one in the corner fainting. Be sure to call ahead for hours.

American Red Cross
11355 Ohio Ave., West Los Angeles
(800) RED-CROSS
www.redcrossblood.org

Huntington Memorial Hospital Blood Donor Center
100 W. California Blvd., Pasadena
(626) 397-5422
www.huntingtonhospital.com/Main/BloodDonorCenter.aspx

**Long Beach Memorial Medical Center
and Miller Children's Hospital Long Beach**
2801 Atlantic Ave., Long Beach
(562) 933-0808
www.memorialcare.org/medical_services/blood-donation/blood-donation-long-beach.cfm

Watts Healthcare Corporation (WHCC)
10300 S. Compton Ave. (between 103rd and 104th Streets in Watts),
Los Angeles
(323) 564-4331
www.wattshealth.org
Hours: Mon through Fri 8 a.m. to 5:30 p.m.; Sat 8 a.m. to 7 p.m.

UCLA Blood and Platelet Center
1045 Gayley Ave., 2nd floor, Los Angeles
(310) 825-0888
www.gotblood.ucla.edu

USC Blood Donor Center
2250 Alcazar St., Los Angeles, CA
(323) 442-5433
www.uscblooddonorcenter.org

Other Ways to Help
The Art of Elysium
3728 Wilshire Blvd., Penthouse, Los Angeles
(213) 389-3201
www.theartofelysium.org
If you are an actor, artist, or musician who'd like to donate your time and talent to kids battling serious medical conditions, The Art of Elysium is for you. They provide workshops in acting, art, comedy, fashion, music, radio, songwriting, and creative writing to children battling serious medical conditions.

Project Angel Food
922 Vine St., Los Angeles
(323) 845-1800
www.angelfood.org
Volunteers deliver nearly 13,000 free and nutritious meals to men, women, and children living throughout Los Angeles with HIV/AIDS, cancer, and other life-threatening illnesses.

WHCC offers OB/GYN, primary and preventive care, pediatric and adolescent care, dental, physical therapy, and pharmacy services. Sliding scale starts at $30. Check website for details on 3 other locations in South Los Angeles.

Westside Family Health Center

1711 Ocean Park Blvd. (at 17th St.), Santa Monica
(310) 450-2191
www.wfhcenter.org
Hours: Mon through Fri 8:30 a.m. to 5 p.m.; Sat 8:30 a.m. to 2 p.m.

The Westside Family Health Center has been providing primary, pediatric, and prenatal care, immunizations, TB screening, HIV testing, and vision and hearing care for nearly 40 years. They handle asthma, diabetes, mammograms, and counseling. All services are provided on a sliding scale price with most costing between $35 and $77. Accessible via the Big Blue Bus or Metro; if you drive, follow the street signs for parking. Make an appointment by calling the number above or e-mailing appointments@wfhcenter.org and putting your name, daytime/cell number, and the nature of your appointment in the e-mail and they will contact you within 24 hours.

FREE **OR** LOW-COST **HOSPITALS**

Cedars-Sinai Medical Center

8700 Beverly Blvd. (1 block before S. San Vicente Blvd.), Los Angeles
(310) 4-CEDARS (423-3277)
www.cedars-sinai.edu

Through the Community Benefit Program, Cedars-Sinai is committed to providing access to essential health care for the uninsured and underinsured. They operate mobile medical units for kids and families to underserved areas; provide free diabetes screenings, education, and prevention programs for seniors; and teach healthy habits to kids in schools. They offer free seasonal flu shots for senior citizens, a psychological trauma center, a teen hot line, and more. Call for more details.

Children's Hospital Los Angeles

4650 Sunset Blvd., Los Angeles
(323) 660-2450
www.chla.org
Hours: Mon through Thurs 8 a.m. to 5 p.m.; Fri 8 a.m. to 4:30 p.m. Appointments made up to 4 months in advance. Consultation before treatment.

Children's Hospital Los Angeles is one of the premier pediatric medical centers in the country, treating more than 93,000 kids per year and 287,000 at its 29 outpatient clinics and laboratories. Among some of their many services, they provide general dentistry for children with disabilities ages 1 to 18, and up to age 7 for healthy children. Children's Hospital Los Angeles takes Medi-Cal and sliding scale as payment. You can also donate platelets here.

Shriners Hospitals for Children

3160 Geneva St. (near S. Virgil Ave.), Los Angeles
(213) 388-3151
www.shrinershq.org

Shriners Hospitals for Children provides pediatric care and treatment to children up to the age of 18 with orthopedic conditions, cleft lip and palate, regardless of their ability to pay. You must fill out an application and schedule an appointment or get a referral. Shriners does not tend to emergency needs.

INSURANCE: FREE TO CHEAP

PPP

PPP, or Public-Private Partnership, is used to describe a government, service, or private business venture funded and operated through a partnership between the government and one or more private sector companies.

Medi-Cal

Medi-Cal is the name of the Medicaid program in California, jointly administered by the California State Department of Health Care Services and the Centers for Medicare and Medicaid Services (CMS)—meaning it is a medical assistance program that falls under the Social Security Act. This public health insurance program meets the health care needs of low-income individuals, including families with children, senior citizens, the disabled, pregnant women, those in foster care, or a low-income individual suffering from tuberculosis, breast cancer, or HIV/AIDS. Under the California Partnership for Long-Term Care, Medi-Cal aims to protect Californians from losing their life savings on long-term health care costs in the event they are needed. Medi-Cal does not offer dental insurance to those over the age of 21, nor does it offer acupuncture, audiology, chiropractic, optician, podiatry, psychology, incontinence, or speech therapy services. If you are enrolled in SSI/SSP, CalWorks (AFDC), Refugee Assistance, Foster Care or Adoption Assistance Program, In-Home Supportive Services (IHSS), or are 65 or older, blind, disabled, under 21, pregnant, in a nursing or intermediate home, on refugee status for a limited time, or have been screened for breast or cervical cancer, you are eligible for Medi-Cal. For more information, visit www .medi-cal.ca.gov.

Healthy Families Program

The Healthy Families Program offers low-cost health, dental, and vision coverage for eligible children up to the age of 19, at $4 to $17 per child per month, with a maximum of $51 per family per month. It covers those who do not have insurance or qualify for Medi-Cal. Coverage includes immunizations, prescription drugs, doctor visits, and hospital care. Visit www.healthy families.ca.gov for more information or call LA Care at (888) 452-2273 to apply.

Access for Infants and Mothers

AIM is insurance for low-income expectant mothers who don't have insurance to cover pregnancy and are not receiving Medi-Cal or Medicare Part A and Part B. AIM can also step in when private insurance health plans have a maternity-only deductible or co-payment greater than $500. Visit www.aim .ca.gov or call (800) 433-2611 for more information Mon through Fri 8 a.m. to 8 p.m. or Sat 8 a.m. to 5 p.m.

LA Care's Healthy Kids

Healthy Kids offers low-cost health coverage, at the rate of $0 to $6 per month, for children under the age of 19 who don't qualify for Medi-Cal or Healthy Families but do meet other eligibility and income requirements. Services included are doctor visits, prescription drugs, hospital care, immunizations, dental and vision care, mental health, ER, and alcohol/drug abuse care. Log on to www.lacare.org or call (888) 452-2273 to see if you qualify.

LA Care Health Plan Medicare Advantage HMO

This program meets the health care needs of low-income seniors in Los Angeles County and can be used in tandem with Medicare to provide better benefits. Eligibility can be met if you are entitled to Medicare Part A, Medicare Part B, do not have end-stage renal disease (ESRD), and have full Medi-Cal benefits. This plan covers doctor, dental, and vision visits and services, worldwide emergency services coverage, nonemergency routine transportation, routine podiatry, and prescription drug benefits. Log on to www.lacare .org or call (888) 839-9909 to inquire for more information.

AIDS Drugs Assistance Program (ADAP)

ADAP exists to provide medication for HIV-positive uninsured and underinsured individuals. ADAP has more than 180 drugs available and 3,000 pharmacies statewide. To qualify you must be a resident of California, infected with HIV, 18 years of age or older, have an income of less than $50,000, a prescription from a licensed California physician, and lack private insurance that covers the medications or do not qualify for no-cost Medi-Cal. Patients with an income below 400 percent of the Federal Poverty Level receive ADAP drugs at no cost. A co-payment is required for those whose income falls between $40,840 and $50,000 annually.

WOMEN'S CLINICS

Alliance Women's Medical Group

1930 Wilshire Blvd., Suite 500 (at Bonnie Brae St. in Filipino Town),
Los Angeles
(213) 353-4971
Hours: Mon through Sat 9 a.m. to 4 p.m.

Available via phone 24 hours a day, the Alliance Women's Medical Group offers comprehensive medical services for women including free pregnancy testing and birth control prescriptions, though the pharmacy determines what you pay when filled. Consultations are $60.

Saint Ana Women's Medical Clinic

Norma C. Salceda, M.D., F.A.C.O.G
937 Alvarado St., #1C, Los Angeles
(213) 639-1050
www.saintanaclinic.com

Saint Ana Women's Medical Clinic offers free pregnancy testing, STD testing, pregnancy care, obstetrics, IUD, infertility, gynecology, and other women's health care to those who qualify. Check out their website for information on additional area locations.

Women's Clinic & Family Counseling Center

9911 W. Pico Blvd., Suite 500, Los Angeles
(310) 203-8899
http://womens-clinic.org
Hours: Mon, Tues, Thurs 8 a.m. to 4 p.m.; Wed 8 a.m. to 6 p.m.; Fri 8 a.m. to 3 p.m. Open the first Sat of every month from 9 a.m. to 1 p.m.

Serving the medical needs of women with low or no income, Women's Clinic & Family Counseling Center offers birth control services, bladder and urinary tract infection treatment, colposcopy, emergency contraception, HIV testing, hormone replacement therapy, pap smears, pregnancy testing, STDs, vaginal and yeast infection treatment, depression, eating disorder and addiction treatment, parenting and gay/lesbian counseling, and more.

Women's Health Center

3620 Martin Luther King Jr. Blvd. (at Imperial Hwy.), Lynwood
(310) 638-9007
www.jwchinstitute.org/wm_health.htm

Low-income clinic for women offering OB/GYN exams, cervical and breast cancer screenings, pregnancy testing and prenatal services, birth control, health education, STD exams, and referrals for other health and social services as needed. Primary care and family planning.

PLANNED **PARENTHOOD**

Planned Parenthood is the nation's leading sexual and reproductive health care provider and advocate, offering abortion and birth control services, emergency contraception, HIV testing, HPV and hepatitis vaccinations, LGBT services, men's health services, patient education, pregnancy testing, STD testing and treatment, and more. All services are free or reduced, depending on your income and ability to pay. They also offer an option to set up payment plans when necessary. For more information on Planned Parenthood, visit www.plannedparenthood.org. Appointments for the centers listed below can be made by calling (800) 576-5544.

Alhambra
Alhambra Health Center, 320 S. Garfield Ave., Suite 126

Burbank
Burbank Health Center, 916 W. Burbank Blvd.

Canoga Park
Canoga Park Health Center, 21001 Sherman Way, #9

El Monte
El Monte Health Center, 4786 N. Peck Rd., Suite B

Lakewood
Lakewood Health Center, 5525 E. Del Amo Blvd. and 5519 E. Del Amo Blvd.

Lawndale
South Bay Health Center, 14623 Hawthorne Blvd., #300

Long Beach
Long Beach Health Center, 2690 Pacific Ave., Suite 370

Los Altos Hills
Foothill College Health Center, 12345 El Monte Rd.

Los Angeles

Bixby Boyle Heights Health Center, 560 S. St. Louis St.
Bixby Health Center, 1057 Kingston Ave.
Dorothy Hecht Health Center, 8520 S. Broadway
Eagle Rock Express Center, 1578 W. Colorado Blvd.
East Los Angeles Health Center, 5068 Whittier Blvd.
Hollywood Health Center, 1014½ N. Vermont Ave.
Planned Parenthood Basics Baldwin Hills/Crenshaw, 3637 S. La Brea Ave.
S. Mark Taper Foundation Center for Medical Training, 400 W. 30th St.

Pasadena

1045 N. Lake Ave.

Santa Monica

Santa Monica Health Center, 1316 3rd St. Promenade, #201

South Bay

South Bay Health Center, 14623 Hawthorne Blvd., #300

Van Nuys

Van Nuys Health Center, 7100 Van Nuys Blvd., #108

Westminster

Westminster Health Center, 14372 Beach Blvd.

Whittier

Whittier Health Center, 7655 Greenleaf Ave.

CHEAPER MEDICINE

In addition to the prescription coverage provided by many of the plans already outlined in this chapter, there are some other awesome options on reduced rates for cheap medicine. In general, it does not hurt to ask your local pharmacy if they have a prescription plan that offers cheaper rates;

many national chains may have something like this but don't advertise it, since they don't want it to spread and become common knowledge.

LARx Prescription Savings Program
(877) FOR-LARX (367-5279)
www.forlarx.com

Okay, the card is free, no registration or qualification required, nor is there a membership fee. If you are in possession of the card, you can obtain discounts of 5 to 40 percent on virtually all brand-name and generic drugs at participating pharmacies. How is this not a win-win situation?

Walmart
4101 Crenshaw Blvd., Los Angeles
(323) 299-8014
www.walmart.com

Certain generic drugs at commonly prescribed dosages are only $4 for a 30-day supply, $10 for a 90-day supply, $9 for certain "women's health and other covered generic drugs" for 30 days, or $24 for 90 days. Check out their website for information on their Panorama City, Rosemead, Torrance, and West Hills locations.

ALTERNATIVE MEDICINE

Get your acupuncture, Chinese herbs, and medical marijuana right here. Eastern medicine has been around far longer than either one of us and can be a great option for you alone, or perhaps in conjunction with Western treatment. Your Chinese herbs are priced by brand and cheaper if you buy them from the manufacturer itself.

Costa Acupuncture
10200 Venice Blvd. (at Jasmine Ave.), #109B, Culver City
(310) 776-5096
www.yoursourceforwellness.org

Acupuncture can relieve your neck, back, and joint pain, PMS, headaches, infertility, digestion problems, depression, insomnia, addiction, cravings, and then some. Costa Acupuncture also offers cupping, herbs, and nutritional supplements. Check out their self-healing techniques online and get started on a brand-new you now! (I really should have been a motivational speaker.) Their services are offered on a sliding scale between $20 and $40. There is an additional $10 fee for your first visit. Closed Tues, Thurs, and Sun.

Emperor's College Graduate School of Traditional Oriental Medicine
1807 Wilshire Blvd. (at 18th St.), Santa Monica
(310) 453-8383
http://emperors.edu

At Emperor College's community clinic, you can pay just $30 to $50 per session for acupuncture treatments lasting 1.5 hours in length. Book your appointment 1 to 3 days in advance for any day but Sunday. Walk-in clinic for 20-minute ear acupuncture to treat pain, indigestion, PMS, stress, anxiety, insomnia, addiction, and weight loss support on Wed afternoons from 12:45 to 4 p.m for just $15 per treatment.

South Baylo University
2727 W. 6th St. (at S. Benton Way in Lafayette Park), Los Angeles
(213) 738-1974
www.southbaylo.edu/en/clinics/la_clinic.htm

Acupuncture is offered 7 days a week at the clinic at South Baylo University for just $20 per session, and lasts 30 minutes to 1.5 hours, depending on your problem. First come, first served. The Anaheim clinic is located at 1126 N. Brookhurst St. (714-535-3886).

Wing Hop Fung
727 N. Broadway, Suite #102 (at Ord St. in Chinatown), Los Angeles
(213) 626-7200
www.winghopfung.com

Wing Hop Fung means "Together Forever Prosper" and is your go-to place for Chinese herbs, arts, crafts, and clothing. Some items can also be purchased online. All herbs are at great prices. Wing Hop Fung is open 7 days a week and will soon be offering wine and champagne-tasting lunches and dinners, along with dim sum lunch events. They have another location in Monterey Park at 725 W. Garvey Ave. (626-227-1688) as well.

CANCER **SUPPORT**

The Angeles Clinic
2001 Santa Monica Blvd. (at 20th), Suite 560W, Santa Monica
(310) 582-7900
www.theangelesclinic.org

Check the website to see which clinical trials the clinic is currently participating in. Free breast cancer-related services for low- to moderate-income
individuals. A second location is at 11818 Wilshire Blvd., West Hollywood
(310-582-7900).

weSPARK Cancer Support Center
13520 Ventura Blvd., Sherman Oaks
(818) 906-3022
www.wespark.org

weSPARK provides free support groups, creative programs, and workshops for
those afflicted with cancer in an effort to heal the mind, body, and spirit of
all whose lives have been affected by it. Go to their website for a list of current programs in grief, tai chi, kundalini yoga, Pilates, support, and more, as
well as a link to online cancer support resources. You will be required to fill
out an intake form before physically participating in any program.

FITNESS, FUN & GAMES:
HAVE FUN WHILE
LOOKING GOOD

"I don't jog. If I die, I want to be sick."

—ABE LEMONS

Los Angeles, with nearly 150 brilliantly sunny days per year, generally pleasant humidity (not counting the September day that reached 112 degrees in 2010), and average monthly temperatures ranging between 57 and 70 degrees, is an outdoor lover and fitness fanatic's paradise. So whether you want to hike it, beach it, or throw it, get started. Get healthy or stay healthy, maybe make and meet some new friends, become one with nature, and hey, at least you'll look good and be able to keep up with the rest of our image-obsessed culture. Botox, anyone?

TAKE A HIKE

Echo Mountain and Inspiration Point
Lower San Gabriel Mountains
Lake Avenue and E. Loma Alta Drive, Altadena

At Echo Mountain and Inspiration Point, you can hike 10.4 miles of mostly upward trail and take in well-preserved historical ruins of a turn-of-the-20th-century hotel along the way. Sort of like *Titanic*. But not a ship. And not on water. The Cobb Estate at the beginning of the trail has equestrian trails and a small botanical garden. As you reach the top, nearly 5 hours later (depending on your speed), shout through the ground-mounted megaphone to hear that echo bounce back to you. Follow signs on your descent for Castle Canyon so you can stop at the Inspiration Point pavilion. This hike is mildly strenuous, so if you're at all an exercise-phobe, you'd best build up your tolerance before attempting this one.

Franklin Canyon Park
2600 Franklin Canyon Dr., Beverly Hills
(310) 858-3090
www.lamountains.com/planning_franklin.html

Turn onto Franklin Canyon Drive from Beverly Drive. You will drive for a mile until you hit Franklin Lake, a giant man-made lake. Check out the many migratory birds that pass through the 605 acres and over 5 miles of hiking trails in Franklin Canyon Park and enjoy a picnic beneath the oak and sycamore trees. Breathe deeply. You can now forget any vacuous thoughts the inhabitants of Beverly Hills below might have.

Griffith Park
4730 Crystal Springs Dr., Los Angeles
(323) 913-4688
www.laparks.org/dos/parks/griffithpk

With the Autry National Center, Los Angeles Zoo, Griffith Observatory, the LA Equestrian Center, bike rentals, golf, swimming, tennis, pony rides, merry-go rounds, invigorating walking (beware rattlesnakes on unmarked paths), and extraordinary views of the LA Basin, San Fernando Valley, and San Gabriel Mountains to be ingested, there's virtually nothing this park doesn't have going for it. Except your presence. So remedy that and head there now. Bronson Caves, located in the southwest corner of the park, have been featured as Batman's hideout in the TV series, and in such classics as *Bonanza, Gunsmoke, Star Trek: Voyager, Star Trek VI: The Undiscovered Country,* and more. What's a cheaper outing than the park? Come on! Don't act like a Borg and be a party-pooper of the galaxy! Get moving. Open year-round 5 a.m. to 10:30 p.m.

Los Angeles State Historic Park
1245 N. Spring St., Los Angeles
(323) 441-8819
www.parks.ca.gov

These 32 acres of park adjacent to Chinatown are an urban oasis in the middle of downtown Los Angeles. Enjoy the view of a skyline from the serenity of nature that surrounds you. Plenty of biking, running, walking, picnicking, and general park-ing pleasure. On-leash dogs are welcome. Open 8 a.m. to sunset.

Malibu Creek State Park
1925 Las Virgenes Rd., Calabasas
(818) 880-0367
www.parks.ca.gov

Park in the second parking lot near the backcountry trailhead. If the peaks of Goat Buttes Summit look familiar and the theme of *M*A*S*H* is running through your head, it's because you recognize those peaks from the opening credits of the television show. The road will become a dirt road after you cross the bridge. When it forks, stay to the right, and then try, just try, not to gasp at the breathtaking beauty that will surround you. The Visitors Center is rarely open, but the trail to your right just before the bridge that crosses to it can take you to massive granite monoliths that served as the backdrop to the original *Planet of the Apes* (1968). Are you enjoying your entertainment history lesson in this chapter? I should hope so. Great camping site with fishing, horseback riding, and bird watching. Located 25 miles from downtown Los Angeles, Malibu Creek State Park also features Century Lake, a man-made lake. Day trippers can avoid the $12 parking fee altogether by parking on Mulholland for free. Open dawn to dusk.

Runyon Canyon Park
Franklin Avenue to Palermo Road, Los Angeles
(213) 485-5572
www.lamountains.com

Just off the 101 Freeway, Runyon Canyon Park offers you 130 acres of urban wilderness. Hollywood runs and walks here, taking in views of the Hollywood sign and Griffith Observatory, Downtown LA, La Brea and Wilshire, the Pacific Ocean, Catalina Island, the Sunset Strip, Hollywood Boulevard, and Baldwin Hills along the way; listen for buzz on the latest deals as you drift by the workout-focused designer sweats-clad power mongers of Tinseltown. You can enter at the south or north entrance. If you enter from the south, you can choose to go clockwise or counterclockwise. The latter is more of a workout. Off-leash dogs love them some Runyon Canyon.

Sandstone Peak
Santa Monica Mountains
West of the Triunfo Pass on Yerba Buena Road, Malibu

Take the Mishe Mokwa Trail for a stunning, 6-mile round trip hike. When you summit at Sandstone Peak, you'll catch your breath and Kodak views of the San Gabriel Mountains, Los Padres National Forest, Pacific Ocean, and Channel Islands.

Santa Anita Canyon
San Gabriel Mountains
Chantry Flats at end of Santa Anita Avenue
www.bigsantaanitacanyon.com

Hop across streams and hear the rush of the 55-foot Sturtevant Falls, feeling like an animated character in a Disney movie all the while. Pretend one of the 80 cabins, built some 70 years ago and counting, belongs to you. Then remember you're not ready to give up your iPhone and modern conveniences, though this hike is a pretty rad way to spend the afternoon. Wear appropriate gear to protect yourself from poison oak and lyme disease. Rattlesnakes, mountain lions, and bear reside in the Santa Anita Canyon, but are not likely to bother you. Over 40 miles of trails to choose from. Parking is free or $5, depending on whether the free lot is full and you have to head to the Pack Station/General Store and use their lot.

Solstice Canyon Park
Off Corral Canyon Road, Malibu

Alder and sycamore trees line Solstice Canyon Park in the Santa Monica Mountains, along with waterfalls and creeks. You're ready for your Cover Girl supermodel shoot in a bikini in nature. Or not. You could just go, fully clothed, and enjoy yourself without the pressure of a modeling shoot. You don't have to be super buff in order to handle this pleasant hike. (I can hear your sigh of relief through the pages of this book.)

Temescal Gateway Park
15601 Sunset Blvd., Pacific Palisades
(310) 454-1395
www.lamountains.com

One mile north of the PCH at the intersection of Temescal Canyon and Sunset Boulevard is this beautiful park, once a meeting place for early-20th-century church groups and spiritual communities. (It's okay, today it doesn't matter which way you swing.) Take in all 141 acres of oak and sycamore canyons. If you take the Temescal Canyon Trail, stay to the right, it's the best! To check out the creek, take a right past the red cabin, a quick left, and then stay straight. Temescal Gateway Park abuts the entrance to the 36 miles of hiking trails in Topanga State Park. So, it's 2 free parks for the price of one.

Will Rogers State Historic Park
1501 Will Rogers Park Rd., Pacific Palisades
(310) 454-8212
www.parks.ca.gov

In the 1930s, Will Rogers was the highest paid actor in Hollywood. There's even a musical called *The Will Rogers Follies*. A vaudeville star, radio personality, philosopher, and columnist, he could do wonders with his rope tricks. His ranch of 186 acres overlooking the Pacific Ocean was turned into a state park in 1944. You can tour his ranch house Thursday through Sunday, watch the Will Rogers Polo Club every April through October weekend, and take trail rides by horse or hike. If you take your laptop within 150 feet of the Ranger Station in the park, you'll be able to surf the Internet and learn that Will Rogers used to play polo here with his friends Clark Gable and Gary Cooper. Inspiration Point has the most stunning views, so don't leave without making it up there!

YOGA

It's Los Angeles, so whether you love it or you've never tried it, at some point in your Los Angeles sojourn, be it the year you live there after college or the moment you realized you were a lifer, you have to give yoga a whirl. It's one of those rare physical activities you can do your whole life (like walking, swimming, tennis, and golf), and its benefits have been documented for centuries. A good yoga class does wonders for any back, shoulder, or neck pain I experience as a result of my relationship with my computer. It could do the same for you, and there are a number of cheap deals you should be taking advantage of, so get ready to give your best downward dog. Om . . .

Basic Hatha Yoga
Memorial Branch Library
4625 W. Olympic Blvd. (at S. Mullen Ave. in Mid-Wilshire/Hancock Park),
Los Angeles
www.lapl.org

Take a free basic hatha yoga class at the Memorial Branch Library on Saturday for 1 hour and 15 minutes and be sure to check out http://artists survivalguide.blogspot.com for more information on free Los Angeles fitness and yoga classes. I love pigeon pose. Really works on those hips that can get tight from all that sitting in traffic!

Bikram Yoga Silverlake

3223 Glendale Blvd. (at Brunswick Ave.), Los Angeles
(323) 668-2500
www.bikramyogasilverlake.com

One week of unlimited yoga for just $20. If you purchase a package within your introductory period, they'll give you 15 percent off. Offer good for first-time students who are residents of the greater Los Angeles area. They also have cash-only donations classes for charity, with a minimum suggested donation of $10.

Black Dog Yoga

4454 Van Nuys Blvd. (near Moorpark St.), Sherman Oaks
(818) 380-0331
www.blackdogyoga.net

Black Dog Yoga offers classes of all levels in hatha yoga, based mostly on the Anusara and Ashtanga Vinyasa systems. Hatha yoga joins the masculine, active energy of the sun with the feminine, receptive energy of the moon to create a more balanced and powerful individual, *you,* if you take advantage of their 2 weeks of unlimited yoga at $30 for Los Angeles residents only. Mid-day power hours at Black Dog Yoga are a steal at $5, and community classes are just $10.

Bryan Kest's Power Yoga

Power Yoga Studio—West: 1410 2nd St., 1st floor, Santa Monica
Power Yoga Studio—East: 522 Santa Monica Blvd., Santa Monica
(310) 458-9510
www.poweryoga.com

Bryan Kest's Power Yoga offers donation-based classes, with the suggested donation at $12, but they want you to give what you can.

Mark Blanchard's 304 Power Yoga

409 W. Olympic Blvd., #304 (between S. Olive St. and S. Grand Ave.),
Los Angeles
(213) 488-0820
www.304poweryoga.com

Take Mark Blanchard's power hour class at 6:30 a.m. or noon for just $11, and increase your strength, flexibility, mental clarity, and awareness, as well as the firmness of your butt. (Hey, it's LA, don't think no one is checking you out.) Ten percent off single sessions for active SAG members, LA City workers, or students with valid photo ID. New students can pay $60 for 1 month of unlimited yoga. This deal must be purchased with your first class. Voted *LA Weekly* Best of 2010.

Runyon Canyon Yoga
2000 N. Fuller Ave. (at Runyon Canyon), Hollywood
(323) 666-5046

Daily free outdoor yoga classes given to yoga enthusiasts of all shapes, sizes, and walks of life in the grassy area of Runyon Canyon Park near the Fuller entrance. Bring a mat or towel and a donation if you please. Commune and become one with nature before you venture out into the world and become one with traffic. Stay up to date with "Runyon Canyon YOGA" on Facebook.

Urth Yoga
2809 W. Sunset Blvd. (near Silverlake Blvd.), Los Angeles
(213) 483-YOGA (9642)
www.urthyoga.com

Urth Yoga is an eco-friendly hatha yoga studio in the heart of Silverlake. Take advantage of their $20 offer of unlimited yoga for 10 days, or $49 for 1 month. Mat rental is free in your introductory period, and you'll receive a 15 percent discount if you purchase any packages in that time. Payment plans and discounted programs offered to those in need, because money should not stand in the way of you and your "Namaste."

The Yoga Collective
1408 3rd St. Promenade, 3rd floor, Santa Monica
(310) 395-0600
http://theyogacollective.com

The Yoga Collective runs great deals such as $30 for unlimited yoga in your first month, or 10 classes for just $100. Located on the entertainment-friendly 3rd Street Promenade, you can pair your yoga with a walk out to the Santa Monica Pier or beach to meet a friend, and you've packed your day with budget-friendly escapades!

Yoga Shelter
12408 Ventura Blvd. (at Rhodes Ave.), Studio City
(818) 691-3000
www.yogashelter.com

Yoga Shelter offers what they call Sanga Yoga. "Sanga" means community, and Yoga Shelter wants yoga to be affordable and accessible to all, so you can invite harmony and balance into your body and life. All classes are open to all strength and experience levels. They offer 1 free week of yoga to first-time yoga students who are also LA County residents, 10 percent off a 36-class pass, 60 days (that's 2 months!) of unlimited yoga for $120, and more. Deals are constantly changing, so check their website for the latest.

YogaWorks for Everybody
Multiple locations
www.yogaworks.com

YogaWorks runs specials all the time to get you to join. For example, does 2 weeks of unlimited yoga for $30 plus a free subscription to *Yoga Journal* sound like a good deal? You bet. Your deal might be something different, but it's guaranteed to be just as awesome. Check their website for information about their many locations in Los Angeles and Orange County.

Yogi's Anonymous
1221 2nd St., Santa Monica
(310) 451-YOGI (9644)
www.yogisanonymous.com

Yogi's Anonymous offers free classes from time to time, and streams classes live on their website. You can also have access to their entire yoga library for just $15/month. Then maybe you, too, can do yoga naked in the privacy of your own apartment. (That one was for my boyfriend. Oh, yeah, I'm talking to you. Now everyone knows. Woops!)

TRADITIONAL **SPORTS**

Angels Gate Park
3601 Gaffey St., San Pedro
(310) 548-7705
www.laparks.org/dos/parks/facility/angelsGatePk.htm

Dribble that ball by foot on the soccer field or by hand on the basketball court. When you're completely tuckered out, take a break to hike over to the Korean Bell of Friendship and Bell Pavilion for a deep breath and views of the Los Angeles Harbor, Catalina Channel, and sea terraces of San Pedro Hill. Even better if you do all of this after a scenic car trip down Palos Verdes Drive on your way there.

Los Angeles, California Volleyball
www.volleyball.org/usa/california/la/index.html

This page will tell you how to get on the listserve for everything you ever needed to know about volleyball in Southern California, from classes and clinics to tournaments, leagues, open gyms, and pickup games, to beach and grass volleyball resources. That's right, you heard me. Volleyball resources. For the best beach volleyball viewing, check out Manhattan and Hermosa Beaches.

Playa Vista Sports Park
13196 W. Bluff Creek Dr., Los Angeles
www.playavistaagents.com/sportspark

Playa Vista Sports Park, located in Los Angeles on the west side, is a 7-acre park boasting a Little League baseball field, soccer field, two half basketball courts, two tennis courts, and a playground. Use of the park is totally free. Visit their website for more information.

TennisLosAngeles.com
www.tennislosangeles.com

Tennis Los Angeles can connect you to tennis players on the courts throughout Westwide Beaches, West LA, Downtown, the San Fernando Valley, and

San Gabriel Valley. For nominal fees, you can join a league, find partners, and play doubles in any season. For a list of free tennis courts in Los Angeles, see Appendix B on p. 297.

Venice Beach Basketball Courts
Off Ocean Front Walk at 17th and 18th Avenues, Venice

If you're serious about basketball, you'll want to shoot hoops with all men who can jump, at one of the 3 full courts at this outdoor basketball institution. Of course, the form played here is a bit more streetball, so the rules are a bit more lax and the show a bit more theatrical, complete with slam dunks and fake-outs.

YMCA
www.ymcala.org

Swimming, cycling, Pilates, volleyball, dancing, and more for some of the cheapest rates around at one of the nearly 25 YMCA locations in metropolitan Los Angeles. Classes are cheapest for members, but still quite reasonable for nonmembers. The Stuart M. Ketchum Downtown YMCA location offers free health classes featuring health officials from organizations such as the American Cancer Society, American Heart Association, and the USC Stroke Center speaking about topical health issues we face individually, in our family, and in our community. See the website for the YMCA location closest to you and for the current schedule of classes.

City of Los Angeles Department of Recreation and Parks

Whether it's swimming, baseball, basketball, flag football, golf, soccer, softball, tennis, or volleyball that gets the blood pumping and your endorphins climbing, the City of Los Angeles Department of Recreation and Parks has a league for you. Fees are usually on a per-team basis, but go a long way toward covering everything you'll need to participate in your chosen sport. You'll sweat, have fun, make new friends, and feel like a kid all over again. Visit **www.laparks.org** for more details.

SKATEBOARDING, **SWIMMING** & OTHER **SPORTS**

Academy of Mixed Martial Science (AMMS)
11671 National Blvd. (at Barrington), West Los Angeles
(310) 795-AMMS (2667)
http://mma-losangeles.com

One Sunday of every month, the Academy of Mixed Martial Science hosts a free 90-minute self-defense workshop as a service to the community. Learn basic and easy-to-use control techniques to hold and subdue an attacker quickly and safely without injuring the opponent, as well as vital area-striking to stop an attack in 5 moves or less. Visit the website to sign up. AMMS also welcomes new students to try a free introductory class in Muay Thai Kickboxing, Brazilian Jiu-Jitsu, Kick-Fit, or Self-Defense. The South Bay location is at 13040 Hawthorne Blvd. and can be reached using the phone number listed above. HI-YA!

Los Angeles Organization of Ultimate Teams (LAOUT)
www.laout.org

In Ultimate Frisbee, you pass a Frisbee among players on two opposing teams, with each team trying to score a goal in the "end zone." Like football or hockey, minus the full-body contact and helmet. LAOUT has teamed up with www.PickUpUltimate.com, which lists all the pickup games, not just in Los Angeles but the world. Joining a league will cost you some money; pickup games are free.

Muscle Beach Gym
Venice Beach Recreation and Parks Office
1800 Ocean Front Walk, Venice
(310) 399-2775
www.musclebeach.net

Eat your heart out, Arnold Schwarzenegger. Pre-CA Governor/Terminator Arnold, the one who won bodybuilding competitions in Austria Arnold, that is. Muscle Beach claims it pioneered the concept of the "outdoor gym" and was the "original birthplace of the physical fitness movement of the 20th century." Catch buff men in their skivvies lifting heavy stuff in full view of your visual pleasure. If you're not into pumping iron, you can watch others do so in many a competition. Buy a 1-day workout pass for $10, and you can start lifting, too. If things get too steamy, you can head into the ocean to cool off following.

Pasadena Ice Skating Center

310 E. Green St., Pasadena
(626) 578-0800
www.skatepasadena.com

All ages can triple salchow to their heart's content at this ice rink for just $8. Skate rentals are $3. They also offer free practice time and guest passes if you purchase one of their reasonably priced ice skating lessons packages. Follow them on Twitter @skBattle for further discounts.

The Santa Monica Stairs

4th Street and Adelaide Drive

Do the wooden stairs, concrete stairs, or the loop, and your toned gluteus maximus will thank you. I don't care how in shape you are. Stairs are tough, and they are a great workout. Take it from the girl who has lived in a 5th-floor walk-up for over 7 years. I know. For you roving eye types, there's some decent eye candy here as well.

Venice Beach Skatepark
1800 Ocean Front Walk, Venice
www.venicebeach.com/article_skatepark.php

Opened in 2009, this is a 16,000-square-foot park that features two bowls, a snake run, and a street section with steps, rails, and platforms. Admission is free. Open 9 a.m. to sunset daily, it is the only skatepark located on a beach. For professionals and amateurs, Venice Skate Park hosts a number of skateboarding events as well. Dude.

West Hollywood Pool
647 N. San Vicente Blvd., West Hollywood
(323) 848-6538
www.weho.org

At $2 for residents and $3 for nonresidents, you can't get a better deal for cooling off. Especially since you don't own that house in the hills with the pool just yet. Seniors and the disabled swim for free, children are just $1, $1.75 if not WeHo residents. Check website for lap and recreational swim times.

World on Wheels
4645 Venice Blvd., Los Angeles
(323) 933-5170
www.amfworldonwheels.com

"I love the nightlife!" you'll scream as you whip around the rink on your roller skates. Hopefully your high school boyfriend won't come up behind you suddenly, send you sprawling on the floor and splitting open your chin, thus ending your night in the ER. (Can't even see the scar anymore.) In general, skating will run you $6 to $12, depending on the night, whether you're a student, and whether you have your own skates. Check website for hours and prices. If you're really into roller skating and can't get enough, check out the Los Angeles Derby Dolls (http://derbydolls.com)—tickets start at $18 for the spectacle.

REI—Pick a Class, Any Class

Recreational Equipment, Inc. (REI), the one-stop shopping store for your outdoor gear, equipment, and clothing needs, offers a number of classes through the REI Outdoor School Greater Los Angeles Area. Choose from climbing, cycling, hiking and camping, navigation, outdoor photography, paddling, and snowsports. Classes for members are $20 less than for nonmembers. A lifetime membership will cost you just $20 (so long as you spend at least $10 per year), and it will earn you the annual REI member refund, typically 10 percent back on eligible purchases, special members-only offers on gears and clothing at REI, as well as savings on adventure travel with REI Adventures. Two locations are at 1800 Rosencrans Ave., Suite E, Manhattan Beach (310-727-0728); and 402 Santa Monica Blvd., Santa Monica (310-458-4370). Visit www.rei.com for more information.

SURF'S **UP**

Balboa Island at Newport Beach
www.balboa-island.com

Beach it, boardwalk it, bike it, and more on Balboa Island, just a $1 ferry ride ($2 if you bring your car) from Newport Beach. Stroll around, hit the beach, spend $2 to $3 for the carousel and Ferris wheel, where you'll catch glimpses of the majestic Pacific. You won't be surfing here—small sandy beaches are perfect for vessel voyeurism or catching up on that novel you've been meaning to finish.

El Porto Beach
Vista Del Mar and 45th Street, Manhattan Beach

Rockin' waves for great surfing and fun volleyball to be had by all. No dogs. Rent bikes or skates at the snack bar. Restrooms with showers so you can look spiffy following your prance in the saltwater. Free residential parking or metered lot parking.

Hermosa Beach
Hermosa Avenue and 33rd Street, and Pier and Hermosa Avenues

Swim, jog, walk, and tan at Hermosa Beach. Take in the league games of beach flag football. Bike nearby. Check out the unique annual Grunion Run during the summer months. Grunion is a species of fish that flops onto the beaches of Southern California each year in a primitive ritual of spawning. If you have a fishing license, you can try catching the slippery little suckers with your hands, which is a feat requiring great sportsmanship and dexterity. Grunions are yummy, and catching them, or trying to, or watching others trying to catch them, is fun and funny. Metered or lot parking will cost you a bit. All main parking is located on 11th Street, 13th Street, or Hermosa Avenue.

Huntington Beach
www.surfcityusa.com

It is here that you will find famous surfing events, as well as the Surfing Walk of Fame, Hall of Fame, and International Surf Museum. Dog Beach, the dog park here along these 8.5 uninterrupted miles of beautiful coast, features dog bakeries, specialty shops, and parks. It is one of the few dog-friendly beaches where dogs can play in the water. Keep walking and you'll catch the volleyball courts as well.

Laguna Beach
Seven miles of Pacific Ocean in Orange County, made most famous by too many reality television shows to count in the past decade. Tide pools with great marine life viewing off Wave Street and the PCH, along with plenty of diving, surfing, and skimboarding. Weekends feature many artists and street musicians on the boardwalk. So romantic! Plenty of free residential parking if you go out of your way just a tad.

Long Beach
Mother's Beach at Marine Park
Appian Way at 2nd Street, Long Beach

Peaceful waters safe for kids, as well as lifeguards and volleyball courts. To rent a kayak on these calm waters for just $9 an hour, visit www.kayak rentals.net, or go there in person at 5411 E. Ocean Blvd., Long Beach.

Manhattan Beach
Pier is at Manhattan Beach Boulevard, Manhattan Beach

Manhattan Beach is where beach volleyball was born. And you thought Tom Cruise and Val Kilmer invented it in *Top Gun*. No entrance fee to plant your towel in the sand; feed the meters on the street or in the lots. Restrooms and showers, but no pets allowed. Particularly busy in August, when Manhattan Beach hosts the Manhattan Beach Open Volleyball Championships, Sand Castle Contest, and Surf Festival. Fish from the pier. Stroll to a nearby cafe or restaurant for a bite to eat at the end of the day. Star sightings always possible, as many live nearby or work at the Manhattan Beach Studios. Park near the pier or underground near The Shade hotel.

Redondo Beach Pier
Enter at intersection of Torrance Boulevard and S. Catalina Avenue
www.redondopier.com

A pretty beach, a fishy smelling pier, free concerts and events in the summer, and relaxed walking and beach gazing to be had. Crowd is a bit older, not so hip or crazy. Tons of free residential parking.

SCAVENGING:
CHIC ON THE CHEAP

"Before beginning a hunt, it is wise to ask someone what you are looking for before you begin looking for it."

—WINNIE THE POOH

In my home office, I have a three-drawer filing cabinet, coffee table, leather inbox with matching pencil holder, and trash bin that were all rescued outside of an office, storage facility, and an apartment. Across the room near the windows sit beautiful candles and candle holders, also rescued from outside that storage facility. Lest you think my office is some swanky wood-paneled spacious room with Berber carpet, a humidifier, stocked beverage refrigerator, and the smell of vanilla wafting from the scented plug-in you saw advertised on TV that day you caught all the morning talk shows because you were home in bed sick from work, please, banish that thought. My office is 5.5 feet from my bed, which makes pajamas permissible attire and my scavenged "found" items all the more chic and sleeker than whatever else I could have conjured up on my limited budget. Los Angeles has some of the trendiest and swankiest neighborhoods on the West Coast, the better to go fishing in, and thanks to a modern world where everyone is online and plugged in, there are a myriad of other possibilities for you to scavenge for those must-have furniture items to decorate your abode to necessity and stylistic perfection!

TROLLING **THROUGH** TRASH

Here is a list of some of LA's primo neighborhoods to troll for upscale trash. Hand sanitizer not necessary, as you won't actually be forced to do any Dumpster diving—you'll simply haul that item away from the curb in your vehicle. Listings are done by day of the week, but remember you'll probably want to go the night before, when the owner hauls the item to the curb in preparation for the next morning's pickup. Technically, individuals removing large items from their house during spring cleaning should arrange a special pickup with the city, but most people do not follow the appropriate course of action. The other alternative is to check out these neighborhoods on the weekend, when people aren't pressed with work schedules and rush-hour traffic in both directions, thereby freeing them up to actually get around to cleaning and lugging those large items to the curb.

TUESDAY

In Eagle Rock/East LA, tool down Colorado Boulevard for a great find on Monday night, in preparation for Tuesday's trash pickup. This area is growing increasingly popular for artists, so you may find some funky stuff that speaks to your slammin' style. If your style is a bit more upscale, then venture over to Pacific Palisades on Hilltree and Latimer, or San Vicente and Bundy in Brentwood. Or head on over to the valley in Studio City, starting on Mulholland in the mountain areas and then head north, checking out Camarillo and Vineland. Peeps with money do tend to live in this area to reduce their commute to work at the television and movie studios. What does this mean for you? Maybe upgrading those hopes for Ikea-like items to something a little more . . . posh.

WEDNESDAY

In Bel-Air, case the joint on North Beverly Glen and Sunset. Practice your answer to "OMG, where did you find this?" to which you'll respond coolly, "Oh, just this little place in Beverly Hills." Head all the way west to Santa Monica for the sleekest and most modern selects on streets south of Adelaide, north of Colorado, and west of Euclid. Yes, it's "The Valley," but get that attitude out of your voice—Sherman Oaks is one of the nicest places to live in Los Angeles. Check out Ventura and Sepulveda Boulevards for your scavenging delight.

THURSDAY

In Beverly Hills and Hollywood, focus on Mount Olympus Drive just above Hollywood Boulevard and off Laurel Canyon to score great finds. The Hollywood Hills are full of people with money and celebrities of all levels, so they are worth twisting, turning, and scouring your way through for disposed items that become your great find! Check out the few miles of Fairfax west to Doheny traversing from West Hollywood, through to the eastern border of Beverly Hills. You can really hit the jackpot here on weekends. Encino is also in "The Valley," yes, but haven't we already spoken about your attitude at least once already? White Oaks and Miranda area exploration can turn up that coffee table or end table you were dying for to complete your living room look.

For Those Large Items

The **Bureau of Sanitation (BOS)** wants you to recycle your bulky items through charitable organizations and thrift stores, so they have less work to do. However, if you simply can't find a way or means to do that, they will pick up those large or bulky household items, such as mattresses and couches, at your curb free of charge, provided you are a resident of the City of Los Angeles and schedule it ahead of time. To make arrangements to have these items removed, dial (800) 773-2489, Mon through Fri, anytime between 7:30 a.m. and 4:45 p.m., and at least one day before your regular collection day. Be very clear when you speak with them about just what it is you need them to remove. You can also fill out a Service Request Form, which will take two days to process. The BOS will not collect your automotive parts, construction materials, commercial materials, or cardboard (only collected if you are moving in or out). For more information, visit **http://san.lacity.org.**

ONLINE **EXCHANGE**

Want free stuff but want to take the physical hunt out of it and leave it to your eyes and fingers to conduct the search from the comfort of your living room? Possibilities are just a click away on your computer.

Craigslist
www.craigslist.org

Your best choice is to opt for items that are accompanied by a photo, unless you're feeling particularly risky. If your budget includes some actual bucks, you can scroll through items listed by category under "For Sale," and check out upcoming "Garage Sales." If you go to "For Sale" and click on "Free," items are listed by neighborhood.

Daily News
www.dailynews.com

Comb the classifieds and feel retro. Isn't that something your parents did? I'd love a new dresser. Let me know what turns up. I'd prefer one that either a) matches the bed frame I'm seeking, b) is orange (I don't know why I feel so strongly about orange in this scenario, but I do), or c) has many deep drawers and comes with people willing to get it into my apartment. Now that you have your assignment, good luck. And thanks!

Domestic Sale
www.domesticsale.com/Classifieds/Los-Angeles_CA/

More free classifieds listed by neighborhood and category. Let your nimble fingers do the combing.

eBay Classifieds
www.losangeles.ebayclassifieds.com

Search by category for a great steal. Items aren't free, but there are often great deals.

Freecycle
www.freecycle.org

The Catch: You have to post something for free in order to see a listing of what else is up for grabs.

I mean, really. Is this so terrible? A wonderful way to help others and recycle objects for a greener environment in the 21st century? Get over yourself. It's awesome. And the organization is worldwide. Wow. Scavenge on a global level.

Furniture 2 Go
www.furniture2go.com

The Catch: Will cost you money, but items are shiny-new and severely discounted.

Come on, you know the swinging bachelor in you has always wanted a brand-new large loveseat and a sofa for under $550 total. Delivery is free, so you're also spared the back pain.

Yard Sales

Yard sales are not just for Granny. They're a great way to find incredible retro or vintage items with which to furnish your pad in a stylish and swinging way. Check Craigslist for extensive listings, or follow the signs and your whimsy as they are posted. Yard sales are usually on Saturday and Sunday, and the earlier you arrive, the better.

In Los Angeles, which neighborhood you go to is going to determine what types of items you might find. Beverly Hills will bring you gilded baroque furniture and mirrors. (Huh. Mirrors in Beverly Hills. Imagine that! As if anyone in this town worries about how he or she looks.) Hancock Park, with its crumbling big houses and mansions and longtime residents, is great for Hollywood Regency and mid-century modern furnishings and decor.

There are two types of people who run yard sales. On one end you have the spring cleaners who are desperate to clean out their homes and make some cash as quickly as possible, and on the other end of the spectrum you have the hoarders, who will fiercely cling to each item until they sell it for the amount of money they believe it's worth.

The key to navigating the yard sale successfully is confidence. Say what you want and what price you are willing to pay for it. If the owner won't budge and you don't like what you hear, be prepared to turn and walk away without hesitation. The owner will usually come running after you as soon as you turn on your heel, and you can strike an acceptable bargain with which you'll both be pleased.

Lafreebee
http://lafreebeee.com/free-services

Lafreebee contains current listings, updated by the minute, of free stuff. People provide an accurate description and include the location of where to find the item, which could be a free sofa, bed, or power drill. You just never know. First come, first served. May the scavenger hunt begin!

Los Angeles Times
www.latimes.com

The *Los Angeles Times* puts their classifieds online and in print, so though the newspaper may be struggling against a slow death, there are still great deals, garage and estate sales to be listed in their classifieds. I'm also in the market for a standing wardrobe or armoire. (Did I mention my bedroom is sans closet?) Can you keep your eye out for me?

Oodle
www.oodle.com

Founded by former Excite and eBay executives, this site has oodles of stuff listed by category, one of which is "free." Use your best judgment in perusal.

Recycler
www.recycler.com

Used cars, pets, appliances, music, sports equipment, real estate deals, and more. Search by category and location. There is a "free" section under "Community," but most items will cost you. However, there are great finds for great prices, most of them with photos, and you can always do your best to exercise your mad bargaining skills.

Swap
www.swap.com

The Catch: Gotta give some to get some. Then again, that's a pretty good and accurate philosophy. Don't worry. I won't get too deep on you.

Swap is for book, video game, CD, movie, and DVD trading. You enter what you have on the "Have List," and the website tells you what you can get for them.

SHOPPING:
PRICE TAG PRAGMATISM

"The only reason a great many American families don't own an elephant is that they have never been offered an elephant for a dollar down and easy weekly payments."

—MAD MAGAZINE

I believe the fierce dynamic duo of a little imagination and a lot of bargain shopping is something to exercise in abundance and be loud and proud about at all times. And with that, I give you your guide to shopping in Los Angeles without breaking the bank and still remaining fashion forward, heck, *everything* forward. Ta-da! Cue runway music.

FEELING **THRIFTY**

Goodwill
Multiple locations
www.goodwill.org

All Los Angeles-area locations open at 9 a.m. Mon through Sat, and at 10 a.m. on Sun. Goodwill Industries International is committed to enhancing "the dignity and quality of life of individuals, families, and communities by eliminating barriers to opportunity and helping people in need reach their fullest potential through the power of work." Shop Goodwill and let the money you spend on your must-have items do some goodwill for those in the world around you. Check out their website for listing information on their other area loctions.

National Council of Jewish Women
Multiple locations
www.ncjwla.org

All locations are open 7 days a week, 9:30 a.m. to 6 p.m. The NCJW is consistently ranked by *Los Angeles Magazine* as having some of the best thrift clothes shopping in Los Angeles.

Out of the Closet
Multiple locations
www.outofthecloset.org

All store locations are open 7 days a week at 10 a.m. Out of the Closet is owned and operated by the Aids Healthcare Foundation (AHF), the largest specialized provider of cutting-edge medicine and advocacy, regardless of ability to pay. Your purchase at Out of the Closet helps fund the medical services AHF provides. Shop with all heart and no guilt. If you're trying to get rid of that large dining room table Grandma gave to you when she downsized and thought you would love, call Out of the Closet at (877) 2-PICK-IT-UP to schedule a large item donation pick up. Say it. Come on, I know you're thinking it. There's absolutely nothing about this system that does not work. Friggin' fabulous. Check out their website for listing information on all LA locations.

Polkadots & Moonbeams
Vintage Boutique: 8367 W. 3rd St., Los Angeles, (323) 651-1746
Modern Boutique: 8381 W. 3rd St., Los Angeles, (323) 655-3880
http://polkadotsandmoonbeams.com

If you want that perfect look that combines both your vintage and super mod and trendy fashion sense, but don't do Goodwill because you're a snob (yeah, I know who you are . . .), check out Polkadots & Moonbeams for great prices and one-of-a-kind finds. Your experience and purchase of their unique items is bound to leave you "fabulous, glamorous, and accidentally sexy." Store opens at 11 a.m. 7 days a week. Both stores are in the 8300 block of W. 3rd Street between Orlando and Kings Road, 1.5 blocks from The Beverly Center.

Salvation Army Thrift Store
Multiple locations
www.salvationarmy.org

I still wear the man's vest I bought for under $2 at the Salvation Army Thrift Store on MacArthur Boulevard in Allentown, Pennsylvania, in high school, and when I do, I look oh-so-hip. What's stopping you? You know you need a snazzy new interview suit you don't want to pay a billion bucks for, not to mention an end table and a Halloween costume. Great deals galore on clothes and more! Check website for a Los Angeles location near you.

Serifos
3814 W. Sunset Blvd. (near Hyperion Ave. in Silver Lake), Los Angeles
(323) 660-SHOP (7467)

Owner Donna Choi is as charming as they come and sells a mixture of original jewelry she herself makes, as well as vintage knickknacks and gifts, all at prices you won't find anywhere else.

Society of St. Vincent de Paul

2010 N. Avenue 21, Los Angeles
(323) 224-6280
www.svdpusa.org

In addition to providing food programs, rent/mortgage assistance, low-cost housing, and free pharmacy services, the Society of St. Vincent de Paul operates thrift stores where the money from your purchase is, once again, put toward a great cause. Another location is at 2750 E. Pacific Coast Hwy. in Long Beach (562-494-9955).

RESALE & **CONSIGNMENT** STORES

Buffalo Exchange

131 N. La Brea, Los Angeles
(323) 938-8604
www.buffaloexchange.com

Buffalo Exchange is dedicated to protecting the environment by reusing and recycling clothing. They buy, sell, and trade clothing and accessories locally with store customers. Bring your unwanted clothes into the buy counter at any time and they'll give you cash or a trade on the spot for any of your items they want. The merchandise is consistently several notches above what you might find in a thrift store, in that they only take on the most desirable items. Clothes are sold for 35 percent of their value or traded for 50 percent of their value. Prices of items vary by condition, designer, and other factors, but most average around $15. Visit the website for additional locations in Los Angeles, Long Beach, Sherman Oaks, Santa Monica, and Costa Mesa.

Crossroads Trading Company

2656 Griffith Park Blvd., Los Angeles
(323) 644-0060
www.crossroadstrading.com

Just like Buffalo Exchange, Crossroads Trading Company sells clothes for 35 percent of their value, or trades (this means you get store credit) them for

Thrift, Resale & Consignment

What is the difference between a thrift store, a resale store, and a consignment shop? Items in a thrift store are donated, while a resale store buys items and resells them. Consignment store merchandise was placed there by people who would like to recover some of the money from the sale of their unwanted items. A consignment store handles the overhead, marketing, and staffing, and once the item is sold, the original owner of the items will share a percentage of the selling price with the store.

You can find great bargains and great items at any of these types of stores. In general, consignment shops tend to carry higher-end designer or jewelry items, but not always, as sometimes people who donate to thrift stores don't recognize the original worth of their item(s). If you're a choosy shopper with a fashion reputation to uphold, the important thing to do is to take your time to comb the racks carefully for those one-of-a-kind treasures.

50 percent of their value. No jewelry. Everything from Gap to Gucci, J. Crew, Diesel, Levi's, Theory, Marc Jacobs, and more, so you're covered for both your day and evening wear. Shazam! All locations open at 11 a.m. Mon through Sat. Check individual locations for Sun hours, which, if they are open, usually start at noon. Visit their website for information on their additional Pasadena, Santa Monica, Studio City, and West Hollywood locations.

Give + Take Swap Boutique
200 Culver Blvd. (near Vista Del Mar Ln. above Tanner's Coffee), Los Angeles
(310) 482-3398
http://giveplustake.com

Okay, this one's an original, so bear with me. For a membership rate of $25/month, you can experience this hybrid between a clothing swap and a secondhand boutique and not spend a penny beyond your membership fee. There are three ways to exchange your clothes: First off, you get a value for what they think your clothes are worth and you are assigned points, with which you can then choose something of the same value from the store. Second, you can bring in a certain number of items and walk away with the same number of items. Lastly, there is a free-for-all basement. They have strange hours, so check the website for most current ones. Swapping and swap parties can also be arranged. You probably already spend hundreds of dollars a year on clothes already, so why not recycle that wardrobe and trade it in for something hot and brand spankin' new without ballooning your budget to something you can't afford?

It's a Wrap

1164 S. Robertson Blvd., Los Angeles
(310) 246-WRAP (9727)
www.itsawraphollywood.com

Have you ever seen the wardrobe department on a movie or television set? Let's just say they do a lot, and I mean A LOT, of shopping. These clothes are worn once or twice, and that's it. And when I say once or twice, I mean maybe for a full day, but sometimes only for a few measly hours. The clothes can't be returned to the store; they've already been worn. They can't keep them around, or the wardrobe department will be overflowing! So what do they do? They sell them to It's a Wrap so you can buy them! Maybe you're wearing the sexy jeans Jennifer Aniston wore in her last romantic comedy, or the shirt Ryan Gosling wore in his last brooding male hero role. Who knows? You pick the duds and let your fantasies do the rest. Halloween shop opens in September every year for great finds (Hollywood does do horror flicks, too, you know). Open Mon through Fri 10 a.m. to 8 p.m., and Sat and Sun 11 a.m. to 6 p.m. A second location is at 3315 W. Magnolia Blvd., Burbank (818-567-7366).

Style on Green

1136 E. Green St., Pasadena
(626) 796-9924

Not always the best of finds here or the cheapest, but a good place to sell your outdated designer clothes you may have owned once upon a time . . . in that other job . . . in another economy . . . in another century.

Wasteland Clothing

7428 Melrose Ave., Los Angeles
(323) 653-3028
www.wastelandclothing.com

Vintage, modern, current, and collectible designer items. Say that ten times really fast. Don't want those duds? Sell them at The Buy Counter, who decides if they want to purchase your clothes, and then pays up to 35 percent of the value of them. (Like Buffalo Exchange and Crossroads.) You can sell up to 60 items at a time, and you may have to wait, so multitask like I do and return some e-mails or call your mom while in line. Hello, spring cleaning! Additional locations are at 325 N. San Fernando Rd., Burbank (818-842-4900); 1338 4th St., Santa Monica (310-395-2620); and 12144 Ventura Blvd., Studio City (818-980-8800). All locations open at 11 a.m. Mon through Sat, and Sun noon to 8 p.m.

FLEA & **ANTIQUES** MARKETS

Long Beach Antique & Collectible Outdoor Market
4901 E. Conant St. (Long Beach Veterans Stadium), Long Beach
(323) 655-5703
www.longbeachantiquemarket.com

For $5 on the third Sun of each month from 6:30 a.m. to 3 p.m. (early admission is an additional $5 at 5:30 a.m.), you can spend quality time at a sporting arena doing some competitive shopping. Long Beach Antique & Collectible Outdoor Market boasts over 800 dealers and 20 acres of stalls with everything from antiques to collectibles, vintage items, and home furnishings for sale at bargain prices. Free parking.

Melrose Trading Post
7850 Melrose Ave. (at Fairfax Ave.), Hollywood
(323) 655-7679, ext. 103
www.melrosetradingpost.org

Every Sun, from 9 a.m. to 5 p.m. and for the price of $2, you can go back to high school. Well, at least the parking lot of Fairfax High School, to be exact, where you'll wind through some 3,000-plus attendees and 200 vendors at the flea market the *Los Angeles Times* calls "A flea market for 'the sexy, hip and groovy crowd." Guess that means I can't just roll out of bed with my retainers and go. (Worked for me in high school!) Sigh. I've got to look good, too. So much pressure! Free live jazz music, too, so you can get your Sunday groove on. Street parking only. That $2 admission fee goes toward funding student programs at Fairfax High School. *LA Weekly* often runs an admission coupon in the events section.

Pasadena City College Flea Market
1570 E. Colorado Blvd., Pasadena
(626) 585-7906
www.pasadena.edu/fleamarket

On the first Sun of each month, from 8 a.m. to 3 p.m., wander among 500 vendors for antiques, collectibles, records, tools, clothes, toys, food (who wants to be hungry while shopping?), and more. The flea market is held in the parking lots along the east side of Pasadena City College's campus on Bonnie Avenue from Colorado to Del Mar. Free admission, and your purchases benefit student scholarships and activities. Street and lot parking.

Roadium Open Air Market
2500 W. Redondo Beach Blvd., Torrance
(310) 532-5678
www.roadium.com

The Roadium Open Air Market features new and used merchandise from 25 to 75 percent off department store prices. If you park at El Camino on the weekend, a free bus will take you directly to the market. Sweet! Open 7 days a week, except for Christmas and New Year's, from 7 a.m. to 4 p.m. Admission ranges from $1 to $1.50, depending on the day of the week, and 50 cents per passenger. Weekday parking is free; weekend parking is on-site.

Rose Bowl Flea Market
1001 Rose Bowl Dr. (at Rose Bowl Stadium), Pasadena
(323) 560-7469
www.rgcshows.com

On the second Sun of each month, from 9 a.m. to 3 p.m., for a measly $8 (children under 12 are free, as is parking), you can wander what feels like miles and miles of a shopper's paradise. The crème de la crème of interior designers are browsing right alongside you, choosing just the right item for a client's home, so you're keeping good company. Die hards can fork over a few extra dollars for early admission.

Don't Let the Bedbugs Bite

I don't want to creep you out, but we do need to have a little discussion. If you're shopping at a flea market or thrift store, you need to take precautions so as to avoid bedbugs.

Bedbugs are smaller than a tick, nocturnal, and can live for long periods of time without food. They're vampires. When they do get the munchies, they don't head to the 7-Eleven, they head straight for your tasty blood. Getting rid of them in your home requires hiring a professional exterminator, cleaning all of your clothing, and throwing out things like your mattress. Yeah. A huge and costly pain you'd like to avoid, right? Following are important tips to abide by when shopping so you, too, can avoid the headache that having to deal with bedbugs causes:

Use the Bedbug Registry. Since 2006, the free online public database of user-submitted bug reports from across the United States and Canada will provide you with recent Los Angeles reports of bedbugs. At press time, there were over 400 total. Ewwww! At **http://bedbugregistry.com.**

Inspect each item you intend to purchase thoroughly. If it's clothing you are shopping for, check all the nooks, crannies, and crevices of the fabric in cuffs, collars, and pockets inside and out. If it's a bag, purse, or wallet and you must, must have it, shake that baby up, down, out, and all around like a 1970s disco dance. If you are buying a furniture item, avoid porous pieces like wicker furniture.

Santa Clarita Open Air Market (Saugus Swap Meet)

22500 Soledad Canyon Rd. (Saugus Speedway), Santa Clarita
(661) 259-3886
http://saugusspeedway.com

At the Santa Clarita Open Air Market, you can browse through 30 acres of bargains—this time not at a stadium, but a racetrack. On your mark, get set, go! (Insert sound of firing gun here.) Find new merchandise, collectibles, antiques, garage sale merchandise, produce, plants, food, and more. Admission is free every Tues and Sat; on Sun adults will fork over $1.50, while

If it's a couch or chair, inspect the fabric of the furniture for brown and black droppings or smears that look something like ink marks. If you see anything like that, run. Run fast.

Place bought items in a double-knotted plastic bag. Placing those bought items in a double-knotted plastic bag ensures no air can get through and that you will kill any unwelcome critters that may have thought they were moving to new digs. Your digs. It is also an important step as you head home and prepare to wash and dry those items, as part of the final killing machine process.

Check your body. When you've finished shopping, pretend you work for TSA and give your body and clothing a thorough inspection on the way out. Those bedbugs are small, but they're feisty and eager. Don't let them party on you.

Place purchases in the trunk of your car. The trunk of your car is easiest to vacuum on a regular basis so as to ensure you are frequently killing any bedbugs dead, alive, or ready to hatch. And really, do bedbugs deserve to ride shotgun?

Wash and dry all items immediately. All thrift store items should go from your trunk to the washer and dryer immediately. Everything should be washed and dried on hot. If it's an evening wear item and you can't put it in a dryer, then it has to be dry cleaned, but stick it in the dryer on hot for 20 minutes first, so you don't risk infesting your local dry cleaners.

For more information on bedbugs, visit http://bedbugger.com.

children under 12 get in free. Market opens at 7 a.m. and closes at 1 p.m. on Tues and Sat and 2 p.m. on Sun. Free parking.

Santa Monica Airport Outdoor Antique & Collectible Market
Airport Avenue off Bundy, Santa Monica
(Exit 10 Freeway Bundy South, right on Airport Avenue at south side of Santa Monica Airport)
(323) 933-2511
http://web.mac.com/davidandlisala/iWeb/Site/Welcome.html

On the first and fourth Sun of each month from 8 a.m. to 3 p.m., come rain or come shine, you can find Victorian to mid-century antiques of everything from furniture to carpets, paintings, jewelry, posters, lighting, vintage clothing, beads, garden furniture, and then some at the Santa Monica Airport Outdoor Antique & Collectible Market. Seniors are discounted, children under 16 can get in for free, dogs are welcome, and a few extra bucks will get you early admission. Also known as the Santa Monica Airport Flea Market. Free parking!

DOLLAR **STORES**

99¢ Only Stores
Multiple locations
www.99only.com

99¢ Only Stores are great for paper plates and napkins, 4th of July tiki torches, and kitchen utensils, as well as holiday decorations. If you must do food, my advice is to stick to the nonperishable items. You may also find some household cleaning supplies, paper towels, scarves, and sunglasses, so you can pretend you're a cleaning lady masquerading as a celebrity going incognito. Or not. Most are open Mon through Sun from 8 a.m. to 9 p.m. All Los Angeles area locations are listed on the website

The Dollar Tree
Multiple locations
www.dollartree.com

The Siamese Twin of the 99¢ Only Store, The Dollar Tree has everything from floral supplies and decor to party supplies, school and office supplies, toys, tableware, and more. Fruit and vegetables at your own risk. Most stores open at 9 a.m. Mon through Sat, and 10 a.m. on Sun. Check website for locations and details.

PETS:
CANINE, FELINE, BOTTOM LINE

"Dogs have owners, cats have staff."

—UNKNOWN

In 1999 my mother called me at work to tell me she was going to have to put my beloved childhood cat, (Virginia) Pearl, "down." At 14, or 98 cat years old, Pearl's unexpected kidney failure was causing her pain and it was only going to get worse. I dropped everything, left work early, and took a bus home to hold her one more time and bid goodbye. Through thick and thin, good times and bad, parental separations and eventual divorce, Pearl, the softest kitty in the world, had always been there for me. If you want your very own Pearl or need to provide care for your Pearl, Los Angeles has a number of shelters, services, and organizations devoted to finding loving homes for furry companions and keeping them healthy, so they, too, will be able to bask in your undivided love and attention.

GET **A** PET

For a modest fee, you can ensure that there will be a tail wagging at your door or a parrot screeching your name for the next 15 years or so of your life. That bundle of joy will also come spayed or neutered, microchipped, and licensed as part of the adoption fee. Animal care shelters also provide emergency medical services to injured or diseased pets. Go ahead, take one look into their eyes and just try to walk away . . . you can't.

Agoura Shelter
29525 W. Agoura Rd., Agoura
(818) 991-0071
http://animalcare.lacounty.gov

Agoura Shelter houses all types of animals, with a high concentration of pit bulls and chihuahuas. Adoption prices range from $30 to $120, depending on how long the animal has been in the shelter. Adoption cost includes vaccinations and microchip; licenses issued for $10 to $25. Spay/neuter is an additional $50 and done in the shelter. Just 5 minutes to adopt the love of your life!

Have you had it with Los Angeles traffic? Is the Agoura Shelter too far for you to make yet another car trip? Do not fear. There are other options closer to you. Below are shelters with similar hours, prices, and services as the Agoura Shelter:

Baldwin Park Shelter, 4275 N. Elton Ave., Baldwin Park; (626) 962-3577

Burbank Animal Shelter, 1150 N. Victory Place, Burbank; (818) 238-3340

Carson Shelter, 216 W. Victoria St., Gardena; (310) 523-9566

Castaic Shelter, 31044 N. Charlie Canyon Rd., Castaic; (661) 257-3191

Downey Shelter, 11258 S. Garfield Ave., Downey; (562) 940-6898

Lancaster Shelter, 5210 W. Avenue I, Lancaster; (661) 940-4191. While in Lancaster, you can also check out the Antelope Valley Adoption Center (Pet Stop), 42116 4th St. E, (661) 974-8309, which houses ready-to-adopt shelter dogs, but is not a shelter itself.

Santa Monica Animal Shelter, 1640 9th St., Santa Monica; (310) 458-8594

City of Los Angeles Department of Animal Services
221 N. Figueroa St., 5th floor, Los Angeles
(888) 452-7381
www.laanimalservices.com

LA Animal Services is devoted to promoting and protecting "the health, safety, and welfare of animals and people." Most care centers are open 6 days a week and closed on Mon. You can adopt a dog for $117 (compared to the $338 average) or a cat for $76 (compared to the $259 average). These costs include spay/neuter, microchip, and license. All care centers can be contacted via phone at (888) 4-LAPET1 or (888) 452-7381. See below for addresses:

North Central: 3201 Lacy St., Los Angeles; 246 kennels with behavior assessment areas and a pasture.

South Los Angeles: 3612 11th Ave., Los Angeles (care center with spay and neuter clinic); 3320 W. 36th St., Los Angeles (Annex); Annex houses animals needing medical care or other special attention.

East Valley: 14409 Vanowen St., Van Nuys (care center with spay and neuter clinic); 165 dog kennels and the largest community room of all the care centers.

Harbor: 957 N. Gaffey St., San Pedro; 79 dog kennels and 72 cat cages as well as community cat rooms, get-acquainted yards for dogs, a large grassy field for pet training, spay/neuter clinic, medical facilities, pet recovery and isolation areas, as well as a special area for rabbits and exotic animals. Meow!

West Los Angeles: 11361 W. Pico Blvd., Los Angeles; community room for cats and get-acquainted yards for dogs, plus a medical suite for special animal care.

West Valley: 20655 Plummer St., Chatsworth; 50,000 square feet of facilities with 152 dog kennels, multiple cat rooms and play areas, and access for dogs to air-conditioned areas to escape the heat of the summer.

Inland Valley Humane Society & SPCA
500 Humane Way (past Pomona Blvd.), Pomona
(909) 623-9777
www.ivhsspca.org

Unaltered dogs are $135, altered dogs $110, unaltered cats $110, altered cats $85. Adoption fee includes first set of shots, de-worming, spay/neuter, rabies vaccination, and 2-week follow-up care appointment. Closed Sun.

Pasadena Humane Society & SPCA
361 S. Raymond Ave. (between Del Mar Blvd. and Bellevue Dr.), Pasadena
(626) 792-7151
www.phsspca.org

Your dog adoption fee of $120 at the Pasadena Humane Society & SPCA includes spay/neuter and vaccinations, a free health exam within 5 days from participating veterinarians, a microchip, and pet tag, 10 percent discount at PHS Pet Store, discount on training class, and a dog DVD. Your cat adoption fee ($70 for one cat or $85 for two) includes the same, except for instead of dog training and a dog DVD, you get a cat carrier and a cat DVD. May I just say that the fact that cats need no training whatsoever is proof that they are highly evolved creatures? Rabbit adoption fees ($30) include spay/neuter, free health exam within 5 days of adoption, microchip, and discount. General information packet provided with all adoptions. Closed Mon.

SPCALA P.D. Pitchford Animal Adoption and Educational Center
7700 E. Spring St. (near the Long Beach Park Ranger Station), Long Beach
(562) 570-7722

SPCALA South Bay Pet Adoption Center

12910 Yukon Ave. (near W. El Segundo Blvd.), Hawthorne
(310) 676-1149 or (213) 678-2839
www.spcala.com

Adopt a dog for $115, a cat for $95, or two fantastic felines for $180. Adoption fee includes spay/neuter surgery, current vaccinations and microchip, health exam, and a leash, or cat carrier. If you already have a family pet, once your adoption is approved, you need to bring that pet to the shelter to meet the new pet you are about to adopt. I see you, whipping out your phone to snap a picture to upload to Facebook to share the cuteness of your new pet with the world.

SPAYING & **NEUTERING** THAT **PET**

Get your pet spayed and neutered as soon as you can so as to avoid an unexpected litter of new puppies and kittens. There are too many pets out there that need great homes; we shouldn't be irresponsibly adding to those numbers. In addition to many of the adoption centers, animal care shelters, and humane organizations, there are a number of Los Angeles veterinary hospitals that offer reasonably priced spay/neuter deals.

Ambassador Dog & Cat Hospital

3684 Beverly Blvd., Los Angeles
(213) 384-1255
http://ambassadorpet.com

Cats are $75 to $95, and dogs $110 to $325 for 75 pounds and over. (Dog prices of spay/neuter is determined by weight.) Pre-surgery exam is required at no cost. Spay/neuter on Mon and Wed are 20 percent off.

Animal Medical Center

2528 W. Martin Luther King Blvd., Los Angeles
(323) 294-6154

Cats are $80 to $100; dogs $120 to $250. They accept $30 to $60 vouchers. For information on how to obtain and qualify for a voucher, read about the free certificate program under "Department of Animal Services" below.

Department of Animal Services
Attn: Low Income Verification and Processing
PO Box 54856
Los Angeles, CA 90054-0856

Senior citizens, the permanently disabled, and low-income residents with a yearly combined household income less than the HUD Very Low Income for the Los Angeles County Area can apply for a $70 certificate to be put toward spaying/neutering a pet. This certificate is available at all animal care centers with presentation of a DWP Bill showing Lifeline or Low Income qualification, or can be obtained by applying directly via mail at the above address. Limited $30 vouchers are available to all at animal care shelters on a first come, first served basis.

East Los Angeles Dog & Cat Hospital
5655 Whittier Blvd., Los Angeles
(323) 723-5611
www.casillasveterinaryhospitals.com

Cats are $100 to $110; dogs are $105 to $150. If the dog is over 5 years old, you must also submit that dog to a $25 exam.

Echo Park Pet Hospital
1739 Glendale Blvd., Los Angeles
(323) 663-1107

Cats are $89 to $115; dogs are $99 to $160. They accept $30 vouchers and offer Free Certificate Spay/Neuter Programs for low income, senior citizen, and permanently disabled Los Angeles residents.

Green Dog & Cat Hospital
1544 W. Slauson Ave., Los Angeles
(323) 753-8440

Cats are $50 to $80; dogs $130 to $170. They do accept vouchers.

Golden State Humane Society
555 E. Artesia Blvd., Long Beach
(562) 423-8406
www.goldenstatehumanesociety.com

Animal Control

To keep your pet safe and out of harm's way, you should go to Animal Control to spay or neuter your pet and get a license. They will require proof of rabies vaccination in order to process your registration. Here is a list of animal control centers near you:

Glendora Animal Control, 150 S. Glendora Ave., Glendora; (626) 914-8275

Hermosa Beach Animal Control/Police, 1035 Valley Dr., Hermosa Beach; (310) 318-0360

Huntington Park Animal Control, (323) 582-6161

Long Beach Animal Control, 7700 E. Spring St., Long Beach; (562) 570-7387

Manhattan Beach Animal Control, 1400 Highland Ave., Manhattan Beach; (310) 545-5621

Monterey Park Animal Control, 320 W. Newmark Ave., Monterey Park; (626) 307-1217

Orange County Animal Care Center, 561 The City Dr. S, Orange; (714) 935-6848

Seal Beach Animal Care Center, 1700 Adolfo Lopez, Seal Beach; (562) 430-4993

South East Area Animal Control Authority (SEAACA), 9777 Seaaca St., Downey; (562) 803-3301

Temple City Animal Control, 5938 Kauffman Ave., Temple City; (626) 285-7187

Cats are $29.50, dogs $39.50 up to 30 pounds, with an additional $1.50 per pound thereafter.

Signal Hill Animal Hospital
3449 E. Pacific Coast Hwy., Long Beach
(562) 597-5533
www.signalhillanimalhospital.com

Cats are $35 to $55; dogs are $65 to $210. Reduced rate on Wed.

DOG-FRIENDLY **PARKS** & BEACHES

Below is a list of outdoor places Sparky can run off some energy. You'll get exercise, the dog will get exercise, you might meet some friendly strangers, figure out how to solve that problem at work, or score a date if you're on the prowl . . . how is this not a howlingly fantastic idea?

BEACHES

Huntington Dog Beach (PCH between 21st and Seapoint Streets): Dogs can be off-leash in water and on wet sand.

Long Beach, Rosie's Dog Beach in Belmont Shore Area (between Argonne and Roycroft Avenues): The only legal, off-leash dog beach in Los Angeles County. One dog per human.

Malibu, Leo Carillo State Park and Beach (north on PCH toward Oxnard until you arrive at El Matador and Leo Carillo State Beaches): Dog on leash no longer than 6 feet. No dogs allowed between Towers 2 and 3.

Malibu, Thornhill Broome Beach in Point Mugu State Park: Dogs on leash no longer than 6 feet.

PARKS
On-Leash

Airport Park, 301 Airport Ave., Santa Monica. Dog must be licensed in Santa Monica.

Angeles National Forest, 701 N. Santa Anita Ave., Arcadia

Charmlee Natural Area and Malibu Bluffs, 2577 Encinal Canyon Rd., Malibu

Coldwater Canyon Park, 12601 Mulholland Dr., Beverly Hills

Elysian Park, 835 Academy Rd., Los Angeles

Laurel Canyon Park, 8260 Mulholland Dr., San Fernando Valley

Rancho Dog Park, 2551 Motor Ave., Los Angeles

Redondo Beach Dog Park, 200 Flagler Lane, Redondo Beach

Runyon Canyon Park, 2000 N. Fuller Ave., Los Angeles. Off-leash off trails in restricted areas.

Rustic Canyon Park, Rustic Canyon Road, Pacific Palisades

Santa Monica Mountains National Recreation Area (from Beverly Hills to Oxnard Plane)

Silverlake Dog Park, 1850 W. Silverlake Dr., Los Angeles

Off-Leash

Alice Frost Kennedy Dog Park, 3026 E. Orange Grove Blvd., Pasadena
Barrington Dog Park, 333 S. Barrington Ave., Brentwood
Brookside Park, 360 N. Arroyo Blvd., Pasadena
Buena Park Dog Park, 7171 8th St., Los Angeles
Calabasas Bark Park, 4232 Las Virgenes Rd., Calabasas
Costa Mesa Bark Park, Arlington and Fairview Avenues in TeWinkle Park (across from Orange County Fairgrounds), Costa Mesa
Culver City Dog Park, (off Jefferson at far corner of Culver City Park), Culver City
Downtown Dog Park, Broadway at Pacific Avenue, Long Beach
El Segundo Dog Park, 600 E. Imperial Ave., Los Angeles
Griffith Park Dog Park, 4730 Crystal Springs Dr., Los Angeles
Hermon Dog Park at Arroyo Seco Park, 5568 Via Marisol, Los Angeles
Huntington Beach Best Friend Dog Park, Edwards Street at Inlet Drive, Huntington Beach
K-9 Corner, at 9th and Pacific, Long Beach
Memorial Park, 1401 Olympic Blvd., Santa Monica. Licensed Santa Monica dogs may use the park leashless during restricted hours.
Pacific Street Park, at Pacific and Main, Santa Monica
Recreation Dog Park, 5201 E. 7th St., Long Beach
Saslow Dog Park, 1004 E. 4th St., Los Angeles
Sepulveda Basin Dog Park, 17550 Victory Blvd., Encino
Studio City, Laurel Canyon Dog Park, 8260 Mulholland Dr., Los Angeles
Uptown Dog Park, 4600 Long Beach Blvd., Long Beach
Wattles Garden Park, 1850 N. Curson Ave., Los Angeles
Westminster Dog Park, 1234 Pacific Ave., Venice
Westridge-Canyonback Wilderness Park, 17500 Mulholland Dr., Los Angeles
Whitnall Off-Leash Dog Park, 5801½ Whitnall Hwy., North Hollywood
William S. Hart Park & Off-Leash Dog Park, 8341 De Longpre Ave., West Hollywood. Off-leash hours are restricted.

Other

Farmers Market, 6333 W. 3rd St., Los Angeles; (323) 933-9211
The Grove, 189 The Grove Dr., Los Angeles; (888) 315-8883
Mildred E. Mathias Botanical Garden, 777 S. Tiverton Ave., Los Angeles
Mount Hollywood Trail, Mount Hollywood Drive, Los Angeles
Pershing Square, 532 S. Olive St., Los Angeles
Westfield Century City Mall, 10250 Santa Monica Blvd., Los Angeles

Exploring in Los Angeles

TOURS:
PUT ON YOUR
SIGHTSEEING SHOES

"I was recently on a tour of Latin America, and the only regret I have was that I didn't study Latin harder in school so I could converse with those people."

—DAN QUAYLE

Hate looking like a tourist? Now is the time to get over yourself. How else are you going to satisfy your natural curiosity and learn about the world you live in? Aren't you even mildly interested in those stars made famous by movies and television all over the world? Don't you want to see how the other half lives, or where they're walking when captured in tabloid photos? Don't you wish I would stop pestering you with questions? Of course you do. I've worked for the other half. They're not like you or me. It's a whole other world entirely. Why do they look amazing when they step off the plane? Because they never once packed or lifted a single piece of luggage, and they flew first class! Los Angeles has got the bus tours, walking tours, delebrities ("dead celebrities"), and just plain random unique-to-Los-Angeles tours that are worth exploring. Here are a few of the best. Read on.

BUS **TOURS**

Beverly Hills Trolley Tour
Start at southeast corner of Rodeo Drive and Dayton Way, Beverly Hills
(310) 285-2442
www.beverlyhills.org

Forty-minute open-air trolley tours depart on the hour Tues through Sun, from 11 a.m. to 4 p.m., through the summer and Nov/Dec holiday season. The rest of the year you can only catch this $10 experience on the weekend. You will get a wonderful debriefing on the fancy schmancy neighborhood, celebrity homes, Rodeo Drive, and famous historical landmarks of Beverly Hills. $5 for children under 12. Hop on, pay driver.

Sightseeing World
Start at 6806 Hollywood Blvd., Los Angeles
(866) 431-1634
www.sightseeingworld.com/location/los+angeles

Spend 2 hours touring Hollywood and Beverly Hills on a double-decker bus for the cheapest rate in Los Angeles; just $20.99 if you buy online. When you're finished, you'll be able to say you've seen Mann's Chinese Theatre, the Walk of Fame, Sunset Boulevard, Santa Monica Boulevard and West Hollywood, Rodeo Drive, the Beverly Wilshire Hotel, and the Miracle Mile. Pretty soon you'll be hanging off the side singing "Clang, clang, clang went the trolley . . . " just like Judy Garland in Hugh Martin and Ralph Blane's score to *Meet Me in St. Louis.* Only I'll be meeting you in Los Angeles. Kids are only $12.99.

STAR **GRAZING**

Forest Lawn
1712 S. Glendale Ave., Glendale
(323) 254-3131
www.forestlawn.com

Forest Lawn Glendale, with its 300 acres, is a cemetery, memorial park, art gallery, and a destination for some architectural and religious pilgrimages. Ronald Reagan married Jane Wyman here, and Regis Philbin also wed at the Wee Kirk 'o the Heather. Over a quarter of a million people are buried here, including many mentioned in Madonna's song "Vogue," as well as Clark Gable, Humphrey Bogart, Mary Pickford, Carole Lombard, Sammy Davis Jr., and Nat King Cole, to name some of those quarter million.

Forest Lawn in the Hollywood Hills (6300 Forest Lawn Dr., 323-254-7251) is a bit easier to self-navigate, but doesn't have as many stars as Forest Lawn Glendale. It is here that you will find the graves of Bette Davis, John Ritter, Buster Keaton, and Freddie Prinze, among others. Forest Lawn does not encourage sightseeing or ogling of the stars' graves, and isn't likely to be particularly helpful. Pick up a map of the grounds at the information kiosk when you first drive through the gates. Whatever you do, do not carry your copy of *Final Curtain* or *Permanent Californians,* and be mindful that all you do is captured on video camera. Come on. It's Hollywood. Of course you're on camera. You're best to check out the virtual tour of the cemetery on www.seeing-stars.com prior to your exploration, so your efforts are not futile.

Hillside Memorial Park

6001 W. Centinela Ave., Culver City
(310) 641-0707
www.hillsidememorial.com

In view from the 405 and in Culver City is Hillside Memorial Park, a Jewish cemetery dotted with cypress trees and classic white buildings. The final resting place for Jack Benny, Milton Berle, Michael Landon, and Shelley Winters, you can get some fresh air, spot the stars (albeit not in their finest form), and ponder the lives of those who gave their heart and soul to entertainment.

Hollywood Boulevard

Start at the intersection of Hollywood Boulevard and Vine Street, Hollywood

It's cheesy, chintzy, and tacky, but there's only one Hollywood Boulevard. Play hopscotch on the stars on the Walk of Fame as you take in the sights of the iconic Capitol Records building, Grauman's Chinese Theatre, The Egyptian Theatre (the first movie palace built in Hollywood), and the Hollywood and Highland Center, which contains the Kodak Theatre, home to the Oscars. If you were a member of the Academy and this book could win an Oscar, would you vote for me?

Hollywood Forever

6000 Santa Monica Blvd., Los Angeles
(323) 469-1181
www.hollywoodforever.com

Founded in 1899, the Hollywood Forever backs up to Paramount Studios. The late and great of Hollywood, from Alfalfa of *Our Gang* fame to Jayne Mansfield, Rudolph Valentino, Cecil B. DeMille, Douglas Fairbanks, Tyrone Power, Johnny Ramone, and the Chandler family, the dynasty that started the *Los Angeles Times*, can all be found at six feet under. Go through the gate, proceed through Pineland, make a left at Maple, another left at Midland for a trip around the man-made lake, and then cross Maple and head toward the Cathedral Mausoleum. Hollywood Forever is on the National Register of Historic Places and holds outdoor movie events in the summer.

Morbid Souvenir Shopping

In search of a unique tchotchke to stand apart from all other tchotchkes? Consider an item from the Los Angeles County Department of Coroner's gift shop, **Skeletons in the Closet,** located at 1104 N. Mission Rd., Los Angeles. No other coroner's office in the nation has its very own gift shop. Don't want to go there in person? You can purchase items such as a glitter body key chain, foot lapel pin, body mouse pad, beach towel, magnet, or T-shirt for a reasonable price online at www.lacoroner.com. The coroner's office doesn't pour dollars into advertising this gift shop (not really in the best of taste now, is it?), and it's not exactly very profitable, but you can help change that now that you are armed with this morbid information.

Holy Cross Cemetery

5835 W. Slauson Ave., Culver City
(310) 836-5500
www.holycrossmortuary.com

Spot the graves of Bing Crosby, Rosalind Russell, John Candy, Jimmy Durante, Rita Hayworth, and such in this Roman Catholic cemetery that also happens to be a beautiful memorial park with ponds, waterfalls, and perfectly manicured grounds. When you enter the gates off Slauson Avenue, choose the fork in the road to your far left so as to make the most of your star sighting adventure at the level of your feet.

Inglewood Park Cemetery

720 E. Florence Ave., Inglewood
(310) 412-6500
www.inglewoodparkcemetery.org

The office at this cemetery will hand you a celebrity list and map, unlike the snooty Forest Lawn Glendale. You'll find Ella Fitzgerald and Gypsy Rose Lee. Hum some jazz under your breath as you depart, out of respect for Ella.

The Lake Shrine

Enter at 17190 or 17080 Sunset Blvd., Pacific Palisades
(310) 454-4114
www.lakeshrine.org

The ashes of Mahatma Gandhi can be found here. No, I'm not lying! That wouldn't be very Gandhi-like of me if I were. The 10 acres of The Lake Shrine (a former movie set) are a picturesque oasis with hillside, a lake, waterfalls, fountains, lily ponds, and an Old Dutch windmill. Most native Los Angelenos, let alone visitors, don't make the time to explore this little spot where Sunset meets the Pacific Ocean. Elvis Presley loved it as much as he loved peanut butter, banana, and bacon sandwiches. Beatles member George Harrison's memorial service was at The Lake Shrine. Take time to tour the meditation gardens and you'll feel closer to Gandhi. Closed Mon, sometimes Sat, and very busy during Sunday morning religious services.

Larchmont Village
Start at Melrose and N. Rossmore Avenues, Los Angeles

Walking down Larchmont feels a little bit like you're in *The Donna Reed Show* or *Leave it to Beaver*. It's this picture-perfect little main street that you would automatically conjure up in your mind's eye if someone said "Picture Main Street, USA." (No, please don't go there with the vanishing of the mom-and-pop shops, this is an upbeat book, for Pete's sake!) Flanked by Paramount Studios on one end and multimillion-dollar homes on the other, you've got high potential for celebrity sightings in between the shops and restaurants that line the walk. Grab a slice at Village Pizzeria (131 N. Larchmont), which won't break the bank and will make your taste buds very happy, park yourself on a bench outside, and take in the view.

Melrose Place
Start at northwest corner of Melrose Place (at intersection of Melrose Avenue), Los Angeles

The name inspired a television show; in reality, Melrose Place inspires some celebs to shop till they drop. Antiques meet A-list celebrities as they shop in the fashionable boutiques that dot the landscape. Stroll down Melrose and when you reach the end, turn south on North La Cienega Boulevard, and then walk half a block to Melrose Avenue. Make a right and head west on the north side of the street. Stop at Urth Caffe for coffee and an organic pastry, and you'll fit right in with the rest of the LA crowd. Keep on strolling all the way through the 7300 section of Melrose Avenue—you may catch Britney Spears or Katie Holmes browsing the racks.

Montana Avenue
Start at 17th Street and Montana Avenue, Santa Monica

Trendy stores and coffee shops line this beautiful pristine street in the heart of Santa Monica, where you'll find entertainment industry execs picking up their weekend coffee and enjoying time with their families. Celebrity sightings abound, and the Aero Theatre on Montana between Euclid and 14th Street shows art house films you can't catch anywhere else.

Pierce Bros. Westwood Village Memorial Park
1218 Glendon Ave., Los Angeles
(310) 474-1579
www.pbwvmortuary.com

If you want to see Hugh Hefner's plot awaiting him directly next to the lipstick-stained kisses adorning Marilyn Monroe's grave, then you should visit the Westwood Village Memorial Park, enshrouded by the high-rise buildings on Wilshire Boulevard's financial district. With its small and intimate layout, it is also easy to see the graves of Rodney Dangerfield, whose epitaph reads "There goes the neighborhood," Billy Wilder ("I'm a writer, but then nobody's perfect,") or, my favorite, Jack Lemmon's, which reads, simply, "Jack Lemmon in," and then you see the beautiful green grass in front of his headstone. Also buried here? Donna Reed, Natalie Wood, Truman Capote, Don Knotts, and more (the cemetery business, after all, is always on the rise). The Hammer Museum is close by.

Robertson Boulevard
Start at The Beverly Center
8500 Beverly Blvd. (at N. La Cienega Blvd.), Los Angeles

More shopping, coffee, and celeb sightings. Sigh. Just another tough day in Los Angeles. Head west on West Beverly Boulevard, and then left on North Robertson. Strut down the street and soak in the eye candy, retail and otherwise. When you get to West 3rd Street, cross to the other side and head back, so you can make sure you didn't miss a thing, or a person. Telltale signs of celebs include lurking photographers and dark SUVs.

Rodeo Drive
Start at Santa Monica Boulevard, Beverly Hills
www.rodeodrive-bh.com

Come on, you've always wanted to retrace the steps of Julia Roberts in *Pretty Woman*. Don your highest pair of high heels and start at Santa Monica Boulevard, walking south in the direction of the palm trees and 100 luxury stores toward Brighton Way, Dayton Way, and stopping at Wilshire. See if you see anyone you might know from, say, the supermarket checkout line. (Oh, don't play dumb. The tabloid you read while waiting for your broccoli to move forward on the conveyor belt. It's okay to admit you read them. I do.)

OTHER **ATTRACTIONS**

Adamson House
Malibu Lagoon Museum
23200 Pacific Coast Hwy., Malibu
(310) 456-8432
www.adamsonhouse.org
Hours: Tues, bus tours only; Wed through Sun 11 a.m. to 3 p.m. (last tour 2 p.m.)
Admission: $5 for 17 and older; $2 ages 6 to 16; free to children 2 and under

Adamson House is a classic home designed in 1930 with killer views surrounding the property, so it's no wonder they host many a wedding here. The house features Malibu Potteries tile and original furnishings. The Malibu Lagoon Museum, adjacent to the Adamson House, will tell you everything you ever wanted to know about the history of Malibu. Of course they don't mention things like when Suzanne Somers house burned down. That's sad and private. This is a museum, people, not the tabloids. Cash only. Every Fri at 10 a.m., you can catch the Gardens Tour, which is included in the price of admission for the House Tour.

Candy Cane Lane
Lubao Avenue and Oxnard Street, Woodland Hills

Every Christmas season, just as you start making your list and checking it twice, those few blocks between Lubao Avenue and Oxnard Street in Woodland Hills light up like the Griswolds' house in *National Lampoon's Christmas Vacation* at their brightest wattage, and are further buoyed by the parade-

Go Los Angeles Card

If you're visiting Los Angeles or you happen to live in the City of Angels but are looking ahead to heavy sightseeing as you will be entertaining your sister, brother-in-law, and two nephews for the upcoming three-day holiday weekend, then you might want to consider investing in the **Go Los Angeles Card,** an "all access attraction pass which offers the ultimate in convenience, cost savings, and flexibility for visitors to the city." The more days you purchase, the greater your savings, and I would really recommend it if your agenda is looking like it will be particularly geared toward family-type entertainment.

Purchasing this card can get you in to up to 40 attractions free, including Legoland, California Science Center, Los Angeles Zoo and Botanical Gardens, Knotts Berry Farm, Six Flags Magic Mountain, Warner Bros. Studio VIP Tour, and Starline Tours: Hollywood Trolley Tour, for example. With the purchase of a 3-, 5-, or 7-day card, they also throw in Universal Studios Hollywood. The price of the card fluctuates slightly and is also sometimes on sale. For instance, the current rate is $143.99 for 3 days. For that I could go to Universal Studios with my nephews on the first day, Magic Mountain in the morning and Double Decker Starline bus on the second day, and Legoland followed by a Spirit Cruise to top off the 3 days. In between all that I could enjoy further discounts, deals, and complimentary food and beverage at various locations. Cards are not honored after 5:30 p.m., so if you are a late sleeper or slow moving, it's probably not the deal for you. It is cheaper and easier to purchase it online. They also have cards for New York, Toronto, Miami, Chicago, Las Vegas, Oahu, San Diego, San Francisco, Seattle, Maui, Orlando, Blue Ridge, and Boston. Visit **www .smartdestinations.com** or call them at (800) 887-9103.

like stature of holiday figures and lawn ornaments in front of the twinkling lights. Whether you walk or drive, if you need a little Christmas, you can get it here.

Christmas Tree Lane

Santa Rosa Avenue (between Woodbury Ave. & Altadena Dr.), Altadena

Each holiday season, volunteers and the Christmas Tree Lane Association string the "Mile of Christmas Trees" with 10,000 lights in what is the largest old-scale Christmas lighting spectacle in Southern California. In 1885 the Woodbury family, founders of Altadena, planted 135 deodar cedar trees, and in 1920, the first organized tree lighting spectacle was held. Oh by gosh, by golly! Come on, ring those bells!

LA Conservancy Tours

(213) 623-2489
www.laconservancy.org

The LA Conservancy doesn't think eight is enough. They offer 8 regularly scheduled walking tours, in addition to a self-guided tour of 7th Street. These tours focus on historic downtown Los Angeles. You can select from Angelino Heights, Art Deco, Biltmore Hotel, Broadway: Historic Theatre and Commercial District, Downtown's Modern Skyline, Historic Core, Downtown Renaissance: Spring & Main, or Union Station. Tours are Sat and Sun and last 2 to 2.5 hours. Tours are $5 for Los Angeles Conservancy members and children 12 and under; $10 for nonmembers. Check online calendar for hours. Reservations are recommended. Membership starts at just $40/year and includes great discounts and perks on tours and events.

Warner Bros. Studio Tour

VIP Tour Center
3400 Riverside Dr., Burbank
(818) 972-8687
http://vipstudiotour.warnerbros.com

The Catch: $48, but the cheapest of all the studio tours. Admission is free and included as part of the deal when you purchase a Go Los Angeles Card.

This is a 2-hour-and-25-minute tour through the backlot, stages, sets, craft shops, and Warner Bros. Museum. If you're 8 years and older, you can attend. Advance reservations recommended. Tours depart continuously from 8:20 a.m. through 4 p.m., with extended spring and summer hours. It's $48, but it's cheaper than the regular price of Universal Studios Hollywood.

WALKIN', BIKIN' & DRIVIN': CITY ADVENTURES

"For my part, I travel not to go anywhere, but to go. I travel for travel's sake. The great affair is to move; to feel the needs and hitches of our life more nearly; to come down off this feather-bed of civilization, and find the globe granite underfoot and strewn with cutting flints."

—ROBERT LOUIS STEVENSON

I am a big fan of walking. Huge. Yes, yes, it's good for us, we all know that, but in our technology-addled world, it also gives us time to breathe a bit more deeply (once you cut through the infamous layer of Los Angeles smog) and, you know, maybe think and plan our day, tomorrow, the company meeting, Saturday's errands, the grand future. If you manage to do it without your phone or iPod in hand, you may even be able to take in the surrounding landscape and notice something you never noticed before. Don't think I don't know that on the rare occasion you do walk a greater distance than the one to your parked car that your head is buried in your bag or transfixed on the e-mail message lighting up your phone screen. You don't need to spend all of your time in your car while living in or visiting Los Angeles. Really. You can walk. A lot. Even more importantly, there are a few jaunts by car worth taking for their breathtaking views that will cost you nothing more than gas money. Cue appropriate car tunes. (I prefer a mix of contemporary, oldies, '80s, and classic rock.) Shall we begin?

ON **FOOT**

Hollywood Sign
http://hollywoodsigntrip.com

The Hollywood sign is one of the most recognizable signs in the entire world. While it's protected by a no-trespassing fence, you can come within 100 yards of it and get a nice workout on your way there. Start at the top of Beachwood Drive and drive through the gates of Sunset Ranch Stables at 3400 Beachwood. Follow the signs to park next to the Holly Ride trailhead. Take the trail, which will have you turning left after only 100 yards, check out the view, pass the bridle path descending to the stables, and voila! The sign will be in view, but still not as close as you wish. Snap a pic at the gravel top area. At the half-mile mark, you will come to a "T." Make a left, follow the lush trail, descend to the paved Mt. Lee Drive, hang a right, going higher and higher, and take in the majestic San Gabriel Mountains. The road will curve left, you'll see the Mt. Lee radio towers, continue to the end, and find that Hollywood sign 100 yards below.

Lake Hollywood Reservoir
www.hollywoodknolls.org/hollywood_reservoir.htm

The Lake Hollywood Reservoir is best reached via the north gate, which you will find directly across from the Department of Water and Power's Toyon Tanks Facility at 2920 Lake Hollywood Dr. The entire perimeter of the reservoir is an exercise-acceptable 3.2 miles, and you'll get slamming views of ducks on the water, trees, homes of the rich, famous, and rich and famous in the Hollywood Hills, and the impressive Mulholland Dam along the way.

Marina Del Rey
Start at Washington and Mildred Avenues, Marina Del Rey
www.visitmarinadelrey.com

The bike and pedestrian park starts at the intersection of Washington and Mildred. You can catch big homes on water (read: yachts) as you stroll toward the pedestrian-only path that will have you winding through Admiralty Park. When you get to the public library, continue on the road behind the library. More panoramic views will abound as you hang a left and continue southeast on the path behind the boats. Cross Bali Way. When you get to Mindanao Way, make a right. Head straight on Mindanao to the cul-de-sac. You will be at the entrance to Burton W. Chase Park.

Santa Monica Pier & Boardwalk
Start at intersection of Wilshire Boulevard & Ocean Avenue, Santa Monica

Starting at the intersection of Wilshire and Ocean, head northwest on the path through Palisades Park. You'll start to feel like you're in a commercial advertising tourism in Southern California, with the sparkling ocean and swaying palm trees in view. When you reach Montana Avenue, take the stairs heading down the sandstone cliffs to the pedestrian bridge that crosses the Pacific Coast Highway. At the parking lot, head west to the boardwalk and then turn southeast. Weave through bikers and skaters and, as you reach the pier, take the walkway next to the boardwalk. At the Santa Monica Pier, ascend the stairs leading up and just west of the boardwalk. Spend a few bucks to ride the Ferris wheel, and your Southern California commercial-making moment is complete.

Silver Lake Reservoir
Silverlake Boulevard, Los Angeles

While the Silver Lake Reservoir does not actually provide water for the residents of Silver Lake (gotcha!), but instead provides water to other South Los Angeles communities (Silver Lake gets their water from Eagle Rock), it does provide a nice 2.2-mile jogging and walking path, as well as a dog park. The upper section is named "Ivanhoe," after the Sir Walter Scott novel, and the lower section is named "Silver Lake" after Herman Silver, a member of Los Angeles's first Board of Water Commissioners. Exciting. The 3 million bird balls you see in the Ivanhoe section? They're there to shade the water and prevent the creation of bromate, a chemical reaction triggered by sunlight. Be on the lookout for the neighborhood regular, a shirtless retired doctor, Marc Abrams, who has been making daily 20-mile treks near the Silver Lake Reservoir while reading a newspaper all the while for the past 30 years.

Sunset Boulevard
Start at W. Sunset Boulevard and N. Doheny Drive, Los Angeles

You've read about The Roxy, The Standard, The House of Blues, Whiskey a Go Go, The Laugh Factory, and The Chateau Marmont. See them in all their glory on Sunset Boulevard, made famous by musicals, rock songs and videos, television, and movies. Starting at the intersection of West Sunset and North Doheny, walk east on West Sunset, and just keep on going. This route is also drivable.

Venice Boardwalk
Start at N. Venice Boulevard and Pacific Avenue, Venice

"I like to rollerblade on the Venice Boardwalk while listening to Eminem. I just go," said the 50-plus-year-old eccentric woman to her coworker and my friend, Steve. "And I know that people are just looking at me because they are jealous. I'm so good, and they want to be me." Venice Boardwalk provides some of the best people watching entertainment anywhere on the planet. Street performers and vendors will vie for your attention. See if you don't spot in-line skater/dancer/electric guitar player Harry Perry, known to all as Guitar Guy, who has been gracing the boardwalk for 37 years, or Lionel Powell, aka Treeman, who frightens passersby with all 8 feet 6 inches of himself on stilts while wearing face paint, shrubbery, and moss pants.

Venice Canals & Abbot Kinney Boulevard
Start at Ocean Avenue and S. Venice Boulevard, Venice

Abbot Kinney, a developer, conservationist, and tobacco giant, modeled the Venice Canals after Italy in 1905. Most of that vision has dissolved into concrete and asphalt, but several saltwater strains remain, peppered with some excellent window shopping along trendy Abbot Kinney Boulevard. Starting at the corner of Ocean Avenue and South Venice Boulevard, head southeast on Ocean Avenue for 3 blocks, hang a right on Linnie Avenue, and continue and cross the bridge over Eastern Canal, taking in the homes that make you feel as though you are in Venice, Italy. Move ahead to Linnie Canal Court, make a right on Dell Avenue, and then at Carroll Canal Court, turn right to take in the Carroll Canal. Eastern Court will be your last canal sighting. Make a left and then a right onto South Venice Boulevard. In a quarter mile you will reach Abbot Kinney. Hang left and drink in all the shopping you could do on someone else's dime.

BIKE **RESOURCES**

BikeMetro
www.bikemetro.com

BikeMetro covers Los Angeles, Orange, San Bernadino, and Riverside Counties, and is looking to expand nationwide. Maps, information, routes, and communities!

City of Los Angeles Department of Transportation Bicycle Information
www.bicyclela.org

Everything you need to know about riding a bike in Los Angeles, including the laws, safety tips, programs, clubs, resources, and maps. You can look at maps online as well as request them by phone or e-mail. One-stop shopping for the biker in you. They also list clubs by Road Bicycle Clubs, Mountain Biking/MTB Clubs, and Velodromes and Other Cycling Clubs (which includes the Tandem Club of America). Stop it. Now you're singing Harry Dacre's "A Bicycle Built for Two." I hear you. Don't pretend you're not.

BIKE **REPAIR** & USED **BIKE** SHOPS

Bicycle Kitchen
706 Heliotrope (near Melrose Avenue), Los Angeles
(323) NO-CARRO (662-2776)
http://bicyclekitchen.com

The Catch: They help you fix your own bike. Upside? You become the Martha Stewart of bicycle repairs and have something new to add to the special skills of your resume.

A nonprofit educational organization run by volunteers, Bicycle Kitchen is filled with tools and stands for working on bikes. They ask for a $7 donation. They offer classes in which they ask for a $30 donation and never turn anyone away for lack of funds. But I don't suggest you mess with your karma, dude, and stiff them. $7 ain't gonna kill you.

There's also an ice cream shop, vegan and Chilean restaurants, coffee shop, and a pizza joint nearby so you can feed yourself when you're ravenous after exercising all of that manual dexterity.

Bike Oven

3706 N. Figueroa St. (near W. Avenue 37), Los Angeles
(323) 223-8020
http://bikeoven.com

Do it yourself repair under the guidance of volunteer mechanics for the price of a suggested donation of $5. You can work on your own bike, or one of theirs. They have a healthy supply of random parts to select from if and when you need them. Open Tues and Thurs evenings 7 to 10 p.m. and Sat and Sun from 1 to 4 p.m.

BikerOWave

12255 Venice Blvd. (between Ocean View Ave. and Grand View Blvd.),
Los Angeles
(310) 230-5236
www.bikerowave.org

Self-service repair for $7 an hour or $4 a half hour. And no, those aren't suggested donations rates, so pay up. (Are you seriously balking? Stop! Nope! Don't want to hear it. Cheap is common sense, not an attitude.) Not-for-profit and volunteer member-run organization. Open Mon through Wed 6:30 to 10 p.m., Thurs 3:30 to 10 p.m., and Sat and Sun 11 a.m. to 5 p.m.

Coco's Variety

2427 Riverside Dr., Los Angeles
(323) 664-7400
www.cocosvariety.com

You can buy a "project" beat-up bike for $40–$50. Translation: This is sort of like buying a "fixer upper" of a house. They also refurbish bikes and resell them for $250, but I wasn't going to share that because it is way out of our budget. However, if I didn't share it, I was afraid you might accuse me of withholding information.

Topanga Creek Bicycles
1273 N. Topanga Canyon Blvd., Topanga
(310) 455-2111
http://labiketours.com

This is a bike shop specializing in mountain and touring bikes, but every Sat at 8:30 a.m. they have an equal-opportunity mountain ride open to all people of all ages and skill levels. You can also use that time as an opportunity to demo a bike from their shop.

Valley Bikery
14416 Victory Blvd., #104, Van Nuys
www.valleybikery.com

Like potluck for bikes, only instead of broccoli casserole and lasagna, you've got mobile bike clinics, urban expedition bike rides, and community bike repair events. Their mission is to "promote cycling as a sustainable, healthy, and fun method of transportation in the San Fernando Valley." Open Tues 7 to 10 p.m. and Sat 1 to 5 p.m.

SCENIC DRIVES

Angeles Crest Scenic Byway
Wind 55 breathtaking miles along the San Gabriel Mountains to see one of the most beautiful sights in all of Los Angeles. A secluded and steep drive climbing to 7,900 feet, those 55 miles might take you 3 well-spent hours, especially if you build in time to step out of the car to take in the views of the San Gabriel Mountains, Angeles National Forest, and Mojave Desert. Further exploration of the Angeles National Forest will have you investigating camping, swimming, biking, fishing, skiing, and horseback riding, depending on the time of year of your visit. If you're limited by time, gear, or taste and won't be hiking, split the difference and stop for a peak (no pun intended) at the Mount Wilson Observatory and the view of the Los Angeles Basin. You won't regret it. To get there, take the 210 to Highway 39/Azusa Avenue exit, and head north. Azusa Avenue will turn into San Gabriel Canyon Road.

AAA Membership: Cheap in the Long Run

AAA—it's no longer something just for your parents or that thing you keep confusing with the AARP (well, maybe that's just me); it's time you consider stepping up to the plate and deciding that maybe it's time to grow up and join. "Why?" you ask. "What does being a member of this club get me, exactly?" I can hear the skeptic in you wondering aloud.

Well, for starters, let's examine the fact that each year you live in Los Angeles, you further increase the likelihood that at some point you are going to run up against some lamentable car woes. I mean, it's just a matter of time until the odds will inevitably catch up with you. For under $70 annually when you first join, you can get towing benefits off that crowded 405 for up to 7 miles, discounted rates for rental cars, emergency fuel delivery, identity theft monitoring, vehicle locksmith service up to $60, a 20 percent discount on vehicle history reporting, a spare key card, free maps, travel planner, and tour books, as well as further discounts at other businesses.

And really, isn't that a relatively small price to pay for the insurance against a potential disaster that's very likely to end up costing you more time and more money if you're the one paying for the emergency fuel delivery or towing during rush hour on a Friday? Or what about when you visit Grandma up the coast and get stuck outside San Francisco? I'm an optimist, so you don't even want to begin to imagine the doomsday scenario. Consider making the investment today. I promise you'll feel very, very adult! Call (877) 428-2277 or visit **www .aaa.com** for more details.

Mulholland Drive

Mulholland Drive is named after William Mulholland, the former head of Los Angeles Department of Water and Power, who, in the early 20th century, built water aqueducts and dams that brought water across the city and allowed it to grow into what it is today. For this he gets his own drive, which happens to have one of the most scenic and quintessential lookout points in all of Los Angeles. And a movie named after it as well. (*Mulholland Drive*, 2001, directed by David Lynch.) Start from the 405 and cruise 7.5 miles to

Highway 101: The Truth About LA Traffic

If you live in Los Angeles or you're just visiting, you don't need to let the traffic rule you and your driving happiness. The most important guiding principle is that unless it's after 9 p.m., it's always going to be your best bet to take a surface street over a freeway. Don't try to convince yourself otherwise. Keep some of these other tips in mind to make your navigation as painless as possible:

Beverly Glen. Taking Beverly Glen to get from the Valley to the Westside will make you a much happier camper.

Canyons are cool. If you can take a street with "Canyon" in the name to get from Point A to Point B, do it. Coldwater can get you from Hollywood to Beverly Hills; Laurel to the Valley, WeHo, or Downtown; Topanga from the San Fernando Valley, Canoga Park, or Chatsworth to Santa Monica.

Fountain Avenue. They don't call it the "Fountain Freeway" for nothing. It's faster than Melrose or Santa Monica. Usually.

Franklin Avenue. Take Franklin Avenue to go east to west in Hollywood.

Highland Avenue. Take Highland to go south to north, except when there are events at the Hollywood Bowl.

Hollywood Bowl. Watch out for traffic around the Hollywood Bowl when they have events. (See above.) You've been forewarned.

Laurel Canyon Boulevard, marveling at the views of the San Fernando Valley, the Hollywood Hills, and the incredible homes.

Ortega Highway and the Palms to Pines Scenic Byway

Spend a Sunday on Highway 74, the Ortega Highway (www.theortegahighway.com), once just Indian trails and fire roads. Winding 25 miles through the Cleveland National Forest in the Santa Ana Mountains between Lake Elsinore and San Juan Capistrano, see who in your car can count the number of bikers at Hells Kitchen the fastest. For a longer drive at 67 miles and to go palms to pines to see the whole spectrum of wildlife and ecosystems at the desert divide, start in Banning on Highway 243 and follow it south to its junction with Highway 74 south and then east to the Palm Desert. You'll

La Brea. Never take a freeway to the Los Angeles Airport (LAX). La Brea will shave minutes off your travel time while boosting your sanity at the same time.

Olympic Boulevard. Take Olympic Boulevard to get from Century City to Downtown. If for some strange reason it's jam-packed, make a right and take Venice Boulevard until you hit South Figueroa Street.

West LA to the Valley. Take Sunset to Bellagio, bearing right on Roscomare Road, which will wind you all the way up to Mulholland. Make a right, then a left at Woodcliff, which will take you down to Valley Vista Boulevard, where you can make a right, and then a left onto Saugus Avenue, which hits Ventura Boulevard.

Pico Boulevard. When available, Pico Boulevard is also an excellent choice to get to the west side.

San Vicente Boulevard. Take San Vicente to travel between Brentwood and Santa Monica.

Sepulveda Boulevard. If it works with your journey, it's a better option than the 405.

6th Street. Take 6th Street to get Downtown.

Sunset Boulevard. Sunset Boulevard is great for driving from the Pacific past West Hollywood.

Venice to the Miracle Mile. Don't take the 10; take Palms Boulevard.

find Idyllwild stoplight free and may want to make an overnight trip out of exploring the San Jacinto Wilderness Area or Joshua Tree National Park in the Palm Desert.

Pacific Coast Highway (PCH)

The PCH conjures images of an open-top convertible, dark sunglasses, hair whipping in the wind, and an endless stretch of white-capped waves crashing on sandy beaches below majestic cliffs. No, I'm not talking about a Danielle Steel novel, I'm talking about California Highway 1, those 485 miles that make up the scenic coast of California. You can do the 20-mile stretch from Santa Monica to Malibu, or you can head all the way north to San Francisco and take your time. If you do that, be sure to build in time to enjoy Big

Sur and the redwood forest, shouting a hearty chorus of "This Land is Your Land" at the top of your lungs. Either way, you can do no wrong.

Palos Verdes Drive from Palos Verdes Estates to San Pedro

More scenic coastlines and sandy beaches, what else do you expect? Along these utopian 14 miles off the coast of the Palos Verdes Peninsula, you'll also spot Frank Lloyd Wright's Wayfarer's Chapel. If you're following Palos Verdes Drive north, take it easy around Portuguese Bend, the stunning 260 acres of unstable land that has been sliding into the beach since 1956.

Rim of the World Scenic Byway

Start at the Mormon Rock Fire Station 1.5 miles west of I-15 on Highway 138, north of San Bernadino. Go east until 138 merges with Highway 18 at Crestline. Follow 18/38 east to the west end dam of Big Bear Lake, staying on 38 all the way around the lake to where the highway ends at the Mill Creek Ranger Station on the border of the San Bernadino National Forest. This 107-mile epic trek will have you weaving through wilderness above the Los Angeles Basin to Big Bear Lake. It's one way you can guarantee you'll see some of the white stuff (snow) in the winter and stay cool in the summer.

Topanga Canyon

Turn onto Topanga Canyon Blvd. from the PCH and discover your inner hippie. With 15 or 20 miles of hairpin turns and little to no cell phone reception, you'll be digging the plunging canyon and artsy-fartsy vibe of the community and galleries here. You could stop at the beautiful Inn of the Seventh Ray, which is a bit pricey, but has an awesome, more reasonably priced brunch. However, the Inn of the Seventh Ray didn't want to be featured in this book, fearing the word "cheap" in the title might not be in line with good karma or energy. Woops. Did I just mention them?

Wilshire Boulevard

Start Downtown and traverse through an education in diversity (from Koreatown to the Orthodox Jewish community making their way to temple on the Sabbath in the Miracle Mile) and architecture (Art Deco, Victorian, Gothic, and Modern) in your 16-mile drive to Santa Monica. To break it up, stop at one of the museums in Museum Row on a free admission day or window shop on Rodeo Drive.

TRANSIT:
MASS TRANSPORTATION &
OTHER CHEAP ALTERNATIVES

"Look at all the buses now that want exact change, exact change. I figure if I give them exact change, they should take me exactly where I want to go."

—GEORGE C. WALLACE

So you're drawn to Los Angeles by the lure of the sun. You've managed to snag some digs for dirt-cheap monthly rent and land that entry-level job you were dying for to get your foot in the door on the production side of the entertainment business, but you forgot to factor in the combined whammy of your car payment, car insurance, and gas, not to mention your carbon footprint and the road rage whose etymology can be traced right to the 405, the 5, the 10, the 101 . . . all of a sudden living in your teenage bedroom doesn't seem so bad. The state of California has some of the highest gas taxes in the entire country, which has you shelling out some serious cash to fill her up. Depending on your commute to and from work, epic Los Angeles traffic, and oh, you know, the fun you are planning to have on occasion, that monthly budget for gas is attempting to rival your rent payment. Los Angeles, with its comprehensive bus and rail system, can actually get you nearly anywhere you need to go, and you can breathe easy and maybe even take in a chapter of that book collecting dust on your nightstand while someone else gets paid to navigate the stressful traffic on your behalf. Plus, you can pack your bike on that bus. Graduate to Greyhound or Amtrak for those weekend getaways, and you'll be living large on a small budget.

BY **BUS** & BY **RAIL**

Los Angeles County Metropolitan Transit Authority
www.metro.net

Running from just after 4 a.m., with the last departure between midnight and 1 a.m., the nearly 200 bus and rail lines of the LA Metro can fit your schedule and lifestyle, whether you're heading to/from Downtown, east or west, north or south, or stretching to South LA, Watts, Huntington Park, or Long Beach. Many of the stations have bike racks and lockers, and over 100 stops have kiss and ride lots, most of which offer free parking, reserved spaces for a fee, or, on the rare occasion, are paid parking only. Log online and use the Metro Trip Planner to figure out the best route, timing, and cost. Visit www.metro.net/around/mobile-resources to get up-to-the-minute information directly on your phone, so you're never at a loss for the next bus or rail.

Fare Information:
$1.50 regular fare for each boarding
35 cents for transfer to municipal lines; not valid on Metro Bus and Metro Rail
70 cents freeway express add-on for Zone 1; $1.40 for Zone 2
$2.45 for the Metro Silver Line, which connects South Bay and the San Gabriel Valley to Downtown Los Angeles

Passes:
$6 for a day pass, up to 8 at a time (savings after 4 boardings in one day)
$20 for a weekly pass (savings after 13 boardings per week)
$75 for a monthly pass (savings after 50 boardings per month)
$22 per zone for a bus only freeway express stamp or an EZ Premium Stamp affixed to an EZ Transit pass
$84 for an EZ Transit pass good on Metro Bus and Metro Rail

Reduced-Price Fare:
All reduced-price fare discounts can be obtained by filling out an application and mailing it to the Metro's Reduced Fair Office (213-680-0054 Mon through Fri 8 a.m. to 4 p.m.), submitted at a Customer Care Center, or mailed to the TAP Service Center (866-TAPTOGO) listed on the application. Balance protection is built in so you can get a replacement card if yours is lost or stolen.
$14 for Senior/Disabled/Medicare Monthly
$9.50 per zone for Senior/Disabled/Medicare EZ Premium Stamp
$36 for college/vocational monthly
$24 for K through 8 and 9 through 12 Student TAP Card

Children:
Two children under the age of 5 may travel free with each fare-paying adult on bus or rail.

LADOT (Los Angeles Department of Transportation) Transit Services
www.ladottransit.com.

LADOT's transit fleet has nearly 400 vehicles in service that operate over 800,000 revenue hours and serve over 30 million Los Angelenos per year. LADOT operates DASH (Downtown Area Short Hop), which has 5 routes running every 5 to 30 minutes and serving Downtown Los Angeles; Commuter

Express, which operates from places like the Valley, Rancho Palos Verdes, Thousand Oaks, Woodland Hills, and more Mon through Fri during peak commuter hours; Cityride, which is a program for those 65 and over or with mobility impairments; an Observatory Shuttle from the Metro Red Line to Griffith Park and the Griffith Observatory as well as a Union Station/Bunker Hill Shuttle; and charter bus services. No matter your transportation need, LADOT will have you humming "The wheels on the bus go round and round . . ." as you gaze out the window, lost in a prework daydream.

DASH Fares:
35 cents regular fare
15 cents for persons 65 and over, with disabilities, or Medicare card holders
Free to LADOT, DASH, EZ transit pass, or metrolink monthly pass holders

Commuter Express:
Fares start at $1.25 for Zone 1 and go up to $3.90 for Zone 4
Senior and disabled fare ranges from 60 cents for Zone 1 to $1.95 for Zone 4
$25 for 20 Zone 1 LADOT trips to $65 for 20 Zone 4 LADOT trips
$50 for monthly Zone 1 LADOT pass to $124 for Zone 4 LADOT monthly pass

A Note on Transfers:
Transfers between Commuter Express routes or to/from DASH can be made with an LADOT pass. Transfers between Commuter Express routes, to/from all DASH routes, and to/from most fixed route transit services in LA County can be made using an EZ Transit pass (see LA Metro). Transfers can also be made to other Commuter Express routes and to/from most other fixed route transit services in LA County by buying a 35-cent Interagency Transfer when you pay your Commuter Express fare (10 cents for seniors/persons with disabilities). Interagency transfers are not valid on DASH.

Children:
Two children under the age of 4 may travel free with each fare-paying adult.

Big Blue Bus
223 Broadway, Santa Monica
(310) 451-5444
www.bigbluebus.com

"Ride blue, go green" is the motto of Santa Monica's Big Blue Bus Company. With nearly 14 lines servicing Santa Monica Boulevard, Wilshire Boulevard, Montana Avenue and Lincoln Boulevard, San Vicente Boulevard and Carlyle

Avenue, Olympic Boulevard, Pico Boulevard, Ocean Park Boulevard, Pacific Palisades, the Freeway Express, Santa Monica College and UCLA Connector, Westwood and Palms, Cheviot Hills, and Bundy Drive and Centinela Avenue, as well as several Rapid routes, is there anything that isn't covered? Fares range from 50 cents to $2. Up to 2 children under the age of 4 can ride free with a fare-paying adult. Monthly passes range from $24 to $60.

Metrolink

700 S. Flower St., Suite 2600, Los Angeles
(800) 371-LINK (5465)
www.metrolinktrains.com

Metrolink is Southern California's commuter rail system that links Orange County with Los Angeles, Riverside, and San Bernadino Counties. Check out online schedules for the Antelope Valley, Burbank Bob Hope Airport, Inland Empire, Orange County, Riverside, San Bernadino, and Venture County routes. Only the Antelope Valley, Inland Empire, Orange County, and San Bernadino lines also operate on weekends. Discount for students, military, senior citizens, youth, and the disabled. Up to 3 children under the age of 5 ride free with an adult using a valid ticket. Their online fare calculator will give you the rate and the savings you're accumulating by opting not to drive. How much do I love seeing my savings flash on the screen?

AMTRAK & **GREYHOUND**

California is vast. It's not like Rhode Island or Delaware, where you can escape for a getaway and be in the next state in a matter of ten minutes. Fortunately, Amtrak and Greyhound offer great deals to get out of town without breaking your wallet, relieving the stress of driving and leaving you free to zone out to your music or catch a snooze.

Amtrak

810 N. Alameda St., Los Angeles
(213) 346-9404
www.amtrak.com

$50 round-trip from Los Angeles to Santa Barbara, $31 each way on the Pacific Surfliner to San Diego, and just over $100 for a leisurely round-trip to and from San Francisco along the coast, so you can cruise with thoughts of wine country and waves crashing against the shore, rather than trouble yourself with the overwhelming stench of cows along the monotonous 5 as you near your glimpse of the Golden Gate Bridge. Amtrak's website will also offer you deals on nearby hotels and activities.

Greyhound
1716 E. 17th St., Los Angeles
(213) 629-8401 or (800) 231-2222
www.greyhound.com

Greyhound's gotten sleek in these past few years in order to compete with the discount bus services cropping up across the country. Now you can cruise with free Wi-Fi to places like Santa Barbara, Sacramento, San Jose, San Diego, and San Francisco (this chapter is brought to you by the letter "S"), for web-only fares of $42 one way ($54 standard) for Rice-a-Roni, the San Francisco treat or San Jose; $54 web only ($62 standard) to Sacramento; $15.84 web only one way ($18 standard) for San Diego; or $14.96 web only one way for San Diego ($17 standard). Additional locations are at 1715 N. Cahuenga Blvd., Hollywood (323-466-6381); 1498 Long Beach Blvd., Long Beach (562-218-3011); and 11239 Magnolia Blvd., North Hollywood (818-761-5119).

CHEAP **WHEELS**

Sometimes, no matter what you do, you simply can't escape the necessity of driving. Here are some methods of doing it the cheap bastard way.

Auto Driveaway
PO Box 17055, Long Beach, CA 90807
(562) 552-7080
Corporate Office: (800) 346-2277
www.autodriveaway.com

Since 1952, Auto Driveaway has been delivering automobiles anywhere in the world. They are what is called a vehicle transportation service. What does this mean for you? Well, if you are at least 23 years of age and can supply an official copy of your moving violation report (MVR) from the Department of Motor Vehicles, which Auto Driveway can help you with for the fee of $12, you can drive that vehicle where it needs to go. Give them a call 1 or 2 weeks prior to your desired departure dates and give them the starting and ending points of your destination in North America. Post a deposit of $350, which you'll receive back in full when you return the car intact, and get free use of a car, a free tank of gas, and sometimes even a gas allowance. Roll that window down and feel the breeze in your hair.

FreeCar Media

11990 San Vicente Blvd., Suite 350, Los Angeles
www.freecarmedia.com

What would America be without its rampant advertising of anything and everything? Now your wheels can hock consumer products, too. FreeCar Media will wrap your vehicle in a boldly colored advertisement for anywhere from a few months to 2 years, and for this head-turning you are agreeing to invite into your life every time you drive your car, you will be paid up to $900 per month. You still have to pay for your own insurance and fuel, but hey, at least now you're getting paid to drive. Sign up now, fill out the web questionnaire to be part of the database that matches drivers to an appropriate ad campaign. You can refuse a campaign if for some reason it doesn't jive with your vibe. I, for instance, don't think I could sell brussels sprouts. Not that the brussels sprout growers of the United States are purchasing advertising for their cause, but, well, you get it.

ZipCar

Corporate Headquarters
25 First St., 4th floor, Cambridge, MA 02141
(866) 4ZIPCAR
www.zipcar.com

For a one-time $25 application fee, an annual fee of $50, no monthly commitment, gas, insurance, and 180 free miles per day included, you've got nothing to lose on this deal. Rent a car by the hour for $8 an hour weekdays, $9 an hour on weekends, or daily rates from $66 on weekdays and $72 on weekends, and you've got wheels as you go, right when you want them. ZipCar operates entirely online for their sign-up and reservations. It's really only easy to reach someone live in the event of an accident, which doesn't apply to you because you're not going to have one.

HORTICULTURAL HAPPENSTANCES:
DIRT CHEAP

"No occupation is so delightful to me as the culture of the earth, and no culture comparable to that of the garden."

—THOMAS JEFFERSON

I kill nearly every plant or flower with which I come into contact. I've decided it's an impressive and remarkable talent; they see me coming and start wilting to their imminent death like the Wicked Witch of the West when met with a bucket of water. Even when I follow watering and sunning directions perfectly, they are not long for this world. For the most part, I prefer to enjoy the beauty of gardens that other, far more highly skilled people tend to, and are there for our personal enjoyment and to make the air we breathe sweeter, the life we lead prettier, and our environment better. Los Angeles has a number of incredibly cultivated gardens for you to meander through like you were the 19th-century aristocracy of some Western European country, and plenty of tips and resources to help you be all that you can be in the world of gardening.

GORGEOUS **GARDENS**

The Arboretum
301 N. Baldwin Ave. (near Stanford Dr.), Arcadia
(626) 821-3222
www.arboretum.org
Hours: Open daily 9 a.m. to 4:30 p.m., except Christmas.
Admission: $8 for adults; $6 seniors and students; $3 children ages 5 to 12; children under 5 free; $4 for the tram; free on the third Tues of each month.

Plants from all around the world, some of them even rare and endangered, can be found in the 127 acres of The Los Angeles County Arboretum and Botanic Garden. Check the website for the many events and classes offered, and be sure to catch the California Philharmonic Concerts on the Green in the summer. No tram riding on the third free Tuesday of the month. Hey, you win some, you lose some.

Beverly Gardens Park
N. Santa Monica Boulevard and N. Beverly Drive (between Doheny and Wilshire), Beverly Hills
(310) 285-2536

Built in 1911 before the city was built up, Beverly Gardens Park is a 2-mile stretch that runs along Santa Monica Boulevard in Beverly Hills. It features a lily pond, towering trees, a jogging path, the Electric Fountain (quite a sight at the unveiling in 1931), many a cacti, and the famous Beverly Hills sign. You'll see City Hall and can hop across the way to Rodeo Drive when you're finished with all that nature. The Bi-annual Affaire in the Garden is held here each May and October, as is the Beverly Hills Food Festival in June. Free parking on the residential streets.

Descanso Gardens
1418 Descanso Dr., La Canada Flintridge
(818) 952-4400
www.descansogardens.org
Hours: 9 a.m. to 5 p.m. daily, except for Christmas.
Admission: $8 general; $6 seniors and students; $3 children ages 5 to 12; children under 5 are free; $3 to $4 for the tram.

The Descano Gardens in the San Rafael Hills comprise 150 acres, but the 5 acres of 3,000 roses are among some of the top sights to behold here. Kids (and adults) can climb aboard a ⅛ replica of a diesel train and tour the Hollywood Regency–style home of E. Manchester Boddy, founder of Descanso Gardens and the former publisher and owner of the *Los Angeles Daily News*. Free parking.

Exposition Park Rose Garden
701 State Dr., Los Angeles
(213) 763-0114
www.laparks.org/exporosegarden/rosegarden.htm
Hours: Closed Jan 1 through Mar 15 for pruning; open daily 9 a.m. to sunset.

It doesn't take a rocket scientist to figure out what is featured in these 7 acres that are on the National Register of Historic Places. If you go on a weekend, see how many brides you can spot taking advantage of this popular photo spot.

Franklin D. Murphy Sculpture Garden
UCLA (part of the Hammer Museum)
Charles E. Young Drive E (near Wyton Dr.), Westwood
(310) 443-7020

So we're expanding our definition of "garden" to include sculpture here. (Hey, the sculptures are outdoors in nature, people.) The Franklin D. Murphy

Sculpture Garden features more than 5 acres of 70 sculptures from around the world by artists such as Auguste Rodin and Henri Matisse.

Mildred E. Mathias Botanical Garden

UCLA (at southeast corner entrance)
Hilgard and Le Conte Avenues, Los Angeles
(310) 825-1260
Hours: Mon through Fri 8 a.m. to 5 p.m. (closed 4 p.m. in winter); Sat 8 a.m. to 4 p.m.; closed Sun and university holidays.

Once the UCLA Botany Department's experimental site for useful subtropical trees in the Southern California landscape, the Mildred E. Mathias Botanical Garden includes an impressive array of eucalyptus, gymnosperms, palms, succulents, aquatics, and camellias. See nearly 5,000 species in 225 families in just 7 acres. Free admission.

South Coast Botanic Garden

26300 Crenshaw Blvd., Palos Verdes Peninsula
(310) 544-1948
www.southcoastbotanicgarden.org
Hours: Open daily 9 a.m. to 5 p.m., except Christmas.
Admission: $8 for adults; $6 seniors and students; $3 children ages 5 to 12; free to children 4 and under; also free the third Tues of each month.

This "Jewel of the Peninsula" has 87 lush acres situated in one of the primo growing spots of the world, known as Sunset's Zone 23. You'll see more than 2,500 different species of plants from around the world, including 100 rare trees and shrubs. A thriving wildlife inhabits this garden, and nearly 200 species of birds are sighted annually. Check out the Dahlia Garden, Rose Garden, Cactus Garden, Garden for the Senses, Children's Garden, and more. Picnic just outside the gates. Free parking.

GREEN **THUMB** RESOURCES

California Friendly Landscape Workshop

(800) 544-4498, press "5"

Diggin' Up Dirt Online

Want to know more about what the term "organic gardening" means? Dying to know how to plant those perennials so they'll flourish? Or maybe you just want a few generic gardening tips. Here are some of your best online resources:

Better Homes and Gardens lives up to its name with a plant encyclopedia, flowers, regional gardening, garden plans, landscaping, lawn and yard care, and store. Visit www.bhg.com.

DoItYourself.com—the Gardening and Outdoor section—has tabs on fences, fertilizer, flower, fruits and vegetables, lawn care, trees and shrubs, outdoor pests, and more. At www.doityourself.com.

Love to Know has a Garden section that will teach all you would love to know about gardening, from berries and fruits, to herbs, mulch, shrubs, vines, and theme gardens. You've hit the gardening jackpot. Visit http://garden.lovetoknow.com.

Martha Stewart, is there anything you can't do? She only sleeps 4 hours a night and wakes before dawn on her farm in Connecticut every day, so it's no wonder she's ahead of us all in her gardening. Click on "Home & Garden" at www.marthastewart.com.

National Gardening Association is the authority on all things garden. With great articles, a plant finder, a weed finder, pest control library, food garden guide, plant care guides, how-to projects, and videos, your gardening needs have been met at www.garden.org.

Organic Gardening is what it says it is: a website about organic gardening. A one-stop resource at www.organicgardening.com.

Learn how to conserve water while also taking care of your lawn and landscaping. Hey, it's Los Angeles. There's always a water shortage, not enough rain, and you've got to conserve. The city encourages residents to collect raindrops in the free rain buckets they hand out. This is serious, people.

Los Angeles Guerrilla Gardening (LAGG)
www.laguerrillagardening.org

Guerrilla Gardeners is a group of volunteers ages 10 to 80, committed to gardening in public spaces as a means to improve the community. Monthly volunteer meetings are held on the first Tuesday of every month.

Master Gardener Technical Assistance
Common Ground Garden Program
University of California Agriculture and Natural Resources
Los Angeles County Cooperative Extension
4800 E. Cesar E. Chavez Ave., Los Angeles
(323) 260-2267
http://celosangeles.ucdavis.edu

Every spring the Master Gardener Volunteer Training Program schools low-income residents in a pay-what-you-can crash course in growing their own food, with an emphasis on organic gardening, vegetables, fruits, flowers, shrubs, trees, soils, composting, pests, and harvesting. Once schooled in this program, the Master Gardeners go out into the world and share their knowledge, providing free gardening workshops in community and school gardens to people like yourself, as well as senior and shelter gardens throughout Los Angeles. (Note: This free assistance is not heavy manual labor.) To submit a request for technical assistance, e-mail ydsavio@ucdavis.edu with the date, time, activity name, sponsoring group, location address and directions, assistance needed, and contact information. The website also provides helpful gardening articles, tips, and resources, as well as information on the Grow LA Garden Victory Initiative, Agriculture, and Environmental Horticulture programs. For a list of nearly 60 public community gardens in Los Angeles, see Appendix F on p. 312.

Smart Gardening Workshop
County of Los Angeles Department of Public Works
Environmental Programs Division
900 S. Fremont Ave., 3rd floor annex, Alhambra
(888) CLEAN LA
http://dpw.lacounty.gov/epd/sg/wk_scheds.cfm

Learn how to reduce yard waste, improve your lawn and garden, how to compost, and discover the benefits and biology of composting. All free for Los Angeles County residents. Workshops last about 1.5 hours. What will you learn in a compost workshop? All about worm composting and grass-cycling, as well as water-wise and fire-wise gardening. Are you taking an advanced workshop? Then you'll learn about landscape design, landscaping with native friendly plants, organic gardening, what good soil is, drought-tolerant plants, and then some. Check online for schedule. Workshops are held at multiple locations.

ART GALLERIES:
PICASSOS FOR PENNIES
OR LESS

"Good art is in the wallet of the beholder."

—KATHY LETTE

Spend an afternoon trolling through an art gallery, and you'll remember that the world is bigger than the dentist appointment you're running late for because your boss needed just one more thing before you left. At least, this is how I feel. Gazing at a piece of art, whether it engages me or I feel I understand it or not, gives me a sense of inner peace, reminding me that not everyone looks at the world through the same set of eyes, beauty is found in all things, and there is an entire experience to be had beyond the suburban carpool or Columbus Day Weekend sale at Macy's. Make a date, whether it's with your daughter, friend, wife, or potential mate. Take in the art, talk about the art, and appreciate the art, even when it doesn't move you. One hundred years from now, some of the art from those galleries will have lived on, and be the few remnants of our civilization to speak volumes about us to our future, so isn't it time you support it and check it out? Plus, it's free entertainment and there are a myriad of art galleries in Los Angeles from which to choose. So put down that remote and venture on down and in.

DIG **IT** DOWNTOWN

Cirrus Gallery
542 S. Alameda St. (near Palmetto St.), Los Angeles
(213) 680-3473
www.cirrusgallery.com
Hours: Tues through Sat 10 a.m. to 5 p.m.

Nestled near Little Tokyo and the Geffen, Cirrus is a fine arts press, publisher, and art gallery focused on the publication and exhibition of work by young California artists. Do you think they would appreciate the awesome clay pinch pot I made in the first grade? Painting, sculpture, drawing, and prints. Parking lot.

Crewest
110 Winston St. (at Werdin Place), Los Angeles
(213) 627-8272
www.crewest.com
Hours: Tues through Thurs noon to 7 p.m.; Fri through Sat noon to 8 p.m.; Sun noon to 6 p.m.

Urban art from underground artists—everything from mixed media to sculpture, watercolors, aerosol, airbrush, and photography. Exhibits rotate every month, so you can, you know, make this a regular thing. You can also shop supplies and art online. Park across the street.

Jancar Gallery

961 Chung King Rd., Los Angeles
(213) 625-2522
www.jancargallery.com
Hours: Wed through Sat noon to 5 p.m.

Tom Jancar and his partner, Richard Kuhlenschmidt, opened this art gallery in 1980. The work of a new contemporary artist is featured every 4 to 5 weeks. Paid parking lot at the end of the street.

Morono Kiang Gallery

213 W. 3rd St. (at S. Spring St. in the Bradbury Building), Los Angeles
(213) 628-8208
www.moronokiang.com
Hours: Tues through Sat noon to 6 p.m.

Over 3,000 square feet of exhibition space featuring cutting-edge contemporary art from around the globe. Strut through international art in rotating exhibits that change every 2 months. The Morono Kiang Gallery also hosts special events such as readings, screenings, and panel discussions. Parking lot across the street.

WOWED **IN** WEHO

Aboriginal Dreamtime Fine Art Gallery
9011 Melrose Ave. (at N. Almont Dr.), West Hollywood
(310) 278-4278
http://aboriginaldreamtimegallery.com
Hours: Tues through Fri 11 a.m. to 6 p.m.; Sat noon to 5 p.m.; Mon by
appointment.

This gallery is what it says it is, specializing in authentic Australian Aboriginal Fine Art. The "Dreamtime" in the name refers to the time when life on earth began, according to the Aboriginals. The gallery has a sister location in Sydney. G'day, mate!

ACME
6150 Wilshire Blvd. (near S. Fairfax Ave.), Los Angeles
(323) 857-5942
www.acmelosangeles.com
Hours: Tues through Sat 11 a.m. to 6 p.m.

Since 1994, ACME has exhibited paintings, prints, sculpture, video, and installations of Los Angeles artists. Exhibits change every 4 weeks. Street parking and validation lot parking.

Manny Silverman Gallery
619 N. Almont Dr. (south of Santa Monica Blvd.), West Hollywood
(310) 659-8256
www.mannysilvermangallery.com
Hours: Tues through Sat 10 a.m. to 5 p.m.

Manny Silverman started as an assistant at the Ernest Raboff Gallery in the 1960s before establishing a successful art framing business and then moving to where his heart was, in art dealing. In 1987 he opened the Manny Silverman Gallery, specializing in American art of the post-war period with a particular emphasis on abstract expressionism.

BOTTICELLLIS **IN** BEVERLY **HILLS**

Anderson Galleries
354 N. Bedford Dr. (near Wilshire Blvd.), Beverly Hills
(310) 858-1644
www.andersongalleries.com
Hours: Mon through Fri 10 a.m. to 6 p.m.

Dealers and agents of museum-quality 19th- and 20th-century paintings, drawings, and sculpture. Exhibits change every 2 months. Public lots nearby with 1 to 2 hours of free parking.

David W. Streets Fine Art, Appraisals, Contemporary Art & Photography
9407 S. Santa Monica Blvd. (at N. Canon Dr.), Beverly Hills
(310) 275-3464
www.davidstreetsbeverlyhills.com
Hours: Tues through Sat 11 a.m. to 5 p.m. or by appointment

An eclectic gallery of photography, sculpture, realist, and contemporary art. David W. Streets, a fine art and celebrity memorabilia advisor and appraiser, represents 35 different artists. Public lots with 2 hours of free parking at North Canon and North Beverly, both only half a block from the gallery.

Galerie Michael
224 N. Rodeo Dr. (at Dayton Way), Beverly Hills
(310) 273-3377
www.galeriemichael.com
Hours: Mon through Sat 10 a.m. to 7 p.m.; Sun noon to 6 p.m.

European paintings, drawings, and prints from the 17th century to the present, and featuring artists such as Henri de Toulouse-Latrec, Marc Chagall, Rembrandt van Rijn, Pablo Picasso, Pierre August Renoir, and more. Two hour free parking on Dayton Way. Amusez-vous bien!

Spencer John Helfen Fine Arts
9200 W. Olympic Blvd., Suite 200 (at S. Palm Dr.), Beverly Hills
(310) 273-8838
www.helfenfinearts.com
Hours: Tues through Sat noon to 6 p.m. or by appointment

All modern California art from the past 70-plus years, from surrealism to realism, magic realism, synchronism, art deco, cubism, and abstraction. The exhibits are often focused on work in California from the 1930s, featuring California Scene, California and American Regionalism, Social Realism, and WPA-inspired works. Parking adjacent to gallery.

VISUAL **IN** THE **VALLEY**

Left Coast Galleries

12324 Ventura Blvd. (at Laurel Grove Ave.), Studio City
(818) 760-7010
www.leftcoastgalleries.com
Hours: Tues through Sat 11 a.m. to 6 p.m.; Sun noon to 5 p.m. or by appointment

Left Coast Galleries showcases contemporary artists across the United States and the globe, with a concentration on classical and modern technique and 21st-century impressionism. Exhibits change every 3 to 4 weeks. Parking structure and street parking.

Nucleus Art Gallery
210 E. Main St., Alhambra
(626) 458-7477
www.gallerynucleus.com
Hours: Sun through Thurs noon to 8 p.m.; Fri and Sat 11 a.m. to 10 p.m.

Nucleus houses original contemporary, illustrated, graphic, commercial, and narrative art of both local and international artists. Nucleus also hosts free workshops as well as benefits, auctions, product signings, music events, and artist lectures, so they're sort of integrative. Cool. Exhibits cycle through every 4 weeks. Street parking and public parking behind the gallery.

SANTA MONICA & VENICE: PAINTINGS NEAR THE PCH

Art One Gallery
1331 3rd St. Promenade (between Arizona Ave. and Santa Monica Blvd.), Santa Monica
(310) 576-1000
www.art-one-gallery.com
Hours: Mon through Thurs 11 a.m. to 7 p.m.; Fri 11 a.m. to 8 p.m.; Sat 11 a.m. to 9 p.m.; Sun noon to 7 p.m.

P-p-p-pop art! A retail gallery that rotates its work weekly, Art One Gallery exhibits the work of Charles Fazzino, famous for his whimsical 3-D style of contemporary art scenes, as well as Steve Kaufman, Susan Rios, Michael Bryan, Linnea Pergola, Romero Britto, and more. Art One Gallery has an impressive collection of animation art as well. Parking structure located behind the gallery . . . it's the Promenade . . . don't expect the parking fairy to make herself known.

Gallery 319
319 Wilshire Blvd., Santa Monica
(310) 899-1499
www.gallery-319.com
Hours: Mon through Sat 11 a.m. to 6 p.m.

For your fine art and custom framing needs, Gallery 319 has a laid-back vibe and a large collection that rotates almost weekly. They showcase prints featuring sports and rock and roll icons, and celebrity artist prints, photos, portraits, and renditions, along with your standard California scenes and more. Two-hour free parking at 4th and Wilshire.

Gebert Gallery

1345 Abbot Kinney Blvd., Venice
(310) 450-9897
www.gebertgallery.com
Hours: Wed through Sun 11 a.m. to 7 p.m.

Gebert Gallery houses abstract contemporary art, painting, and sculpture. Exhibits change every 4 to 6 weeks. It looks like a man . . . screaming in pain . . . because . . . he accidentally stepped on a thumb tack! No? What do you think? Parking lot in back of gallery.

CANVASES **IN** OR **NEAR** THE **CANYONS**

Barnsdall Art Park

4800 Hollywood Blvd., Los Angeles
(323) 660-4254
www.barnsdallartpark.com

Barnsdall Art Park is the Swiss Army knife of attractions, offering a world-class art gallery, 299-seat theater available for rental, a Junior Arts Center to promote arts and education among youth, and Frank Lloyd Wright's Hollyhock House, all rolled into one. The Los Angeles Municipal Art Gallery showcases 10,000 square feet of paintings, sculpture, photography, architecture, design, video, sound, electronic, performance, and installation works of artists from Los Angeles and all of Southern California. The Hollyhock House, with its Mayan Revivalism large stones, introverted windows, courtyards, and ornate accompaniments, can be toured on the hour at 12:30, 1:30, 2:30, or 3:30 p.m. Wed through Sun. Cash only. $7 general admission, $3 for seniors, $2 for those 17 and under; however, if you are 17 and under and come with an adult, you get in free. See? It *is* cheaper to hang out with your parents.

Topanga Canyon Gallery
Pine Tree Circle
120 N. Topanga Canyon Blvd., Suite 109, Topanga
(310) 455-7909
www.topangacanyongallery.com
Hours: Tues through Sat 10 a.m. to 6 p.m.; Sun 11 a.m. to 5 p.m.

Open since the 1980s, Topanga Canyon Gallery currently features more than 40 well-known and emerging artists from the greater Los Angeles area, with over half from Topanga Canyon. Paintings, sculpture, ceramics, and more. Come with a full tank of gas—no gas stations in the canyon! They also have a presence downtown at the Brewery at 618D Moulton Ave.

MUSEUMS:
GET YOUR ART ON

"That which, perhaps, hears more nonsense than anything in the world, is a picture in a museum."

—EDMOND DE GONCOURT

Are you sitting down?

I'll wait.

Comfy?

Do you need a cushion?

Okay. (Drum roll, please.) Los Angeles has some of the best museums in the country. I know! Thankfully, it's absolutely true. From natural history to modern and contemporary art to science and more, Los Angeles has got everything under the sun. A lot of the museums are free admission every day, or at least one day a week or month, and the ones that do charge are fairly reasonable and well within the real or imagined limitations of your wallet. Whether you're living the Los Angeles Vida Loca and compiling your cultural bucket list to mix up those days spent surfing, hiking, and weighing your options of grapefruit diet versus watermelon diet with some art, or merely passing through town briefly in your exploration of the star-studded and sunshine-filled city, a museum visit is a must-do companion piece attraction in any itinerary.

ALWAYS **FREE**

California African American Museum

Exposition Park

600 State Dr., Los Angeles

(213) 744-7432

www.caamuseum.org

Hours: Closed Mon; open Tues through Sat 10 a.m. to 5 p.m.; Sun 11 a.m. to 5 p.m.

The Catch: Parking is $8. For parking, turn west into Exposition Park on 39th Street from Figueroa. To double your parking value and museum pleasure, see more than one museum in your visit to Exposition Park. Sort of like a happy hour deal at a bar, but not, because there's no actual food or alcohol involved.

The California African American Museum (CAAM) opened in 2003 and is committed to highlighting the African-American perspective and experience through Black history, art, and culture year-round. Check website for details on current exhibits and special events.

California Science Center
700 Exposition Park Dr., Los Angeles
(323) SCIENCE (724-3623)
www.californiasciencecenter.org
Hours: Open daily 10 a.m. to 5 p.m.

The Catch: The permanent exhibition galleries are free, but ticket prices apply to the IMAX theater as well as the High Wire Bicycle, Motion-Based Simulator, and Ecology Cliff Climb. IMAX is $8.25 for adults, $5 for children ages 4 to 12, $6 for children ages 13 to 17, students with valid photo ID, and seniors over the age of 60. Individuals who meet height and weight requirements can purchase the "Attraction Pack" to partake in each of these three experiences. Parking is $8 per car, $25 per oversize vehicle. Cash only. For parking, turn west into Exposition Park on 39th Street from Figueroa.

The California Science Center, the West Coast's largest hands-on science center, is dedicated to stimulating curiosity and inspiring science learning in adults, children, families, and school groups through hands-on events and special exhibits attractions including Air and Space and Ecosystems. Children under the age of 7 will love the Discovery Rooms in Creative World and World of Life. Best time to visit is weekend and weekday afternoons.

The Getty
The Getty Center of Los Angeles
1200 Getty Center Dr. (enter via main gate at N. Sepulveda Blvd.),
Los Angeles
(310) 440-7300
www.getty.edu
Hours: Closed Mon; open Tues through Fri, 10 a.m. to 5:30 p.m.; Sat 10 a.m. to 9 p.m.; Sun 10 a.m. to 5:30 p.m.

The Catch: Parking is $15 per car, but free after 5 p.m. and for evening public programming. Your alternative to avoiding the parking fee is to take the Metro Rapid Line 761, which stops at the main gate on Sepulveda Boulevard.

Take in a stunning view of Los Angeles surrounded by modern architecture and beautiful gardens, all the while immersing yourself in an impressive collection of Western art, including European paintings, drawings, manuscripts, sculpture, decorative arts, and European and American photographs.

The Getty Villa Malibu

17985 Pacific Coast Hwy., Pacific Palisades
(310) 440-7300
www.getty.edu
Hours: Open Wed through Mon 10 a.m. to 5 p.m.

The Catch: *Parking is $15 per car or motorcycle, free after 5 p.m. for evening public programming. You can only enter The Getty Villa Malibu from the northbound right-hand lane of the Pacific Coast Highway. Your alternative to avoiding the parking fee is to take the Metro Bus 534.*

Delight in Greek, Roman, and Etruscan antiquities arranged by theme including Gods and Goddesses, Dionysus and the Theater, and Stories of the Trojan War amidst architecture paying homage to the Romans and gardens paces from the Pacific Ocean.

Griffith Observatory

2800 E. Observatory Rd., Los Angeles
(213) 473-0800
www.griffithobservatory.org
Hours: Closed Mon and Tues; open Wed through Fri noon to 10 p.m.; Sat and Sun 10 a.m. to 10 p.m.

The stars (the actual physical ones in the sky) in Griffith Park and free admission align for a red-letter day in your horoscope when you select The Griffith Observatory. Have the heavens opened up and angels wielded their trumpets in a hearty chorus of "Hallelujah"? Limited free parking, and a small charge if you want to see shows in the Samuel Oschin Planetarium. Weekends are busy! Be ready for the uphill climb to the entrance.

Hollywood Bowl Museum

2301 N. Highland Ave., Los Angeles
(323) 850-2058
www.hollywoodbowl.com/visit/museum.cfm
Hours: Open all concert nights; Tues through Sun 10 a.m. to showtime in summer; Sun 4 p.m. to showtime in summer; Tues through Fri 10 a.m. to 5 p.m. in off-season; Sat by appointment.

Check out the history of iconic Hollywood Bowl amphitheater through photographs, computers, exhibits, and audio and video clips. Combine your visit to the museum with $12 cheap seats and a picnic, and you've got a great cheap and awesome evening excursion planned! Parking is free, unless you stick around for an evening concert.

MOCA Pacific Design Center

8687 Melrose Ave. (at Norwich Dr.), West Hollywood
(213) 626-6222
www.moca.org
Hours: Closed Mon; Tues through Fri 11 a.m. to 5 p.m.; Sat and Sun 11 a.m. to 6 p.m.

The Catch: *Metered street parking is your best bet. "High end" parking options include the Pacific Design Center Parking Garage on Melrose Avenue, just east of San Vicente Boulevard. Depending on time spent in the museum and the day of the week, parking in the garage will run you between approximately $4 and $13.50. However, this is the only one of the three MOCA buildings that is always free, so what's a little parking?*

The MOCA Pacific Design Center has rotating exhibits of architecture and design. It is located within the Pacific Design Center, which is the West Coast's leading resource for fine traditional and contemporary contract and residential furniture and design needs, and also houses a theatre, two Wolfgang Puck restaurants (not in most people's budget), and a conference center.

SOMETIMES **FREE**

Craft and Folk Art Museum

5814 Wilshire Blvd. (near S. Stanley Ave.), Los Angeles
(323) 937-4230
www.cafam.org
Hours: Closed Mon; Tues through Fri 11 a.m. to 5 p.m.; Sat and Sun noon to 6 p.m.
Admission: $7 for general admission; $5 for students and seniors; children under 10 are free. Also free the first Wed of every month.

The Craft Art and Folk Museum bridges the gap between local and global cultures, featuring a wide variety of art made in social and cultural contexts, from photojournalism to body art to ancient cave paintings. If you're still scratching your head over the exact definition of folk art, repeat after me: Ordinary people express themselves through the creative combination of utilitarian or indigenous objects that have meaning within their culture; the design has a special significance that tells us a great deal about the particular culture or society that art came from, which, in turn, tells us all a little bit about ourselves. Okay, so I sort of added that last part . . . but now you know! The Craft Art and Folk Museum also sponsors free programs and workshops for families. Free 2-hour street parking or paid lot parking.

The Geffen at The Museum of Contemporary Art, Los Angeles
Moca Grand Avenue
250 S. Grand Ave., Los Angeles
(213) 626-6222

The Geffen Contemporary at MOCA
152 N. Central Ave., Los Angeles
(213) 626-6222
www.moca.org
Hours: Closed Tues and Wed; Mon and Fri 11 a.m. to 5 p.m.; Thurs 11 a.m. to 8 p.m.; Sat 11 a.m. to 9 p.m.; and Sun 11 a.m. to 6 p.m.
Admission: $10 general admission, $5 for students with photo ID and seniors over 65, children 12 and under and jurors with photo ID free. Free every Thurs from 5 to 8 p.m., courtesy of Wells Fargo. They also sometimes offer discounts to those who arrive via public transportation, so be sure to ask when you arrive.

The Catch: Parking for MOCA Grand Avenue is at the Walt Disney Concert Hall garage. Enter from Lower Grand Avenue or 2nd Street. $9 flat rate with MOCA validation. $20 deposit upon entry, $11 refund post validation. Parking for The Geffen Contemporary at MOCA can be found at the Advanced Parking System lot on the corner of 1st Street and Central Avenue and will bleed you $6.50. Public Parking Lot 7 on Judge John Aiso Street is an $8 weekday flat rate and $7 after 4 p.m. and on weekends.

If you want to see only contemporary art, the MOCA is your destination, as it is devoted exclusively to the collection, presentation, and interpretation of work produced in all media since 1940. The museum opened its doors in 1979 and now has over 5,000 works and is still expanding. It is housed in separate buildings in different areas of Los Angeles, so read below to take your pick and decide which one you'll tackle first. Balance your artistic and practical (aka parking) desires in making your decision.

MOCA Grand Avenue houses the administrative offices of the museum, as well as a cafe, underground galleries, and the flagship MOCA store. If you're short on time, aim for this one.

Once a police car warehouse in Little Tokyo, The Geffen Contemporary at MOCA has been open since 1983 and offers 40,000 square feet of exhibition space, as well as a branch of the MOCA Store. The biggest of the MOCA buildings with the most diverse forms of media are presented here.

Hammer Museum
10899 Wilshire Blvd., Los Angeles
(310) 443-7000
http://hammer.ucla.edu
Hours: Tues, Wed, and Fri 11 a.m. to 7 p.m.; Thurs 11 a.m. to 9 p.m.; Sun 11 a.m. to 5 p.m.
Admission: $7 adults; $5 seniors and UCLA alumni with ID; free to museum members, students with ID, faculty, staff, military personnel, and visitors under 17 accompanied by an adult; free on Thurs.

The Hammer Museum exhibits showcase contemporary and historical work in all media of the visual arts on UCLA's campus. As a cultural center, the Hammer Museum also has a full program of rich lectures, screenings, music performances, readings, and lunchtime art talks, wherein they host an intellectual forum to explore topical cultural, political, and social issues.

The Huntington
1151 Oxford Rd., San Marino
(626) 405-2100
www.huntington.org
Hours: Mon, Wed, Thurs, Fri noon to 4:30 p.m.; Sat and Sun 10:30 a.m. to 4:30 p.m.; closed Tues
Admission: $15 for adults ($20 on weekends); $12 for seniors ($15 on weekends); students with ID and youth $6; free to children under 5; free to all on the first Thurs of every month with advance tickets. Hours on free day are the same as weekend hours.

The Huntington is part library, part art collection, and part botanical garden. You'll find it all here and with free parking. The Huntington Art Gallery has one of the most comprehensive collections of 18th- and 19th-century British and French art. The 120-acre garden includes a Desert Garden, Japanese Garden, Rose Garden, and Chinese Garden. The library has all those rare books and manuscripts you need for your research paper on British and American history and literature.

Los Angeles County Museum of Art (LACMA)

5905 Wilshire Blvd., Los Angeles

(323) 857-6000

www.lacma.org

Hours: Mon, Tues, and Thurs noon to 8 p.m.; Fri noon to 9 p.m; Sat and Sun 11 a.m. to 8 p.m.; closed Wed

Admission: $15 for adults; $10 for seniors over 62 and students over 18 with photo ID; children under 17 free; free the second Tues of every month, members and Los Angeles County permanent residents with proof of residency after 5 p.m. Target also sponsors several "free Mondays." Check website for details. $10 parking in the Pritzker Garage.

The Los Angeles County Museum of Art (LACMA) is gigantic, proudly boasting more than 100,000 objects in its collection, from ancient times to the present, from the geographic world to the entire history of art. Its top strengths include Latin art, Islamic art, and Asian art. LACMA is the largest museum in the western United States. Housed in 7 buildings on 20 acres in the heart of Los Angeles, halfway between the ocean and downtown, the campus is currently undergoing a 10-year expansion project called Transformation. LACMA is to The Met as The Louvre is to The Hermitage. What does this mean? It means you shouldn't visit or admit you live in Los Angeles without checking it out. I mean, really. It's embarrassing. Go already!

Museum of the American West—The Autry

4700 Western Heritage Way, Los Angeles

(323) 667-2000

www.theautry.org

Hours: Open Tues through Fri 10 a.m. to 4 p.m.; Sat and Sun 11 a.m. to 5 p.m.

Admission: $9 for adults; $5 for students with photo ID and seniors over 60; $3 for children ages 3 to 12; free to Autry Members and on the second Tues of every month.

Gene Autry spent a large part of his life as a popular singing cowboy in radio, movies, and television, and is oft remembered crooning Christmas classics that waft over the airwaves every December. The Autry National Center was formed in 2003 by the merger of the Autry Museum of Western Heritage with the Southwest Museum of American Indian and the Women of the West Museum. Voices of the Native American experience, the history of the West, and the myths and conflicts surrounding it, as well as the "imagined" West as depicted in movies, books, and more, converge into one dynamic intercultural shebang. Check the website for details on special events, which include $7 Sizzling Summer Nights on Thursday in July and August, where you can mambo, charanga, and salsa your hips into sundown with live music, tacos and margaritas, and complimentary (yes, that's free!) dance lessons. Kids dance separately on their own dance floor, so your style won't be toddler-inhibited. There is also a western music jam held on the third Sunday of each month that is free with admission.

Natural History Museum of Los Angeles
900 Exposition Blvd., Los Angeles
(213) 763-DINO
www.nhm.org
Hours: Mon through Sun 9:30 a.m. to 5 p.m.
Admission: $9 for adults; $6.50 for seniors (62+), students 18 and over with ID, and children ages 13 to 17; $2 for children ages 5 to 12; children 4 and younger are free; free to USC students, except on game days, and free to all on the first Tues of each month.

Step back in time to trace and to learn about the Earth's biodiversity and the 35 million specimens dating back 4.5 billion years (older than the real or falsified combined ages of all Hollywood actors) that The Natural History Museum of Los Angeles presents.

Orange County Museum of Art
850 San Clementine Dr., Newport Beach
(949) 759-1122
www.ocma.net
Hours: Closed Mon and Tues; open Wed through Sun 11 a.m. to 5 p.m.; Thurs 11 a.m. to 8 p.m.
Admission: $12 for adults; $10 for seniors 65 and older and students with ID; free to members, children under 12, and on the second Sun of the month.

Modern and contemporary, dahling. They've had Picasso and Pollock before, so don't turn your nose up just because it's Orange County. The Orange County Museum of Art is also host to the California Biennial.

Pacific Asia Museum
46 N. Los Robles Ave. (at E. Union St.), Pasadena
(626) 449-2742
www.pacificasiamuseum.org
Hours: Open Wed through Sun 10 a.m. to 6 p.m.

Admission: $9 general admission; $7 students and seniors; free to children ages 11 and under, members, and visitors on the fourth Fri of the month.

One of four US institutions dedicated to the arts and culture of Asia and the Pacific Islands, the Pacific Asia Museum has more than 15,000 objects spanning more than 4,000 years and the region extending from Persia to the Pacific Islands. The museum held the first North American exhibition of contemporary Chinese Art after the Revolution, as well as the first exhibition of Aboriginal art in the United States.

Page Museum at La Brea Tar Pits

5801 Wilshire Blvd. (at S. Curson Ave.), Los Angeles
(323) 934-PAGE (7243)
www.tarpits.org
Hours: Open daily 9:30 a.m. to 5 p.m.
Admission: $7 for adults, $4.50 for children ages 13 to 17, students with photo ID, and seniors over 62; $2 for children ages 5 to 12; free to members and children under 5. Free admission on the first Tues of every month.

The Catch: Parking costs $1.50 every 20 minutes up to a maximum of $9, or $7 with museum validation or on weekends and holidays. Parking lot is located directly behind the museum at the corner of Curson Avenue and 6th Street. Don't try to get around the parking charge by parking on Wilshire Boulevard on weekdays prior to the museum's morning opening or between 4 and 7 p.m., or you'll get towed.

Located in the heart of Los Angeles, The Page Museum at the Rancho La Brea Tar Pits is unique—there is nothing like it in the world. Fossils rule here. Learn all about what Los Angeles was like during the last Ice Age (no, much further back than Joan Rivers' first face-lift) between 10,000 and 40,000 years ago when mammoths and saber-toothed cats prowled the Los Angeles Basin. Gawk at Ice Age plants and animals from around the world, watch excavators clean and repair bones through the windows of the working laboratory, and check out the life-size replicas of extinct mammals in Hancock Park just outside the museum.

ALWAYS A FEW BUCKS

All are always a few bucks, though once in a while the kiddies do get free admission.

Los Angeles Maritime Museum

Berth 84, foot of 6th St., San Pedro
(310) 548-7618
www.lamaritimemuseum.org
Hours: Closed Mon; open Tues through Sun 10 a.m. to 5 p.m.
Admission: $3 for adults; $1 youth and senior citizens; free for children 7 and under.

Everything related to the sea. That's what maritime means! Examples of past exhibits include "Caught, Canned, and Eaten," "20,000 Jobs Under the Sea," "Wooden Boats, Copper Quotes: Duncan Gleason's Etchings" and "Hollywood to Honolulu: The Los Angeles Steamship Company."

Petersen Automotive Museum

6060 Wilshire Blvd., Los Angeles
(323) 964-6331
www.petersen.org
Hours: Closed Mon; open Tues through Sun 10 a.m. to 6 p.m.
Admission: $10 for adults; $5 for students and seniors over 65 with photo ID; $3 for children ages 5 to 12; free to members and children under 5. Save $1 on admission by printing your e-ticket from home. Parking will cost you approximately $2 to $8, depending on the length of your visit.

Open to the public since 1994, the Petersen Automotive Museum is dedicated to the history of the automobile and features more than 150 rare and classic cars, trucks, and motorcycles. A permanent exhibit traces the history of the automobile. Great for kids!

Watts Towers and Art Center

1761–1765 E. 107th St., Los Angeles
(213) 847-4646
www.wattstowers.us
Hours: Wed through Sat 10 a.m. to 4 p.m.; Sun noon to 4 p.m.
Admission: $7 general; $3 for seniors and young adults ages 13 to 17; children under 12 are free.

Simon Rodia, born Sabato Rodia in Italy in 1879, immigrated to the United States in the shadow of his brother and found work in rock quarries, logging, and railroad camps as a construction worker. In 1921 he purchased the lot at 1761–1765 107th St. and spent 34 years building his towers without machinery, scaffolding, bolts, rivets, welds, or drawing board designs, but instead used simple tools like pipe fitter pliers, a window-washer's belt and buckle, adorning the towers with broken glass, pottery, and seashells. The tallest tower is just shy of 100 feet. Stand in awe of one man's vision. Watts Towers is also the site of the annual Simon Rodia Watts Towers Jazz Festival and the Watts Towers Day of the Drum Festival.

MULTICULTURAL & SEASONAL CELEBRATIONS: DIVERSITY ON A DIME

*"We all should know that diversity makes for
a rich tapestry, and we must understand that
all the threads of the tapestry are equal in value
no matter what their color."*

—MAYA ANGELOU

Diversity is what makes the world and this country great. Thankfully, Los Angeles itself is a melting pot representative of what America has evolved to be. Different ethnicities hold annual celebrations in the form of fairs, festivals, or parades to celebrate their individual and unique heritage. Don't miss out. There's too much fun to be had in exploring the world and its people beyond ourselves.

FEBRUARY

The Golden Dragon Parade and Festival
Along North Broadway in Chinatown, Los Angeles
(213) 617-0396 (Chinese Chamber of Commerce)
www.lagoldendragonparade.com

Every February, to celebrate the ringing in of the Chinese (Lunar) New Year, firecrackers, a festival spirit, and a spectacular parade, complete with nearly two dozen floats and marching bands, float jubilantly along North Broadway in Chinatown. It's a parade, so it's free. Yay! Some 110,000 people attend the over-112-year tradition. Don't you want to be one of them?

MARCH

LA County Irish Fair and Musical Festival
The Fairplex in Pomona
1101 W. McKinley Ave., Pomona
www.la-irishfair.com

If you want to kick off your St. Patrick's celebration earlier in March, get in on the action of the LA County Irish Fair and Musical Festival in Pomona, so you get your Irish fix of keg tossing, dance, music, and, you know, all that Irish-y stuff. Prices are the same at The Great American Irish Fair & Music Festival, so you might say they're twins.

APRIL

Russian Style Festival
West Hollywood Park
647 N. San Vicente Blvd., West Hollywood
www.russianstyle.us

Did you know nearly 20 percent of West Hollywood residents speak Russian? Otlichno! ("Excellent!" in Russian.) Enjoy Russian food, entertainment, crafts, and jewelry at the Russian Style Festival every April. Co-presented by the City of West Hollywood and the Russian Advisory Board. Free.

MAY

Fiesta Broadway
Broadway, from 1st St. to Olympic, downtown Los Angeles
(310) 914-0015 (office of All Access Entertainment)
www.fiestabroadway.la

Fiesta Broadway is the largest Cinco de Mayo celebration in the entire world. (Disclaimer: The celebration itself takes place on a weekend day very close to the 5th of May, which is not likely to be on the 5th itself. How many fingers am I holding up?) Plenty of food, entertainment, games, and good old-fashioned fun can be had as half a million people rock out on 24 city blocks in Downtown Los Angeles. Free and open to the public.

JUNE

Great American Irish Fair & Music Festival
Irvine Meadows next to the Verizon Wireless Amphitheatre
8800 Irvine Center Dr., Irvine
www.irishfair.org

Traditional harp, fiddle, bag pipes, Gaelic singers, music, poetry, folk dancing, sword fights, and arts and crafts, including Celtic jewelry, are part of this annual 2-day 40-year-old fair held in June every year. This website also promotes events for . . . you guessed it, St. Patrick's Day! At the fair, you'll be mesmerized by the Step Dancing Championship and Sheep Herding Demonstration, and then maybe your office job won't seem so bad. $18 for adults ($15 if you buy in advance), $15 for seniors and students. Children 12 and under are free, and you also get a discount if you love it so much you buy the full 2-day pass to make the most out of your weekend of everything Irish. Go early, stay late, it's worth it. Be one of the 30,000 to shout at the top of your lungs, "Éirinn go Brách!" That's Gaelic for "Ireland forever!"

Los Angeles Pride
San Vicente Boulevard between Santa Monica Boulevard and Melrose Avenue, West Hollywood
(323) 969-8302
www.lapride.org

A celebration of the historical Stonewall Rebellion that took place at the Stonewall Inn on Christopher Street in Greenwich Village, New York City, in June of 1969, LA Pride features musical stars (past headliners have included Olivia Newton John and Joss Stone), food, drink, and a party atmosphere in the heart of West Hollywood. $20 for the day or $15 in advance online.

AUGUST

Nisei Week Japanese Festival
237 S. San Pedro St. (in Little Tokyo), Los Angeles
(213) 687-7193
www.niseiweek.org

Konnichiwa! That's "Hello!" in Japanese. The Nisei Week Japanese Festival was first held in 1934, in an effort to bolster business in Little Tokyo during the dark times of the Great Depression. Interrupted only by World War II, it also became a tool with which "to expose the non-Japanese audience out there to the Nisei's message that the successors to the Issei were a generation of Americans." A "Nisei" is a person born in the United States whose parents emigrated from Japan; an "Issei" is a Japanese immigrant, in this case a Japanese immigrant in the United States. Tea ceremonies, art galleries, film, Japanese floral arrangements, martial arts, fashion shows, talent programs, and ondo (Japanese folk) dancing, are just some of the many rich cultural sights to take in, beyond your standard carnival rides, parade, and food. Some of my favorite Japanese food includes takoyaki (octopus ball) and okonomiyaki (pancake). Hmmm. My mouth is watering now. Seventy-plus years old and counting, the festival is held every August. Free!

LABOR **DAY** WEEKEND

Long Beach Greek Festival by the Sea
Assumption Greek Orthodox Church
5761 E. Colorado St., Long Beach
(562) 494-8929
www.lbgreekfest.org

The festival is held over Labor Day weekend each year and raises money for the church. Enjoy the entertainment and choose from traditional Greek fare like gyros, moussaka, and souvlaki. (Don't eat a gyro if you're on a date. Too messy. Tried this one before with little success, so if this festival is one of your first dates, you can learn from my mistake.) There are a number of other Greek festivals held throughout the year in Los Angeles.

SEPTEMBER

Annual Festival of Philippine Arts and Culture
807 Paseo Del Mar (Point Fermin Park), San Pedro
(213) 380-3722
http://filamarts.org

Delving deeper into its third decade of this annual festival, the traditions of Filipino art and culture are celebrated through music, dance, spoken word, comedy, painting, book readings, kite-making, authentic costumes, and martial arts demonstrations and workshops for one weekend in early September. $7 to enter the festival. Children under 5 and parking are free. On your way home, take the time to explore San Pedro's Sunken City on the 6 acres adjacent to Point Fermin Park.

Brazilian Street Carnival
Long Beach Promenade
205 The North Promenade, Long Beach
(562) 508-4504
http://2010.carnaval.org

Held in September every ear, this event is a Brazilian Independence Day Celebration and carnaval. Featured entertainment includes Brazilian bands and music, including the samba, as well as food and culture booths. Go early and make a day of it; general admission is $20 and senior citizens gain entry with $15. Children under 12 are free.

SEPTEMBER & OCTOBER

Los Angeles Korean Festival Foundation
Seoul International Park
3250 San Marino St., Los Angeles
(213) 487-9696
www.lakoreanfestival.com

For nearly 40 years, at the end of every September/very beginning of October in Seoul International Park, the Los Angeles Korean Festival shares its rich Korean culture and traditions with the Los Angeles community in an effort to promote racial harmony, propel the vibrant culture forward to future generations, and celebrate the Harvest Moon, also known as "Hangawe," or Korean Thanksgiving. Great food, music, dance, clown shows, singing, youth talent shows, the Miss High-Teen Korea Contest, tae kwon do demonstrations, and more. Plenty of the attractions can be enjoyed free of charge.

Oktoberfest!

833 W. Torrance Blvd., Torrance
(310) 327-4384
www.alpinevillagecenter.com

Down your German beer under the big tent any Fri, Sat, or Sun in Sept and Oct while you fill your belly with German grub and listen to authentic oom pah pah bands direct from Germany. Do all this, and be only 10 miles from the nearest beach in Southern California. Admission is $10. Runs 6 p.m. to 1 a.m. Fri and Sat; Sun is more of a family-oriented day and runs 1 to 6 p.m. Check website for other information on salsa and open mic nights held weekly throughout the year.

WorldFest—LA's Largest Earth Day Festival

Woodley Park (at the northern end)
6350 Woodley Ave., Lake Balboa
www.worldfestevents.com

WorldFest hosts this event, which covenes environmental, humanitarian, and animal welfare nonprofits along with great music, speakers, and fun for the kids on this 1-day celebration. Bring your old printer and ink cartridges to recycle and attend a lecture on sustainable living. Adults are $7, seniors $5, children under 12 free, and parking is $5. Or you could skip the parking charge and arrive by bike, which would be good for the environment, your body, and your budget. Aha!

ZOOS, INSECTS &
OTHER WILDLIFE:
SCIENCE CLASS
THE WAY NATURE INTENDED

"If nature were not beautiful, it would not be worth knowing, and if nature were not worth knowing, life would not be worth living."

—HENRI POINCARE

I love to look at the animals and remember, thankfully, that we're not the only ones sharing planet Earth. Colossal mammoths, saber-toothed cats, and giant ground sloths were just some of the animals that roamed prehistoric Los Angeles some 25,000 years ago. Their Ice Age fossils may be on view at the Page Museum La Brea Tar Pits, but the only living and breathing animals you're going to see will be at the Los Angeles Zoo and its various aquariums and other natural wildlife settings. Young or old, nature has no age limit on who can enjoy it, so why don't you try this phrase on for size: "I'm going to the zoo today!"

ALWAYS **FREE**

Ballona Wetlands
Start at southwest corner of Lincoln and W. Jefferson Boulevard
Playa del Rey to Venice
(310) 306-5994
www.ballona.org

You can't enter the fenced-in preserve except twice a month on a docent tour. Call the number above to get details on upcoming tours. You can, however, for free and at any point in time, enjoy a long walk along the perimeter of Los Angeles County's only remaining wetlands in order to catch a glimpse of a disappearing coastal ecosystem. Read the signs as you go, and you'll learn how the wetlands were a rich ecosystem once fed by the Los Angeles River, Centinela Creek, and Ballona Creek. You'll see cattails, blue heron, western grebes, red-winged blackbirds, and catch a glimpse of about 175 other types of birds darting in between the cottonwood and sycamores. You'll catch views of the Pacific Ocean all the while, so you can't say your free stroll isn't easy on the eyes.

Bolsa Chica Conservancy
3842 Warner Ave. (PCH at Seapoint Ave.), Huntington Beach
(714) 846-1114
http://bolsachica.org
Hours: Open daily from sunrise to sunset. No dogs, bikes, or horses.

See this beautiful 300-acre coastal sanctuary for wildlife and migratory birds free of charge. Cross over the tidal inlet via the wooden bridge, and you just may feel like the Shoshonean Native American Indians who lived on the bluffs overlooking these wetlands some 8,000 years ago. Be sure to make time in your visit to do the 1.5-mile trail loop and play a game of "I spy." Revel in the sights, part of Southern California's only 13,000 acres of remaining wetlands. RV camping at Bolsa Chica State Beach as well as biking, jogging, and surf fishing.

El Dorado Nature Center
7550 E. Spring St., Long Beach
(562) 570-1745
www.longbeach.gov/naturecenter
Hours: Trails, Tues through Sun 8 a.m. to 5 p.m.; museum, Tues through Fri 10 a.m. to 4 p.m.; Sat and Sun 8:30 a.m. to 4 p.m.

The Catch: Admission to the Nature Center is free, but they'll charge you $5 for your vehicle during the week, $7 on the weekends, and $8 on holidays. Bike entry is free.

The El Dorado Nature Center encompasses nearly 100 acres of a sanctuary for animals and plants, including 2 miles of dirt trails and a 0.25-mile paved trail winding around two lakes, a stream, and forested area. Check website for special events and volunteer opportunities.

Ferndell Nature Museum / Western Canyon
5375 Red Oak Dr., Los Angeles
(323) 666-5046
www.laparks.org/dos/parks/griffithpk/ferndell.htm
Hours: 6 a.m. to 10 p.m. daily.

Spot more than 50 fern species beneath the sycamore trees on this twisty trail located at the Western Canyon entrance of Griffith Park. Gorgeous. And free. Thus, even more gorgeous.

Shipley Nature Center
17851 Goldenwest St. (south of Slater Ave.), Huntington Beach
(714) 842-4772
www.shipleynature.org
Hours: Mon through Sat 9 a.m. to 1 p.m.; closed on Sun and all major holidays.

Explore 4,000 feet of trails in an 18-acre fenced-in area and wile away the hours through several habitats, including oak woodlands, Torrey pines, meadows, and Blackbird Pond, a natural freshwater wetland with mature willows and sycamores.

SOMETIMES **FREE**

Aquarium of the Pacific
100 Aquarium Way, Long Beach
(562) 590-3100
www.aquariumofpacific.org
Hours: 9 a.m. to 6 p.m. every day of the year except Christmas and the Grand Prix of Long Beach in Apr of every year.

With more than 500 species that fill 19 major habitats and 32 focus exhibits that take visitors through the Pacific Ocean's three regions of Southern California/Baja, the Tropical Pacific, and the Northern Pacific, both adults and kids get an amazing experience. Adult tickets are $24.95, children ages 3 to 11 are $12.95, and seniors 62 and over, $21.95. If you purchase your tickets online, you save $5 on the adult entry fee. The Aquarium offers discount AAA and military admissions, as well as free Seniors Day, Nonprofit Free Days, and Veteran's Day free admission to military personnel. Check website for details. Purchase an Aquarium/Zoo combination ticket for great savings, or add on a Behind-the-Scenes Tour for ages 7 and up, a Sea Life Cruise, Harbor Tour, or ride on the Queen Mary. Parking costs $8 and up.

The Insect Zoo at The Natural History Museum
900 Exposition Blvd. (between Vermont Ave. and Figueroa St.), Los Angeles
(213) 763-DINO (3466)
www.nhm.org
Hours: Mon through Sun, 9:30 a.m. to 5 p.m.

Did you know that, in general, the nearly $250 million of chemicals we spend each year to control cockroaches are far more dangerous than cockroaches themselves? Learn all you ever wanted to know and then some about the things we like to call "bugs," of which there are some 1.5 million species and millions more that have yet to be categorized. Are you feeling creepy, crawly, and itchy yet? $9 for adults, $6.50 for seniors, students with ID and children ages 13 to 17, and $2 for children ages 5 to 12. Children 4 and younger are free, as well as USC students, except on game days, and free to all on the first Tues of each month. Great for kids!

ALWAYS A FEW BUCKS

Cabrillo Marine Aquarium
3720 Stephen M. White Dr., San Pedro
(310) 548-7562
www.cabrillomarineaquarium.org
Hours: Tues through Fri noon to 5 p.m.; Sat and Sun 10 a.m. to 5 p.m.;
closed Mon, Veteran's Day, Thanksgiving, and Christmas.

Juxtaposed to Cabrillo Beach Coastal Park and the Port of Los Angeles, the Cabrillo Marine Aquarium displays the largest collection of Southern California marine life in the world. Suggested donation of $5 for adults and $1 for kids and seniors. Pair it with a walk in the park next door and view the tide pools, beaches, and a salt marsh. Low tides are the best times to explore tide pools! Parking will cost you $1 per hour. $20 to whale-watch Dec through Mar.

Heal the Bay: Santa Monica Pier Aquarium
1600 Ocean Front Walk (on the Pacific Ocean), Santa Monica
(310) 393-6149
www.healthebay.org
Hours: Tues through Fri 2 to 6 p.m. in summer and 2 to 5 p.m. in winter; weekends 12:30 to 6 p.m. in summer and 12:30 to 5 p.m. in winter; closed for major holidays.

You'll see purple sea urchins, hermit crabs, sea stars, abalone, tube worms, and more at this 4,500-square-foot interactive marine center, which is home to more than 100 species of marine animals and plants all found in the Santa Monica Bay. Admission is free to kids 12 and under; suggested donation of

$5 per person, with a minimum of $3 to gain entry. Groups of 10 or more, $2 per person. Great for the kids!

Los Angeles Zoo & Botanical Gardens
5333 Zoo Dr. (Griffith Park at the intersection of the 5 and Ventura 134),
Los Angeles
(323) 644-4200
www.lazoo.org
Hours: 10 a.m. to 5 p.m. every day of the year except Christmas. The zoo starts putting animals in for the night around 4 p.m. so get there early to enjoy a full day. Ticket sales end 1 hour prior to closing.

Whether its koalas, chimpanzees, orangutans, Komodo dragons, pigs, Sumatran tigers, snow leopard, birds, gorillas, kangaroos, wallabies, or reptiles, the 133 acres of the Los Angeles Zoo has something for you among its 250 species, 29 of which are endangered. The Rainforest of the Americas exhibit will open in 2012. Children under 2 and parking are free, seniors 62 and over just $11, and adults 13 and over only $14. $3 off your admission if you arrive by the Metro 96 bus. If you find yourself humming "Yaba-daba-daba-doo! All the monkeys in the zoo . . . know that I love you!" a bit more zealously than natural, then perhaps you may want to check out their volunteer program.

APPENDIX A:

THE SABAN FREE CLINIC LOCATIONS

Appointments can be made by dialing (323) 653-1990.

Hollywood
Hollywood Wilshire Health Center
5205 Melrose Ave., Los Angeles, CA 90038
Hours: Mon through Fri 8:30 a.m. to 5 p.m. for medical

School Based Health Center at Hollywood High School
1521 N. Highland Ave., Los Angeles, CA 90028
Hours: Mon through Thurs 9 a.m. to 1 p.m. for medical; Tues and Wed 9 a.m.
to 3 p.m. for behavioral health services

The S. Mark Taper Foundation Health Center
6043 Hollywood Blvd., Los Angeles, CA 90028; (323) 462-4158
Hours: Mon, Wed, Fri 8:30 a.m. to 5 p.m., Tues and Thurs 8:30 a.m. to 7 p.m.
for medical; Tues, Thurs, Fri 8:30 a.m. to 11:45 a.m. for showers

The Wallis Annenberg Children and Family Health Center
5205 Melrose Ave., 2nd floor, Los Angeles, CA 90038
Hours: Mon through Thurs 2 to 9 p.m., Sat 8 a.m. to noon for medical; Mon
through Thurs 2 to 9 p.m., Sat 8 a.m. to 5 p.m. for dental

West Hollywood
Beverly Health Center, Seniel Ostrow Building
8405 Beverly Blvd., Los Angeles, CA 90048; (323) 653-8622
Hours: Mon through Thurs 8 a.m. to 8 p.m. and Fri noon to 4:30 p.m. for
medical; Mon, Tues, Thurs 8 a.m. to 8:30 p.m., Wed noon to 8:30 p.m. and
Fri 8 a.m. to 4:30 p.m. for dental; Mon through Thurs 8 a.m. to 3 p.m., Fri
10 a.m. to 3 p.m. for showers

PUBLIC TENNIS COURTS

Alhambra
Alhambra Park, 500 N. Palm Ave.; 5 courts
Story Park, 210 N. Chapel Ave.; 2 courts

Arcadia
Camino Grove Park, 1420 S. 6th Ave.; 3 courts, lighted
Live Oak Park, Glickman Avenue and Bogue Street; 7 courts, lighted
Newcastle Park, 101 W. Colorado Blvd.; 2 courts
Orange Grove Park, N. Baldwin and W. Orange Grove Avenues; 5 courts

Burbank
Brace Canyon Park, 2901 Haven Way; 4 courts, lighted
Burbank High School, 902 N. 3rd St.; 6 courts, lighted
John Burroughs High School, W. Verdugo Avenue and N. Parish Place; 8 courts, lighted
Mountain View Park, 751 S. Griffith Park Dr.; 2 courts
Verdugo Park, 3281 W. Verdugo Ave.; 2 courts

Canoga Park
Lanark Rec Center, 21816 Lanark St.; 4 courts, lighted
Chatsworth
Chatsworth High School, 10027 Lurline Ave.; 4 courts
Chatsworth Park South, 22360 Devonshire St.; 2 courts, lighted

Covina
West Covina High School, 1609 E. Cameron Ave.; 11 courts
Culver City
Fox Hills Park, 5809 Green Valley Circle; 3 courts
Veterans Park, 4117 Overland Ave.; 2 courts

El Segundo
El Segundo Rec Park, 401 Sheldon St.; 7 courts
Encino Park, 16953 Ventura Blvd.; 2 courts, lighted

Gardena
Arthur Johnson Park, 1201 W. 170th St.; 4 courts, lighted

Glendale
Glorietta Park, 2801 N. Verdugo Rd.; 4 courts
Hoover Senior High School, 651 Glenwood Rd.; 4 courts, lighted
Montrose Rec Center, 3529 Clifton Place; 2 courts
Oakmont View Park, 2940 Oakmont View Dr.; 2 courts
Scholl Canyon Tennis Center, 3800 E. Glenoaks Blvd.; 10 courts

Granada Hills
Granada Hills Recreation Center, 16730 Chatsworth St.; 4 courts, lighted

Hawthorne
Del Aire Park, 12601 Isis Ave.; 4 courts, lighted
Memorial Park, 12632 Prairie Ave.; 3 courts, lighted

Hermosa Beach
Pier Avenue Courts, 710 Pier Ave.; 6 courts, lighted

La Habra
La Habra Tennis Center, 351 S. Euclid St.; 12 courts

Lake View Terrace
Lake View Terrace Rec Center, 11075 Foothill Blvd.; 2 courts, lighted

Long Beach
El Dorado Tennis Center, 2800 N. Studebaker Rd.; 15 courts, lighted

Los Angeles
Barrington Rec Center, 333 S. Barrington Ave.; 4 courts, lighted
California State University, Circle Drive and Campus Road; 9 courts
Eagle Rock Rec Center, 1100 Eagle Vista Dr.; 3 courts
Echo Park, 1632 Bellevue Ave.; 6 courts, lighted
Jill Gilliam Rec Center, 3970 S. La Brea Ave.; 4 courts, lighted
Lincoln Park, 3900 Selig Place; 4 courts
LMU, Ignatius Circle and Loyola Boulevard; 6 courts

Mar Vista Rec Center, 11430 Woodbine St.; 6 courts, lighted
Panorama Park, 8600 Hazeltine Ave.; 4 courts
Penmar Rec Center, 1341 Lake St.; 6 courts, lighted
Playa Vista Courts, 13290 Bluff Creek Dr.; 2 courts
Plummer Park, 1200 N. Vista St.; 4 courts, lighted
Queen Anne Rec Center, 1240 West Blvd.; 4 courts, lighted
Rancho Cienega Rec Center, 5001 Rodeo Rd.; 12 courts, lighted
Shatto Rec Center, 3191 W. 4th St.; 4 courts, lighted
Stoner Park, 1835 Stoner Ave.; 6 courts, lighted
University of Southern California, 1026 W. 34th St.; 12 courts

Malibu
Pepperdine University, 24437 Pacific Coast Hwy.; 10 courts, lighted

Marina Del Rey
Glen Alla Park, 4601 Alla Rd.; 2 courts

Monterey Park
Elder Park, 1950 Wilcox Ave.; 4 courts
Highlands Park, 200 Casuda Canyon Dr.; 2 courts

North Hollywood
North Hollywood High School, 5231 Colifax Ave.; 5 courts
North Hollywood Rec Center, 5301 Tujunga Ave.; 5 courts, lighted

Northridge
Dearborn Park, 17141 Nordhoff St.; 2 courts, lighted
Northridge Rec Center, 18300 Lemarsh St.; 4 courts, lighted

Pacoima
Bradford Park, 13310 Branford St.; 2 courts, lighted
Richie Valens Park, 10731 Laurel Canyon Blvd.; 2 courts, lighted

Pasadena
Brookside Park, 360 N. Arroyo Blvd.; 5 courts, lighted
Eaton Blanche Park, 3100 E. Del Mar Blvd.; 2 courts, lighted
Grant Park, 232 S. Michigan Ave.; 2 courts, lighted

Pasadena Muir High School, 1905 Lincoln Ave.; 10 courts
South Pasadena High School, 1401 Fremont Ave.; 6 courts
Washington Park, 700 E. Washington Blvd.; 2 courts, lighted

Pomona
Ganesha High School, 1151 Fairplex Dr.; 12 courts
Pomona College, 333 N. College Way; 10 courts

Redondo Beach
Alta Vista Park, 801 Camino Real; 8 courts, lighted
Anderson Park, 2229 Ernest Ave.; 2 courts

Reseda
Reseda High School, 18230 Kittridge St.; 4 courts
Reseda Rec Center, 18411 Victory Blvd; 4 courts, lighted

Rowland
Rowland Heights Park, 1570 Banida Ave.; 2 courts, lighted
Rowland High School, 2000 Otterbein Ave.; 6 courts

San Dimas
San Dimas High School, 800 W. Covina Blvd.; 8 courts, lighted

San Fernando
Sepulveda Rec Center, 8801 Kester Ave.; 4 courts, lighted

San Gabriel
San Gabriel High School, 801 S. Ramona St.; 9 courts
Smith Park, 300 W. Broadway; 2 courts, lighted

San Marino
San Marino High School, 2701 Huntington Dr.; 5 courts, lighted

Santa Monica
Clover Park, 25th St. and Ashland Ave.; 2 courts, lighted
Douglas Park, 1155 Chelsea Ave.; 2 courts
Los Amigos Park, 6th Street and Hollister Avenue; 1 court

Marine Park, Marine Street and Paula Drive; 3 courts, lighted
Memorial Park, 1401 Olympic Blvd.; 4 courts, lighted
Ocean View Park, 2701 Barnard Way; 6 courts
Santa Monica High School, 601 Pico Blvd.; 7 courts

Studio City
Studio City Rec Center, 12621 Rye St.; 4 courts

Sun Valley
Sun Valley Park, 8133 Vineland Ave.; 2 courts, lighted

Sylmar
El Cariso Reg. Park, Hubbard Street and Garrick Avenue; 11 courts, lighted

Valley Glen
LA Valley College, 5800 Fulton Ave.; 17 courts

Van Nuys
Van Nuys Rec Center, 14301 Vanowen Ave.; 3 courts, lighted

West Hollywood
West Hollywood Park, 647 N. San Vicente Blvd.; 2 courts

Westlake Village
Westlake Village Tennis & Swim Club, 32250 Triunfo Canyon Rd.; 13 courts, lighted

Woodland Hills
Pierce College, 6201 Winnetka Ave.; 13 courts
Shoup Park, 5858 Shoup Ave.; 2 courts
Warner Center, 6336 Canoga Ave.; 13 courts

APPENDIX C:

BRANCHES OF THE LOS ANGELES PUBLIC LIBRARY

All locations offer free Wi-Fi unless noted otherwise.

Alma Reaves Woods–Watts, 10205 Compton Ave., Los Angeles, CA 90002; (323) 789-2850. No free Wi-Fi offered at this branch.

Angeles Mesa, 2700 W. 52nd St., Los Angeles, CA 90043; (323) 292-4328

Arroyo Seco Regional, 6145 N. Figueroa St., Los Angeles, CA 90042; (323) 255-0537

Ascot, 120 W. Florence Ave., Los Angeles, CA 90003; (323) 759-4817

Atwater Village, 3379 Glendale Blvd., Los Angeles, CA 90039; (323) 664-1353

Baldwin Hills, 2906 S. La Brea Ave., Los Angeles, CA 90016; (323) 733-1196

Benjamin Franklin, 2200 E. 1st St., Los Angeles, CA 90033; (323) 263-6901

Cahuenga, 4591 Santa Monica Blvd., Los Angeles, CA 90029; (323) 664-6418

Canoga Park, 20939 Sherman Way, Canoga Park, CA 91303; (818) 887-0320. Also offers computers for the visually impaired.

Chatsworth, 21052 Devonshire St., Chatsworth, CA 91311; (818) 341-4276

Chinatown, 639 N. Hill St., Los Angeles, CA 90012; (213) 620-0925

Cypress Park, 1150 Cypress Ave., Los Angeles, CA 90065; (323) 224-0039

Donald Bruce Kaufman–Brentwood, 11820 San Vicente Blvd., Los Angeles, CA 90049; (310) 575-8273

Eagle Rock, 5027 Caspar Ave., Los Angeles, CA 90041; (323) 258-8078

Echo Park, 1410 W. Temple St., Los Angeles, CA 90026; (213) 250-7808. No free Wi-Fi offered at this branch.

Edendale, 2011 W. Sunset Blvd., Los Angeles, CA 90026; (213) 207-3000

El Sereno, 5226 S. Huntington Dr., Los Angeles, CA 90032; (323) 225-9201. Also offers computers for the visually impaired.

Encino–Tarzana, 18231 Ventura Blvd., Tarzana, CA 91356; (818) 343-1983

Exposition Park–Dr. Mary McLeod Bethune Regional, 3900 S. Western Ave., Los Angeles, CA 90062; (323) 290-3113

Fairfax, 161 S. Gardner St., Los Angeles, CA 90036; (323) 936-6191

Felipe de Neve, 2820 W. 6th St., Los Angeles, CA 90057; (213) 384-7676

Frances Howard Goldwyn–Hollywood Regional, 1623 N. Ivar Ave., Hollywood, CA 90028; (323) 856-8260

Granada Hills, 10640 Petit Ave., Granada Hills, CA 91344; (818) 368-5687

Harbor City–Harbor Gateway, 24000 S. Western, Harbor City, CA 90710; (310) 534-9520

Hyde Park–Miriam Matthews, 2205 W. Florence Ave., Los Angeles, CA 90043; (323) 750-7241

Jefferson, 2211 W. Jefferson Blvd., Los Angeles, CA 90018; (323) 734-8573

John C. Fremont, 6121 Melrose Ave., Los Angeles, CA 90038; (323) 962-3521

John Muir, 1005 W. 64th St., Los Angeles, CA 90044; (323) 789-4800

Junipero Serra, 4607 S. Main St., Los Angeles, CA 90037; (323) 234-1685

Lake View Terrace, 12002 Osborne St., Sylmar, CA 91342; (818) 890-7404

Lincoln Heights, 2530 Workman St., Los Angeles, CA 90031; (323) 226-1692

Little Tokyo, 203 S. Los Angeles St., Los Angeles, CA 90012; (213) 612-0525

Los Feliz, 1874 Hillhurst Ave., Los Angeles, CA 90027; (323) 913-4710

Malabar, 2801 Wabash Ave., Los Angeles, CA 90033; (323) 263-1497

Mar Vista, 12006 Venice Blvd., Los Angeles, CA 90066; (310) 390-3454. Also contains a bookstore for used books.

Mark Twain, 9621 S. Figueroa St., Los Angeles, CA 90003; (323) 755-4088

Memorial, 4625 W. Olympic Blvd., Los Angeles, CA 90019; (323) 938-2732

Mid-Valley Regional, 16244 Nordhoff St., North Hills, CA 91343; (818) 895-3650

North Hollywood Regional, 5211 Tujunga Ave., North Hollywood, CA 91601; (818) 766-7185

Northridge, 9051 Darby Ave., Northridge, CA 91325; (818) 886-3640

Pacoima, 13605 Van Nuys Blvd., Pacoima, CA 91331; (818) 899-5203

Palisades, 861 Alma Real Dr., Pacific Palisades, CA 90272; (310) 459-2754

Palms–Rancho Park, 2920 Overland Ave., Los Angeles, CA 90064; (310) 840-2142

Panorama City, 14345 Roscoe Blvd., Panorama City, CA 91402; (818) 894-4071

Pico Union, 1030 S. Alvarado St., Los Angeles, CA 90006; (213) 368-7545

Pio Pico–Koreatown, 694 S. Oxford Ave., Los Angeles, CA 90005; (213) 368-7647

Platt, 23600 Victory Blvd., Woodland Hills, CA 91367; (818) 340-9386. Also contains a bookstore for used books.

Playa Vista, 6400 Playa Vista Dr., Los Angeles, CA 90094; (310) 437-6680

Porter Ranch, 11371 Tampa Ave., Porter Ranch, CA 91326; (818) 360-5706. Also contains a bookstore for used books.

Robert Louis Stevenson, 803 Spence St., Los Angeles, CA 90023; (323) 268-4710

Robertson, 1719 S. Robertson Blvd., Los Angeles, CA 90035; (310) 840-2147

San Pedro Regional, 931 S. Gaffey St., San Pedro, CA 90731; (310) 548-7779. No free Wi-Fi offered at this branch.

Sherman Oaks, 14245 Moorpark St., Sherman Oaks, CA 91423; (818) 205-9716

Silver Lake, 2411 Glendale Blvd., Los Angeles, CA 90039; (323) 913-7451

Studio City, 12511 Moorpark St., Studio City, CA 91604; (818) 755-7873

Sun Valley, 7935 Vineland Ave., Sun Valley, CA 91352; (818) 764-1338

Sunland–Tujunga, 7771 Foothill Blvd., Sunland, CA 91042; (818) 352-4481. Also contains a bookstore for used books.

Sylmar, 14561 Polk St., Sylmar, CA 91342; (818) 367-6102

Valley Plaza, 12311 Vanowen St., North Hollywood, CA 91605; (818) 765-9251

Van Nuys, 6250 Sylmar Ave., Van Nuys, CA 91401; (818) 756-8453. No free Wi-Fi offered at this branch.

Venice–Abbot Kinney Memorial, 501 S. Venice Blvd., Venice, CA 90291; (310) 821-1769

Vermont Square, 1201 W. 48th St., Los Angeles, CA 90037; (323) 290-7405

Vernon–Leon H. Washington Jr. Memorial, 4504 S. Central Ave., Los Angeles, CA 90011; (323) 234-9106

Washington Irving, 4117 W. Washington Blvd., Los Angeles, CA 90018; (323) 734-6303

West Los Angeles Regional, 11360 Santa Monica Blvd., Los Angeles, CA 90025; (310) 575-8323. Also offers computers for the visually impaired.

West Valley Regional, 19036 Vanowen St., Reseda, CA 91335; (818) 345-9806

Westchester–Loyola Village, 7114 W. Manchester Ave., Los Angeles, CA 90045; (310) 348-1096. Also contains a bookstore for used books.

Westwood, 1246 Glendon Ave., Los Angeles, CA 90024; (310) 474-1739

Will & Ariel Durant, 7140 W. Sunset Blvd., Los Angeles, CA 90046; (323) 876-2741

Wilmington, 1300 N. Avalon Blvd., Wilmington, CA 90744; (310) 834-1082

Wilshire, 149 N. Saint Andrews Place, Los Angeles, CA 90004; (323) 957-4550

Woodland Hills, 22200 Ventura Blvd., Woodland Hills, CA 91364; (818) 226-0017

COUNTY OF LOS ANGELES PUBLIC LIBRARY LOCATIONS

Acton
Acton/Agua Dulce Christopher Colombo Brevidoro Library, 33792 Crown Valley Rd.; (661) 269-7101

Agoura Hills
Agoura Hills Library, 29901 Ladyface Court; (818) 889-2278

Arcadia
Live Oak Library, 4153–55 E. Live Oak Ave.; (626) 446-8803

Artesia
Artesia Library, 18722 S. Clarkdale Ave.; (562) 865-6614

Avalon
Avalon Library, 215 Sumner Ave.; (310) 510-1050

Baldwin Park
Baldwin Park Library, 4181 Baldwin Park Blvd.; (626) 962-6947

Bell
Bell Library, 4411 E. Gage Ave.; (323) 560-2149

Bell Gardens
Bell Gardens Library, 7110 S. Garfield Ave.; (562) 927-1309

Bellflower
Clifton M. Brakensiek Library, 9945 E. Flower St.; (562) 925-5543

Carson
Carson Library, 151 E. Carson St.; (310) 830-0901
Dr. Martin Luther King, Jr. Library, 17906 S. Avalon Blvd.; (310) 327-4830

Claremont

Claremont Library, 208 N. Harvard Ave.; (909) 621-4902

Compton

Compton Library, 240 W. Compton Blvd.; (310) 637-0202

Covina

Charter Oak Library, 20540 E. Arrow Hwy.; (626) 339-2151

Cudahy

Cudahy Library, 5218 Santa Ana St.; (323) 771-1345

Culver City

Culver City Julian Dixon Library, 4975 Overland Ave.; (310) 559-1676

Diamond Bar

Diamond Bar Library, 1061 S. Grand Ave., Diamond Bar, CA 91765; (909) 861-4978

Duarte

Duarte Library, 1301 Buena Vista St.; (626) 358-1865

El Monte

El Monte Library, 3224 N. Tyler Ave.; (626) 444-9506
Norwood Library, 4550 N. Peck Rd.; (626) 443-3147

Gardena

Gardena Mayme Dear Library, 1731 W. Gardena Blvd.; (310) 323-6363
Masao W. Satow Library, 14433 S. Crenshaw Blvd.; (310) 679-0638

Hacienda Heights

Hacienda Heights Library, 16010 La Monde St.; (626) 968-9356

Hawaiian Gardens

Hawaiian Gardens Library, 11940 Carson St.; (562) 496-1212

Hawthorne

Hawthorne Library, 12700 Grevillea Ave.; (310) 679-8193
Wiseburn Library, 5335 W. 135th St.; (310) 643-8880

Huntington Park

Huntington Park Library, 6518 Miles Ave.; (323) 583-1461

La Cañada Flintridge

La Cañada Flintridge Library, 4545 N. Oakwood Ave.; (818) 790-3330

La Crescenta

La Crescenta Library, 2809 Foothill Blvd.; (818) 248-5313

La Mirada

La Mirada Library, 13800 La Mirada Blvd.; (562) 943-0277

La Puente

La Puente Library, 15920 E. Central Ave.; (626) 968-4613

La Verne

La Verne Library, 3640 D St.; (909) 596-1934

Lakewood

Angelo M. Iacoboni Library, 4990 Clark Ave.; (562) 866-1777
George Nye, Jr. Library, 6600 Del Amo Blvd.; (562) 421-8497

Lancaster

Lancaster Library, 601 W. Lancaster Blvd.; (661) 948-5029

Lennox

Lennox Library, 4359 Lennox Blvd.; (310) 674-0385

Littlerock

Littlerock Library, 35119 80th St. E; (661) 944-4138

Lomita

Lomita Library, 24200 Narbonne Ave.; (310) 539-4515

La Puente

Sunkist Library, 840 N. Puente Ave.; (626) 960-2707

Los Angeles

A C Bilbrew Library, 150 E. El Segundo Blvd.; (310) 538-3350
Anthony Quinn Library, 3965 Cesar Chavez Ave.; (323) 264-7715
City Terrace Library, 4025 E. City Terrace Dr.; (323) 261-0295
East Los Angeles Library, 4837 E. 3rd St.; (323) 264-0155
El Camino Real Library, 4264 E. Whittier Blvd.; (323) 269-8102
Florence Library, 1610 E. Florence Ave.; (323) 581-8028
Graham Library, 1900 E. Firestone Ave.; (323) 582-2903
View Park Library, 3854 W. 54th St.; (323) 293-5371
Willowbrook Library, 11838 Wilmington Ave.; (323) 564-5698

Lynwood

Lynwood Library, 11320 Bullis Rd.; (310) 635-7121

Malibu

Malibu Library, 23519 W. Civic Center Way; (310) 456-6438

Manhattan Beach

Manhattan Beach Library, 1320 Highland Ave.; (310) 545-8595

Maywood

Maywood Cesar Chavez Library, 4323 E. Slauson Ave.; (323) 771-8600

Montebello

Chet Holifield Library, 1060 S. Greenwood Ave.; (323) 728-0421
Montebello Library, 1550 W. Beverly Blvd.; (323) 722-6551

Newhall

Newhall Library, 22704 W. 9th St.; (661) 259-0750

Norwalk

Alondra Library, 11949 Alondra Blvd.; (562) 868-7771
Norwalk Library, 12350 Imperial Hwy.; (562) 868-0775

Palmdale

Lake Los Angeles Library, 16921 E. Ave. O; (661) 264-0593

Paramount

Paramount Library, 16254 Colorado Ave.; (562) 630-3171

Pico Rivera

Pico Rivera Library, 9001 Mines Ave.; (562) 942-7394

Quartz Hill

Quartz Hill Library, 42018 N. 50th St. W; (661) 943-2454

Rancho Dominguez

East Rancho Dominguez Library, 4205 E. Compton Blvd.; (310) 632-6193

Rosemead

Rosemead Library, 8800 Valley Blvd.; (626) 573-5220

Rowland Heights

Rowland Heights Library, 1850 Nogales St.; (626) 912-5348

San Dimas

San Dimas Library, 145 N. Walnut Ave.; (909) 599-6738

San Fernando

San Fernando Library, 217 N. Maclay Ave.; (818) 365-6928

San Gabriel

San Gabriel Library, 500 S. Del Mar Ave.; (626) 287-0761

Santa Clarita

Canyon Country Jo Anne Darcy Library, 18601 Soledad Canyon Rd.; (661) 251-2720
Valencia Library, 23743 W. Valencia Blvd.; (661) 259-8942

South El Monte

South El Monte Library, 1430 N. Central Ave.; (626) 443-4158

South Gate

Hollydale Library, 12000 S. Garfield Ave.; (562) 634-0156

Leland R. Weaver Library, 4035 Tweedy Blvd.; (323) 567-8853

Temple City

Temple City Library, 5939 Golden West Ave.; (626) 285-2136

Walnut

Walnut Library, 21155 La Puente Rd.; (909) 595-0757

West Covina

West Covina Library, 1601 W. Covina Pkwy.; (626)962-3541

West Hollywood

West Hollywood Library, 715 N. San Vicente Blvd.; (310) 652-5340

Westlake Village

Westlake Village Library, 31220 W. Oak Crest Dr.; (818) 865-9230

Whittier

Los Nietos Library, 11644 E. Slauson Ave.; (562) 695-0708

Sorensen Library, 6934 Broadway Ave.; (562) 695-3979

South Whittier Library, 14433 Leffingwell Rd.; (562) 946-4415

APPENDIX E:

BRANCHES OF LA LAW LIBRARY IN COURTHOUSES & PUBLIC LIBRARIES

Compton, 240 W. Compton Blvd, Compton, CA 90220; (310) 637-0202
Hours: Closed Sun, Mon, Fri; Tues through Thurs 10 a.m. to 8 p.m.; Sat 8 a.m. to 6 p.m.

Lancaster, 601 W. Lancaster Blvd., Lancaster, CA 93534; (661) 948-5029
Hours: Closed Sun, Mon; Tues through Thurs 10 a.m. to 8 p.m.; Fri and Sat 8 a.m. to 6 p.m.

Long Beach, 415 W. Ocean Blvd., Long Beach, CA 90802; (562) 983-7088
Hours: Closed Sat and Sun; Mon through Thurs 8:30 a.m. to 4 p.m.; Fri 8:30 a.m. to 2 p.m.

Norwalk, 12720 Norwalk Blvd., Norwalk, CA 90650; (562) 807-7310
Hours: Mon through Fri 10 a.m. to 2 p.m.

Pasadena, 285 E. Walnut St., Pasadena, CA 91101; (626) 744-4066
Hours: Mon through Thurs 9 a.m. to 9 p.m.; Fri and Sat 9 a.m. to 6 p.m.; Sun 1 to 5 p.m.

Pomona, 400 Civic Center Plaza, Pomona, CA 91766; (909) 784-1961
Hours: Mon through Fri 10 a.m. to 2 p.m.

Santa Monica, 1725 Main St., Santa Monica, CA 90401; (310) 260-3644
Hours: Mon through Fri 9 a.m. to 1 p.m.

Torrance, 825 Maple Ave., Torrance, CA 90503; (310) 222-8816
Hours: Mon through Fri 10 a.m. to 2 p.m.

Van Nuys, 6230 Sylmar Ave., Van Nuys, CA 91401; (818) 374-2499
Hours: Mon through Fri 8:30 a.m. to 4 p.m.

LOS ANGELES COUNTY PUBLIC COMMUNITY GARDENS

Self-maintained and policed, community gardens are open to all who apply and occupy three categories of land: private land with short-term leases, public land with short-term leases, and garden-owned land. Maintaining a vacant lot is expensive, so leasing the land for a community garden until it is needed for development is both practical and pleasant.

Alhambra (Winston Smoyer Memorial), 1006 Clay Court, Alhambra, CA 91801

Altadena, 3330 N. Lincoln Ave., Altadena, CA 91001

Arleta, 8800 Canterbury, Arleta, CA 91331

Baldwin Park, 13067 Bess Ave., Baldwin Park, CA 91706

Baldwin Park WIC, 3601 Puente Ave., Baldwin Park, CA 91706

Bell Gardens, 7800 Scout Ave., Bell Gardens, CA 90201

Bougainvillea, across from 2000 102nd Street, Watts, CA 90002

Columbia Park, 4045 190th St., Torrance, CA 90504

Crenshaw, 1423 Crenshaw Blvd., Los Angeles, CA 90019

CSUN Hille, California State University Northridge Campus

Culver City, 10860 Culver Blvd., Culver City, CA 90230

Dan McKenzie, 4324 160th St., Lawndale, CA 90260

Downtown Long Beach, 525 E. 7th St., Long Beach, CA 90813

Eagle Rockdale Community Garden and Art Park, 1003 to 1100 Rockdale Ave., Eagle Rock, CA 90041

Eastwind Garden, 110 E. Eastwind St., Marina Del Rey, CA 90292

El Sereno, 5454 Huntington Dr., El Sereno, CA 90032

Enrique Noguera, 6614 Fountain Ave., Hollywood, CA 90028

Fountain Avenue, 5620 Fountain Ave., Los Angeles, CA 90028

Francis Avenue, 2910 Francis Ave. in MacArthur Park, Los Angeles, CA 90005

Franklin Hills (Norman Harriton), 2037 Sanborn Ave., Franklin Hills, CA 90027

Good Earth, corner of Clyde Avenue and Boden Street, Baldwin Hills, CA 90016

Granada Hills Salad Bowl Garden Club, 16003 Rinaldi St., Granada Hills, CA 91344

Howard Finn, 7747 Foothill Blvd., Tujunga, CA 91042

Hudson, adjacent to 2335 Webster (at Hill) behind Hudson Park, Long Beach, CA 90810

Jardin del Rio, 2363 Riverdale Ave., Echo Park, CA 90031

John S. Gibson Senior Garden, 1401 S. Harbor Blvd., San Pedro, CA 90731

La Madera, 3805 La Madera Ave., El Monte, CA 91732

La Mirada, 13518 Biola Ave., La Mirada, CA 90638

Lago Seco, 3920 235th St., Torrance, CA 90504

Lakewood, at 5200 Carfax on Candlewood, Lakewood, CA 90713

Long Beach, 7600 Spring St., Long Beach, CA 90815

Mansfield, 1300 N. Mansfield Ave., Los Angeles, CA 90028

Manzanita Street, 4107 W. Sunset Blvd., Silverlake, CA 90029

Mar Vista, 5075 Slauson Ave., Culver City, CA 90230

Milagro Allegro, 115 S. Ave. 56 at Figueroa, Highland Park, CA 90042. Milagro Allegro sometimes hosts a free "Garden Swap." E-mail Master Gardener Milli Macen-Moore at milli@modernsustainability.com for more information. They also run free "Fresh from the Garden" nutrition workshops and cooking demonstrations on the fourth Saturday of every month.

Monterey Eco-Community Garden East, 870 Monterey Rd., Glendale, CA 91206

Monterey Eco-Community Garden West, 824 Monterey Rd., Glendale, CA 91206

Mothers of East LA, 1020 S. Fickett St., Los Angeles, CA 90023

Norman Harriton (Franklin Hills), 2037 Sanborn Ave., Franklin Hills, CA 90027

North Hollywood, 11800 Weddington St., North Hollywood, CA 91601

North Long Beach, 6895 N. Myrtle Ave., Long Beach, CA 90805

Norwalk, 12739 Studebaker Rd., Norwalk, CA 90650

Norwich, 417 Norwich Dr., West Hollywood, CA 90048

Oakland, at Oakland and Maple, Pasadena, CA 91101

Ocean View Farms, 3300 Centinela Ave., Mar Vista, CA 90066

Orcutt Ranch, 23600 Roscoe Blvd., West Hills, CA 91304

Palmer Park, 610 E. Palmer Ave. (at Glendale), Glendale, CA 91205

Paramount, 7200 Cortland Ave., Paramount, CA 90723

Parkman, 20800 Burbank Blvd., Woodland Hills, CA 91367

Pico Rivera, 8606 Beverly Rd., Pico Rivera, CA 90660

Project Youth Green, 12467 W. Osborne St., Pacoima, CA 91331

Proyecto Jardin, 1718 Bridge St., Boyle Heights, CA 90033

Raymond Avenue Neighborhood Garden, 2632 Raymond Ave. (between Adam and 27th), Los Angeles, CA 90007

Rosemary & Thyme, 10161 Jordan Ave., Chatsworth, CA 91311

Rosencrans Farms, across from 561 146th St. between Figueroa and Harbor Freeway, Gardena, CA 90248

Rosewood, 4160½ Rosewood Ave., Koreatown, CA 90004

San Pedro, 1400 N. Gaffey St., San Pedro, CA 90731

Santa Fe Springs, 10145 Pioneer Blvd., Santa Fe Springs, CA 90670

Santa Monica (Park Drive), 2337 Broadway, Santa Monica, CA 90404

Santa Monica (Euclid Park), 1525 Euclid Ave., Santa Monica, CA 90403

Santa Monica (Main Street), 2300 Main St., Santa Monica, CA 90405

Sepulveda, 16633 Magnolia Blvd., Encino, CA 91316

Solano Canyon, 545 Solano Ave., Silverlake, CA 90012

Stanford-Avalon, 658 E. 111th Place, Los Angeles, CA 90059

Union Avenue Cesar Chavez Peace Garden, 1136 S. Union Ave., Westlake, CA 90015

Van Nuys Airport, 16400 Chase St., North Hills, CA 91343

Verdugo Park, 1621 Canada Blvd., Glendale, CA 91208

Vermont Square, 4712 and 4717 S. Vermont, South Los Angeles, CA 90037

Vista Hermosa, 1590 E. 114th St., Watts, CA 90026

Wattles Farm, 1714 Curson Ave., Hollywood, CA 90046

Winston Smoyer Memorial (Alhambra), 1006 Clay Court, Alhambra, CA 91801

Wrigley Village, 2044 Pacific Ave., Long Beach, CA 90806

Yamazaki Memorial Community Garden, 961 S. Mariposa, Los Angeles, CA 90006

INDEX